The Appomattox
Generals

The Appomattox Generals

*The Parallel Lives of
Joshua L. Chamberlain, USA, and
John B. Gordon, CSA,
Commanders at the Surrender
Ceremony of April 12, 1865*

JOHN W. PRIMOMO

McFarland & Company, Inc., Publishers
Jefferson, North Carolina, and London

LIBRARY OF CONGRESS CATALOGUING-IN-PUBLICATION DATA

Primomo, John W., 1952–
   The Appomattox generals : the parallel lives of Joshua L. Chamberlain, USA, and John B. Gordon, CSA, commanders at the surrender ceremony of April 12, 1865 / John W. Primomo.
      p.   cm.

   Includes bibliographical references and index.

   ISBN 978-0-7864-7632-9
   softcover : acid free paper ∞

   1. United States—History—Civil War, 1861–1865—Biography. 2. Chamberlain, Joshua Lawrence, 1828–1914. 3. Gordon, John Brown, 1832–1904. 4. Generals—United States—Biography. 5. Generals—Confederate States of America—Biography. 6. United States—History—Civil War, 1861–1865—Campaigns. I. Title.
E467.P9 2013
355.0092'2—dc23
[B]   2013018878

BRITISH LIBRARY CATALOGUING DATA ARE AVAILABLE

© 2013 John W. Primomo. All rights reserved

No part of this book may be reproduced or transmitted in any form or by any means, electronic or mechanical, including photocopying or recording, or by any information storage and retrieval system, without permission in writing from the publisher.

Front cover: Generals John B. Gordon, CSA (left; National Archives and Records Administration) and Joshua L. Chamberlain, USA (Maine Historical Society).

Manufactured in the United States of America

McFarland & Company, Inc., Publishers
   Box 611, Jefferson, North Carolina 28640
      www.mcfarlandpub.com

For Marilyn, Meredith and Mallory

Table of Contents

Preface 1
Introduction 3

1. Honor Answering Honor 9
2. Early Years 17
3. Outbreak of the War 24
4. The Peninsula Campaign 32
5. Antietam 38
6. Fredericksburg 50
7. Chancellorsville 57
8. Gettysburg 64
9. Interlude of Winter 1863-64 89
10. The Wilderness 95
11. Spotsylvania Courthouse 103
12. North Anna to Petersburg 109
13. Monocacy River and the Shenandoah Valley ... 120
14. Winter 1865 to Fort Stedman 131
15. Quaker Road to Five Forks 141
16. Appomattox 154

17. Going Home 167
18. After the War 176

Afterword 195
Notes 197
Bibliography 215
Index 219

Preface

The Civil War was the defining event in the history of the post–Revolution United States. Historians have calculated that at least 620,000, and as many as 750,000, men lost their lives in the bloody, devastating war. Ultimately, the Civil War also determined that slavery would no longer be tolerated in this country. However, it was secession that caused most men to choose to fight either for the United States of America or the Confederate States of America. The armies were made up of all types of men from all walks of life. In my many years of Civil War studies, no two soldiers presented stories as fascinating and with such remarkable similarity as those of Joshua Lawrence Chamberlain of Maine and John Brown Gordon of Georgia.

Both men volunteered for military service, feeling a strong need to fight for the cause of their respective sections. They entered the army as low-level officers with no formal military training. Repeatedly, they exhibited exceptional aptitude and command, rising through the ranks as they received the glowing accolades of their superiors. Yet, they remained humble and continually demonstrated exceptional courage, which earned them the respect of their men. Ultimately, as fate would have it, their heroism and leadership culminated in their meeting as the commanders of the Union and Confederate armies at the Appomattox Courthouse surrender. At Chamberlain's command, the Union army saluted the Confederates as they laid down their arms and flags. In turn, Gordon ordered his men to return the noble gesture of respect.

While others have written about Chamberlain and Gordon individually, the comparison of the lives of these two remarkable soldiers in one manuscript is original and compelling. This book traces the lives of Chamberlain and Gordon from their youths to the outbreak of the Civil War. It recounts the battles in which they engaged, including the Peninsula Campaign, Antietam, Fredericksburg, Chancellorsville, Gettysburg, the Wilderness, Spotsylvania Courthouse, Petersburg, the Monocacy River and Shenandoah Valley, Fort Stedman, Quaker Road to Five Forks, and, finally, Appomattox. The book also discusses the lives of Chamberlain and Gordon after the Civil War as both men, whose heroics had made them popular figures, entered politics in their respective states.

Information for this book was obtained from the Official Records of the Union and Confederate Armies, the recollections of Chamberlain and Gordon, and descriptions of both men by soldiers who fought with them and those who fought against them. The high esteem in which both men were held is reflected in the fact that material was drawn not only from the superior officers they served but also from the men who served under them. Additionally, works of various noted historians contributed to this effort.

While, inevitably, troop movements and battle maneuvers must be addressed in any work of this kind, I have attempted to minimize and simplify those discussions and focus instead on the characters of Chamberlain and Gordon that made them such extraordinary men and soldiers. Also, any explanation which did not involve Chamberlain and Gordon but which was necessary for purposes of completeness and context has been abbreviated. Justifiably, some readers will find these men flawed; e.g., Gordon apparently belonged to the Ku Klux Klan for a brief period after the Civil War. This book is about two good — not perfect — men, whose faults should be judged according to the time in which they lived. By the standards of yesterday and today, the positive attributes of Chamberlain and Gordon that made them so remarkable are unsurpassed and deserve imitation by every American, whether living on Main Street, working on Wall Street, or, perhaps most important, serving in a state or the federal government.

Introduction

Wednesday April 12, 1865, dawned chilly and gray as the ragged and exhausted remnants of the surrendered Army of Northern Virginia folded their tents and broke camp for the last time. With heavy hearts, they reluctantly prepared to march from the banks of the Appomattox River through the village of Appomattox Courthouse, Virginia, to relinquish their flags and arms to the victorious Union army. It was four years to the day, almost to the very hour, since military forces of the Confederate States of America inaugurated the American Civil War by firing upon Fort Sumter in Charleston Harbor, South Carolina. They had come to this bitter point not through any failure of spirit, but only because further resistance would have proved futile. Commanded by Lieutenant General Robert E. Lee, the Army of Northern Virginia had suffered through a nine-month siege around Petersburg and Richmond, Virginia, at the hands of the Union Army of the Potomac and the Army of the James led by Lieutenant General Ulysses S. Grant. Confederate lines, continuously lengthened and defended by fewer and fewer soldiers, finally collapsed in early April 1865 under the weight of implacable Federal assaults. Within a week, Lee's retreating army of 27,000, most of whom were too feeble to fight, was trapped at Appomattox Courthouse by well-fed and well-equipped Union forces numbering in excess of 60,000.

Lee and Grant met in the home of Wilmer McLean on April 9, Palm Sunday, and agreed to the terms of surrender. Though Lee wished that the Confederates be allowed to simply leave their arms and flags in their camp and go home, Grant felt that a formal surrender ceremony was necessary to demonstrate proper respect for the United States. Neither Grant nor Lee would be present for that event, however. Leading the Confederate

General Joshua L. Chamberlain, date unknown (National Archives and Records Administration, 111-B-4934).

procession would be Major General John Brown Gordon of Georgia, who entered the war in April 1861 as a lowly captain of volunteers yet now commanded the Second Corps of the Army of Northern Virginia. Despite his having had no military training when the war began, Gordon's bravery and skill in battle soon garnered the attention of his superiors and the respect of his men. At the Battle of Antietam in September 1862, he was wounded five times — once, grievously, through the face. Promotions and accolades followed Gordon throughout the war until, by April 1865, he was one of Lee's most trusted confidants.

Before departing, Grant designated an even less likely subordinate than Gordon to command the ceremony on behalf of all Union forces. He was Brigadier General Joshua Lawrence Chamberlain of Maine. Chamberlain had left his position as a professor at Bowdoin College to begin his military career in August 1862 as lieutenant colonel of the 20th Maine Regiment. As with Gordon, Chamberlain had no previous military experience and either taught himself military tactics or learned the art of war in battle. Chamberlain also demonstrated exceptional valor and leadership, eventually receiving the Medal of Honor for heroism in the defense of Little Round Top at the Battle of Gettysburg. Chamberlain was wounded several times during the Civil War, the most seriously near Petersburg on June 18, 1864, when he was shot through both hips. On April 12, 1865, he commanded the First Division of the Fifth Corps of the Army of the Potomac.

Both Chamberlain and Gordon led simple lives before the war. Gordon tried his hand at practicing law but gave it up. Eventually, he went into business with his father producing coal. The bright spot of his legal career was not what he did but who he met, Fanny Rebecca Haralson, the sister-in-law of one of his law partners, who became his love, wife and life partner. Prior to the war, Chamberlain, a seminary graduate, taught rhetoric, oratory and modern languages at Bowdoin College in Brunswick, Maine. He met, fell in love with, and married Frances Caroline Adams, also called Fanny, the adopted daughter of the local church pastor.

Neither man entered the war for personal gain, money or power. Chamberlain and Gordon joined their respective armies because, in their hearts, they believed in the causes for which the North and the South were fighting. They valued those causes above their own lives and were willing to risk all they loved to achieve victory. Both men came to the war with views about the conflict consistent with those of the regions in which they lived. Though slavery was repugnant to Chamberlain, he, as did most Union volunteers, fought to preserve the Union, not to free the slaves. Gordon, on the other hand, believed that slavery was morally, politically and socially right, and that the property rights of Southerners in their slaves must be protected. He saw a threat to slavery as a threat to Southern liberty. During the war, though, Chamberlain and Gordon rarely gave much attention to political issues. They focused on the task at hand, the means to achieve victory. At Appomattox, that issue was finally determined.

Two more fitting soldiers and leaders could hardly have been chosen

General John B. Gordon, date unknown (Civil War Collection, Prints & Photographs Division, Library of Congress, LC-DIG-cwpb-06014).

for the momentous occasion at Appomattox Courthouse. Courage and exceptional leadership skills were only two of their many attributes. They were noble, unselfish and humble. They sought no elevation in rank for themselves and were embarrassed when promotion was bestowed upon them. Chamberlain and Gordon would not abuse their authority and treated ordinary soldiers with respect and dignity. They inspired men with their words and deeds. After one battle, one of Gordon's men, in all seriousness, stated that he wished Gordon would never speak before battle again. When asked why, he replied, "Because he makes me feel like I could storm hell." Accolades for these two leaders came from those they served and those who served them. They were honorable, moral, decent men who behaved mercifully towards soldiers and civilians who honored the opposing flag. At Appomattox and afterward, Chamberlain and Gordon, both of whom had believed so deeply and fought so hard and so long for victory, readily embraced the end of the fighting without hatred for their former adversaries and fostered the peace necessary to heal the division of the country.

As Gordon prepared to lead the Army of Northern Virginia up the Richmond-Lynchburg Stage Road through Appomattox Courthouse at sunrise on April 12, 1865, and as Chamberlain and the Union army awaited their arrival, emotions on both sides ran deep. Chamberlain and Gordon strongly believed in the justice of their respective causes. They had seen many men, their own beloved comrades, suffer and die. Gordon's brother Gus was counted among the Confederate dead at Chancellorsville. After four long years of arduous struggle and painful sacrifice, not only were Southern soldiers being required to come to terms with the loss of their cause, they were also now parting with the man who was the living embodiment of all that they had fought for, their beloved leader, Robert E. Lee. They were being compelled to surrender the blessed emblems of their cause and return home to an uncertain fate. The Northern soldiers had also fought mightily and, though victorious, paid a price no less dear. Thoughts of fallen comrades who would not be present for this final ceremony touched hearts on both sides.

President Abraham Lincoln advised compassion in dealing with the fallen South, and the terms of surrender offered to Lee by Grant were magnanimous. It remained to be seen how others in the Union would treat the defeated secessionists, and how the Southerners, defeated yet staunchly proud, would respond. When the Confederates marched within arms length of their Union foe on the road through Appomattox Courthouse, and the eyes of the victor met the eyes of the vanquished, how would the men react? Would the Union soldier look down upon his beaten enemy, gloating on the triumph and hating the Rebels for the suffering of the past four years begun at Fort Sumter? Would the Confederate soldier, believing no less now than he did in 1861 in the justness of his cause, knowing all that he had sacrificed and lost, be able to make the long, painful walk through the Union ranks without succumbing to the will to again fight his hated Yankee foe?

Commanders on both sides could expect that their men would perform their difficult task in good order, though some may have feared that the proximity of the armies might lead to an exchange of verbal, if not physical, hostility. Yet no one, save Chamberlain, knew what was really coming. As Gordon and the Army of Northern Virginia approached, Chamberlain gave the order for his men to salute the defeated Confederates. Gordon, though caught by surprise, immediately ordered his men to return the salute to their former foe. Both men knew the gesture was not a recognition of either side's cause, but a show of respect for the chivalry of soldiers both Northern and Southern, living and dead. Chamberlain's and Gordon's grace and dignity set the example, not only for the men under their commands but also for a divided nation. The war was over. Soldiers and citizens, both North and South, were countrymen once again. The Civil War began in an atmosphere of hatred and distrust. It would end with honor answering honor.

Chapter 1

Honor Answering Honor

"That night we slept as we had not slept in four years," recalled Brigadier General Joshua Lawrence Chamberlain — commander of the First Brigade in the First Division of the Fifth Corps of the Army of the Potomac — of the night of Sunday, April 9, 1865. That day, Lieutenant General Ulysses S. Grant, commander of all Union forces, accepted the surrender of what remained of the Army of Northern Virginia from General Robert E. Lee at Appomattox Courthouse, Virginia. Lee's surrender did not end the Civil War; other Confederate armies remained in the field. However, it was evident to all, except the Confederate president, Jefferson Davis, and a handful of others who refused to accept the inevitable, that the end had come. It was only a matter of time before the last battle was fought and the remaining Southern forces laid down their arms.

Southern states began seceding soon after the election of Abraham Lincoln as president of the United States. The Civil War began in earnest at Fort Sumter in Charleston Harbor, South Carolina, on April 12, 1861. Many people in the North and South did not believe it would last long. They were wrong. Over 620,000 American soldiers lost their lives in a bloody, devastating war. Finally, at Appomattox Courthouse, the primary armies of the United States and the Confederacy met for the final time. The superior numbers of men and materiel of the North inevitably overwhelmed the will of the South, forcing Lee to surrender on April 9.

The next day, April 10, at Appomattox Courthouse was unlike any other in the four adversarial and bloody years since the war began. Soldiers visited between camps and traded, "exchanging compliments, pipes, tobacco, knives and souvenirs." Hungry Confederates sought food most of all. The practice became so widespread as to cause alarm among the armies' commanders. Eventually, restrictions on intermingling were imposed. Before then, however, the soldiers got a good look at the men they had been fighting. Noting how thin the common Confederate soldier had become, one man of the 20th Maine commented, "No wonder we didn't kill more of them; either one of them would split a minie-ball if it should strike him." Captain Thomas Chamberlain, General Chamberlain's brother and provost marshal of the First Division, saw Major General John Brown Gordon, commanding Lee's Second Corps, and described him as "the best-looking soldier I ever saw in my life!" Of Gordon, one of his own men had said, "It'ud put fight into a whipped chicken just to look at him." Union soldier Morris Schaff described Gordon as "a man of natural eminence. Above medium height, he had a soldier's port, raven-black hair, a noticeably deep scar across his left cheek and as fierce and nearly cruelly blue eye as I ever looked into."[1]

Gordon, Lieutenant General James Longstreet, and Brigadier General W.N. Pendleton were designated by Lee to carry into effect the surrender stipulations, while Grant had appointed Major Generals Charles Griffin, Wesley Merritt, and John Gibbon as commissioners to oversee the formal surrender. The generous terms reflected the leniency that President Lincoln insisted be extended to Southern soldiers. On April 10 they signed the following agreement:

Appomattox Courthouse, Va.
April 10, 1865

1st. The troops shall march by brigades and detachments to a designated point, stack their arms, deposit their flags, sabers, pistols, &c., and from thence march to their homes under charge of their officers, superintended by their respective division and corps commanders, officers retaining their side arms, and the authorized number of private horses,

2d. All public horses and public property of all kinds to be turned over to staff officers designated by the United States authorities,

3d. Such transportation as may be agreed upon as necessary for the transportation of the private baggage of officers will be allowed to accompany the officers, to be turned over at the end of the trip to the nearest U.S. quartermasters, receipts being taken for same.

4th. Couriers and mounted men of the artillery and the cavalry, whose horses are their own private property, will be allowed to retain them.

5th. The surrender of the Army of Northern Virginia shall be construed to include all the forces operating with that army on the 8th instant, the date of commencement of negotiation for surrender, except such bodies of cavalry as actually made their escape previous to the surrender, and except also such pieces of artillery as were more than twenty miles from Appomattox Court-House at the time of surrender on the 9th instant.[2]

On the night of April 10, Chamberlain was summoned to headquarters. There, Griffin and Gibbon told Chamberlain that Grant had chosen him to command the formal ceremony at which Confederate guns and flags would be surrendered. Whatever else went through his mind at that time, Chamberlain thought of the men with whom he had served. He began the war as lieutenant colonel of the 20th Maine regiment and commanded the Third Brigade after the Battle of Gettysburg. Chamberlain asked Griffin if he might be reassigned from command of the First Brigade to his old Third Brigade, which included the 20th Maine, so that he might share the surrender ceremony with them. Griffin gladly granted his request.[3]

Chamberlain believed that Griffin, who had a great admiration for Chamberlain, had "something to do" with Grant's choice. Undoubtedly this is so, yet Grant himself was quite familiar with Chamberlain's battlefield heroics. Grant immediately promoted Chamberlain to brigadier general after he was severely wounded at Rives' Salient near Petersburg, Virginia, on June 18, 1864. As his rationale for doing so, Grant noted that Chamberlain was gallantly leading his brigade at the time, as he had been in the habit of doing in all the engagements in which he had previously been involved.[4]

Perhaps, in pondering his selection, Chamberlain identified many of the very reasons why he was chosen: "I never thought of claiming any special merit, nor tried to attract attention in any way, and believed myself to be socially unpopular among the 'high boys.' I had never indulged in loose talk, had minded my own business, did not curry favor with newspaper reporters, did not hang around superior headquarters, and in general had disciplined myself in self-control and the practice of patience, which virtue was not prominent among my natural endowments." Most significant, however, was that Chamberlain was aware that, in being selected to preside at the formal surrender of the Army of Northern Virginia, he and the Fifth Corps had been granted an honor and a privilege to be accepted "not as for any preeminent work or worth of ours, but in the name of the whole noble Army of the Potomac; with loving remembrance of every man, whether on horse or foot or cannon-caisson, whether with shoulder-strap of office or with knapsack of every man, whether his heart beat high with the joy of this hour, or was long since stilled in the shallow trenches that furrow the red earth from the Antietam to the Appomattox!"[5]

Chamberlain was described as a man of medium height, his form being perfectly proportioned, well-knit, neither slender nor stout, and always erect and graceful. Morris Schaff accurately explained what made Chamberlain the right choice to lead the formal surrender ceremony:

Appomattox Courthouse, Virginia (present day), the spot at which Chamberlain ordered a salute of Confederate soldiers and Gordon ordered his men to return the salute (author's photograph).

"[T]he selection of Chamberlain to represent the Army of the Potomac was providential, in this, that he, in the way he discharged his duty, represented the spiritually-real of this world. And by this I mean the lofty conceptions of what in human conduct is manly and merciful, showing in daily life consideration for others, and on the battlefield, linking courage with magnanimity and sharing an honorable enemy's woes."[6]

Gordon would lead the Confederate procession to stack arms and lay down battle flags. His task was not enviable in the least. Gordon could not forget the emotions of his soldiers:

> When the proud and sensitive sons of Dixie came to a full realization of the truth that the Confederacy was overthrown and their leader had been compelled to surrender his once invincible army, they could no longer control their emotions, and tears ran like water down their shrunken faces. The flags which they still carried were objects of undisguised affection. These Southern banners had gone down before overwhelming numbers; and torn by shells, riddled by bullets, and laden with the powder and smoke of battle, they aroused intense emotion in the men who had so often followed them to

victory. Yielding to overpowering sentiment, these high-mettled men began to tear the flags from the staffs and hide them in their bosoms, as they wet them with burning tears. A great majority of them were duly surrendered; but many were secretly carried by devoted veterans to their homes, and will be cherished forever as honored heirlooms.

On many a battlefield, Gordon had spoken to his men, suppressing their natural fears and inspiring them with their passion and thoughts of loyalty for and love of the South and the defense of their families back home. As he had led them into victory, now he must lead them in defeat. Gordon proved no less effective in consoling men's grief than he had been in rousing their emotions for battle. The following words were delivered to one of his brigades prior to the formal surrender:

> Headquarters, Second Corps
> Army of Northern Virginia
> April 11, 1865
>
> In parting with the Louisiana Brigade of this army I cannot omit to offer this tribute which is due to as heroic a devotion as ever illustrated the armies of any people. Coming with glorious ardor into the support of a cause seemed in itself doubly consecrated to-day by its dead. You have carried your enthusiasm into a hundred battles, filling your comrades and your countrymen with pride and your enemy with fear. Steady and unshaken have you passed throughout the struggle with untarnished record. Your name is without the shadow of a stain. Your conduct in the closing hour is as lofty as when with full ranks you struck and exulted in victory. Take with you, soldiers, in parting, the unfeigned admiration of my heart.
>
> J.B. GORDON
> Major-General, Commanding Second Corps[7]

Chamberlain's men formed for the surrender ceremony at sunrise on April 12, 1865, four years to the day after the Civil War began. Though given command of the Third Brigade for this day, he would, in effect, lead the entire First Division. The Third Brigade, facing north, was aligned down the principal street from the bank of the Appomattox River on the right to the courthouse on the left. Slightly behind the Third Brigade, the First Brigade was posted, while the Second Brigade formed on the opposite side of the street facing the Third. They watched as the Army of Northern Virginia broke camp for the last time and slowly formed ranks. Gordon's Second Corps had been assigned the lead in the surrender column. Chamberlain saw "[t]he dusky swarms forge forward into gray columns of march. On they come, with the old swinging route step and swaying battle-flags." Chamberlain was greatly impressed by the momentous occasion and determined to mark it accordingly. For as he noted, "Our acquaintance had been peculiarly intimate and deep, and we had for them a strong personal regard. The 'causes' were wide apart, but the manhood was the same."[8]

Although Thomas Chamberlain believed Gordon was the best-looking soldier he had ever seen, he did not appear so on this occasion. Gordon's head was bowed, with downcast eyes and an expression of supreme dejection. The defeated Confederate army followed him in silence. Some looked defiant, others apathetic, while others, as Gordon, were understandably depressed. Chamberlain was posted on the extreme right of the Third Brigade, and Gordon approached from Chamberlain's right. As he neared, Chamberlain turned and gave the command for the bugler to sound the "carry arms" — the marching salute.[9] Chamberlain described the moment that Gordon neared his position:

> Instructions had been given; and when the head of each division column comes opposite our group, our bugle sounds the signal and instantly our whole line from right to left, regiment by regiment in succession, gives the soldier's salutation ... the marching salute. Gordon at the head of the column, riding with heavy spirit and downcast face, catches the sound of shifting arms, looks up, and taking the meaning, wheels superbly, making with himself and his horse one uplifted figure, with profound salutation as he drops the point of his sword to the boot toe; then facing to his own command, gives word for his successive brigades to pass us with the same position of the manual — honor answering honor. On our part not a sound of trumpet more, nor roll of drum; not a cheer, nor word nor whisper of vain-glorying, nor motion of man, standing again at the order, but an awed stillness rather, and breath holding, as if it were the passing of the dead!

For his unexpected and uplifting show of respect, Gordon called Chamberlain "[o]ne of the knightliest soldiers of the Federal army." Gordon described the exchange of salutes as "a token of respect from Americans to Americans, a final and fitting tribute from Northern to Southern chivalry."[10] Chamberlain, who had not requested permission for the salute, was well aware that his action might engender criticism, and he sought no forgiveness. He explained that he did not salute the Confederate cause: "Before us in proud humiliation stood the embodiment of manhood: men whom neither toils and sufferings, nor the fact of death, nor disaster, nor hopelessness could bend from their resolve; standing before us now, thin, worn, and famished, but erect, and with eyes looking level into ours, waking memories that bound us together as no other bond;— was not such manhood to be welcomed back into a Union so tested and assured?" The Union soldiers had won and they celebrated the end of the war, though not the defeat of so worthy an adversary.[11]

The ceremony lasted all day. The Confederate units marched between

Chamberlain's men and halted, maintaining good order despite their weariness and hunger. They fixed bayonets on their muskets and stacked arms, then hung their cartridge boxes on the pile. It was most difficult for the Confederate soldiers to part with their flags. Chamberlain watched as, "lastly — reluctantly, with agony of expression — they tenderly fold their flags, battle-worn, and torn, blood-stained, heart-holding colors, and lay them down; some frenziedly rushing from the ranks, kneeling over them, clinging to them, pressing them to their lips with burning tears." Sometimes, as Gordon noted, they ripped the flags from their staffs, tore them and hid the pieces in their shirts. Though the Union men held steady in their lines, Chamberlain noticed that they, too, were moved by the scene. He saw face muscles twitch and tears fall on their battle-bronzed cheeks.[12]

As one weeping Confederate delivered his flag, he poured out his emotions in seemingly agitating words: "Boys, this is not the first time you have seen that flag. I have borne it in the front of battle on many a victorious field and I had rather die than surrender it to you." Chamberlain could see that the man did not wish to offend and only described what every Union color-bearer felt about the significance of his own flag. Chamberlain responded in words of understanding and consolation: "My brave fellow, I admire your noble spirit, and only regret that I have not the authority to bid you keep your flag and carry it home as a precious heirloom."[13]

As the soldiers of the Union and the Confederacy passed almost within arm's length of one another, they looked into each other's eyes and thought of prior battles where they had met: Manassas (twice), the Peninsula, Antietam, Fredericksburg, Chancellorsville, Gettysburg, the Wilderness, Spotsylvania Courthouse, Cold Harbor, and Petersburg. When Chamberlain saw John Bell Hood's men, he remembered how the 20th Maine struggled with regiments from that division at Little Round Top on July 2, 1863. More than 270 men of the 15th and 47th Alabama who had fought that day surrendered to Chamberlain and the Third Brigade on April 12, 1865. He wondered whether some of the men marching past him now were present at Rives' Salient on June 18, 1864, when a minie ball from one of their rifles almost took his life. Nevertheless, it was not hatred but compassion that filled his heart: "We could not look into those brave, bronzed faces, and those battered flags we had met on so many fields where glorious manhood lent a glory to the earth that bore it, and think of personal hate and mean revenge."[14] Perhaps Morris Schaff summed it up best:

> It was not mere chance that Chamberlain was selected, and that he called on the famous corps to salute their old intrepid enemy at this last solemn ceremonial. Chance, mere chance! No, for God, whenever men plough the

fields of great deeds in this world, sows seed broadcast for the food of the creative powers of the mind. What glorified tenderness that courtly act has added to the scene! How it, and the courage of both armies, Lee's character and tragic lot, Grant's magnanimity and Chamberlain's chivalry, have lifted the historic event up to a lofty, hallowed summit for all people. I firmly believe that Heaven ordained that the end of that epoch-making struggle should not be characterized by the sapless, dreary commonplace; for with pity, through four long years, she had looked down on those high-minded, battling armies, and out of love for them both, saw to it that deeds of enduring color should flush the end.[15]

Gloriously, the war was over. Yet, for Chamberlain, it also brought sadness. Serving as a Union soldier had given meaning to his life. Now, he said, "We are left alone, and lonesome. We miss our spirited antagonists in the game, and we lose interest. The weight is taken out of the opposite scale, and we go down. Never are we less gay." The euphoria that victory brought to the Union soldiers was short-lived when, on April 16, news reached them of the assassination of President Lincoln. For Gordon, defeat was bad enough. Now the South would face the repercussions of a United States government vehemently angry about both the Civil War and the assassination of the man who held the country together during its most trying time.[16]

Chapter 2

Early Years

Joshua Lawrence Chamberlain was born in Brewer, Maine, on September 8, 1828, the first of five children begotten by Joshua Chamberlain and Sarah Dupee Brastow. Originally "Lawrence Joshua," he changed the order in adulthood to Joshua Lawrence, the name by which history knows him. His family, though, called him Lawrence throughout his life. Chamberlain's famous military career was foreshadowed by his ancestors. His mother's father and grandfather and his paternal grandfather and uncles served as soldiers in the American Revolution. Chamberlain's father served as a lieutenant colonel of militia in the bloodless Aroostook War, and he wanted his eldest son to also follow a military career. However, Chamberlain's mother intended a spiritual path. In retrospect, it is clear that both parents influenced the man Chamberlain would become — a determined and focused, yet compassionate and understanding soldier.[1]

Chamberlain's early years were spent working the family farm, clearing fields for plowing, chopping wood, and harvesting. He learned to shoot and hunt but never enjoyed killing. He was undoubtedly influenced by his father's direct approach to problem solving. Once faced with an immovable rock, the no-nonsense response Chamberlain received upon appealing to his father for advice was simply, "Move it!" He learned that failure was simply not an option, so he found a way to move the rock. His desire for help in clearing the wheel of a wagon stuck between two large stumps met with the same blunt answer.

Chamberlain remembered and valued the life lessons he learned from these incidents. His leadership on the battlefield would reflect his awareness of the need to coolly assess his situation, and the realization that he alone was responsible for arriving at and implementing a solution to the problem at hand.[2]

In accordance with his father's intended career path, Chamberlain attended Whiting's Military and Classical School at the age of 14. Despite his father's hope that this experience would lead to the United States Military Academy at West Point, Chamberlain leaned toward his mother's desire that he would become a minister, though not in the traditional sense. He wanted to become a missionary in a foreign country where he could teach and spread the word of Christianity. Before he could enter a theological seminary, however, it was necessary to acquire a college education. Bowdoin College in Brunswick was his choice.[3]

Entry into Bowdoin required a knowledge of Greek. Chamberlain already spoke French, a compulsory subject at Whiting, and some Latin, but he knew no Greek. With the same concentrated determination he would later direct toward military tactics and strategy, he learned Greek and was accepted into Bowdoin in February 1848 at the age of 19. Chamberlain did very well in college, overcoming a tendency to stammer when pronouncing certain words. This impediment contributed to his shyness, and his eventual ability to overcome it undoubtedly increased his self-confidence and further strengthened his character.[4]

Chamberlain's college life at Bowdoin was almost short-lived. He and some classmates, many of whom had been drinking, were reported to college faculty by local citizens offended by their impudent behavior. Bowdoin's President Leonard Woods questioned Chamberlain about the incident and the participants. Chamberlain, who had attempted to minimize the

Joshua L. Chamberlain, 1859 (George J. Mitchell Department of Special Collections & Archives, Bowdoin College Library, Brunswick, Maine).

disruption, denied that he engaged in objectionable behavior but, honoring his loyalty to his classmates, refused to identify those who had. Declaring that Chamberlain's reluctance rose from a false sense of honor, President Woods suspended him from school. Chamberlain's classmates refused to allow him to suffer the fate they deserved and belatedly confessed. President Woods relented on Chamberlain's punishment, imposing only a reprimand on the participants.[5]

During his time at Bowdoin, Chamberlain attended the First Parish Church, near the campus. Another who attended that church was Harriet Beecher Stowe, wife of Bowdoin professor Calvin Stowe. It was in March of 1851, as Harriet Beecher Stowe attended a communion service there, that she became inspired to write *Uncle Tom's Cabin*. Her depiction of slavery contributed to the ever-increasing tension between North and South that would culminate in the American Civil War. Chamberlain was among a group of young people who visited the Stowe home to listen to Mrs. Stowe read from her work. The extent to which his views about slavery were influenced by Harriet Beecher Stowe is unknown. What is certain is that Chamberlain's attention was strongly drawn to the adopted daughter of the church pastor.[6]

Frances Caroline Adams, Fanny as she was called, was born August 12, 1826, to elderly Ashur Adams and Amelia Wyllys Adams of Boston. Inexplicably, they sent Fanny at an early age to live with and to be raised by Dr. George E. Adams, Ashur Adams' nephew, and his wife, Sarah Ann Folsom, in Brunswick. Dr. Adams was, thus, Fanny's cousin, but he and Sarah loved Fanny as their own child. In his junior year at Bowdoin, Chamberlain courted and soon fell deeply in love with Fanny, and she with him. The courtship

Fanny Chamberlain (George J. Mitchell Department of Special Collections & Archives, Bowdoin College Library, Brunswick, Maine).

Chamberlain residence, Brunswick, Maine (George J. Mitchell Department of Special Collections & Archives, Bowdoin College Library, Brunswick, Maine).

met with the disapproval of Dr. Adams but neither Chamberlain nor Fanny could be dissuaded. Chamberlain's plan was to graduate from Bowdoin, enter Bangor Theological Seminary and marry Fanny.[7]

In the fall of 1852, Chamberlain and Fanny became engaged, and he entered the seminary. She then departed for Milledgeville, Georgia, where she pursued her interest in music by giving voice and piano lessons. They would not see each other again for almost three years. During this time, Fanny, in part to advance the date of their marriage and in part due to her reluctance to be the wife of a minister, encouraged Chamberlain to seek a career other than the ministry. Her efforts came to nought, and Chamberlain graduated from the seminary in August 1855. Near the beginning of August 1855, Fanny returned to Brunswick.[8]

Though prepared for the religious life as a minister, Chamberlain returned to Bowdoin to represent his class and give the Master's Oration at commencement. His presentation on "Law and Liberty" so impressed the Bowdoin faculty and administration that he was invited to become an instructor in logic and natural theology for the 1855-56 school year. Chamberlain accepted. He would remain at Bowdoin until 1862, later teaching rhetoric and oratory and becoming a professor of modern languages.[9]

On December 7, 1855, Chamberlain and Fanny were married by Dr. Adams in the First Parish Church of Brunswick. Their first child, Grace Dupee, called Daisy by Chamberlain, was born October 16, 1856. After the loss of a second child, Harold Wyllys was born to Chamberlain and Fanny on October 10, 1858. To accommodate his new family, Chamberlain purchased a home close to the campus, previously occupied by Henry Wadsworth Longfellow and his bride. Even with the advent of the Civil War in 1861, little changed for Chamberlain and his family until mid-1862. Then, the quiet life of this seminarian turned college professor would change dramatically and forever.[10]

John Brown Gordon was born in Upson County in central Georgia on February 6, 1832, to Zachariah and Malinda Cox Gordon and was the fourth of their twelve children. In addition to being a prominent Baptist minister, Zachariah owned and ran a large plantation. Around 1840, Zachariah moved his family to Walker County near Lafayette in northwestern Georgia, where he built a summer resort hotel. Gordon Springs, as Zachariah named it, became a popular destination for visitors wishing to take advantage of the medicinal value of springs on the property. Ironically, the area came to be better known for one of the bloodiest battles of the Civil War. More than 35,000 Union and Confederate soldiers suffered as casualties at the Battle of Chickamauga, a battle fought September 19 and 20, 1863, in the fields where John Brown Gordon spent his adolescent years.[11]

Fanny Gordon about 1850 (John Brown Gordon papers, Manuscript, Archives and Rare Book Library, Emory University).

Dissatisfied with the education John received from area schools, Zachariah established his own school for his son's instruc-

John B. Gordon, date unknown (Civil War Collection, Prints & Photographs Division, Library of Congress, LC-DIG-cwpb-06185).

tion. From there, Gordon attended Pleasant Green Academy and then the University of Georgia. So well had he performed at the academy he entered the University of Georgia as a second semester sophomore. One of his specialties was oration, an attribute that would serve him well in his years as a leader of soldiers in the Civil War. Despite his excellent scholastic record, Gordon left the University of Georgia in the fall of his senior year in 1852, presumably to help his father with family business affairs. In 1854,

Gordon moved to Atlanta, where he studied law and passed the bar, never having obtained a college degree. He joined a law firm but did not practice law for long. His brief association with the firm led, however, to one of the greatest joys of his life. There he met Fanny Rebecca Haralson, the sister-in-law of a partner in the firm. After a short courtship, Gordon, at the age of 22, married Fanny on September 18, 1854, Fanny's 17th birthday.[12]

In late 1855, Gordon left the practice of law and became a journalist in Milledgeville, then Georgia's capital. Ironically, Gordon and Fanny moved to Milledgeville shortly after Chamberlain's Fanny, after living three years there, moved from Milledgeville back to Brunswick. Journalism as a profession for Gordon was also short-lived. In March 1856, Gordon and Fanny resettled in northwestern Georgia, where Gordon and his father formed the Castle Rock Coal Company. Although mining was an industry, not yet well-developed, Gordon prospered. The mountainous areas of northwestern Georgia, northeastern Alabama and eastern Tennessee, where Gordon lived and worked, included few slaveholders and few slaves. Nevertheless, when tensions over slavery increased, Gordon used his oratory skills to speak out in favor of the right of Southerners to retain their slaves. He believed that slavery was "morally, politically and socially right."[13]

In July 1860, months before Abraham Lincoln was elected president of the United States, Gordon spoke at Oglethorpe University near Milledgeville, declaring, "African slavery is the mightiest engine in the universe for the civilization, elevation and refinement of mankind — the surest guarantee of the continuance of liberty among ourselves. Then let us do our duty, protect our liberties and leave the consequences with God, who alone can control them." He envisioned that in the not too distant future the Southern flag would fly from the Gulf of Panama to the coast of Delaware, over Cuba, and even from the "guilded turrets of Mexico's capitol." Gordon believed "the well clad, well fed, Southern Christian slave shall beat his tamborine and banjo amid the orange-bowered groves of Central America." He foresaw the need for successful resistance to the aggressions of the North. As the voices in the South advocating secession grew louder in early 1861, Gordon used his oratorical skills in both Alabama and Georgia to convince Southerners that their liberty was at stake.[14]

Chapter 3

Outbreak of the War

While, to this day, the debate over the cause of the Civil War depends upon whether one favors the North or the South, Gordon acknowledged, after the war, an important fact: "[I]t is fair to say that had there been no slavery there would have been no war." In postwar reconciliation years, Gordon perhaps stated most succinctly what each side believed as the Civil War began:

> The South maintained with the depth of religious conviction that the Union formed under the Constitution was a Union of consent and not of force; that the original States were not the creatures but the creators of the Union; that these States had gained independence, their freedom, and their sovereignty, from the mother country, and had not surrendered these on entering the Union; that by the express terms of the Constitution all rights and powers not delegated were reserved to the States; and the South challenged the North to find one trace of authority in that Constitution for invading and coercing a sovereign State.
>
> The North, on the other hand, maintained with the utmost confidence in the correctness of her position that the Union formed under the Constitution was intended to be perpetual; that sovereignty was a unit and could not be divided; that whether or not there was any express power granted in the Constitution for invading a State, the right of self-preservation was inherent in all governments; that the life of the Union was essential to the life of liberty; or, in the words of Webster, "liberty and union are one and inseparable."[1]

In his retrospective wisdom, Gordon concluded that "both sides fought and suffered for liberty as bequeathed by the Fathers — the one for liberty in the union of the States, the other for liberty in the independence of the States."[2]

In the Democratic convention of 1860, Northern Democrats wanted persons in territories to decide for themselves whether to allow slavery. Southern Democrats, on the other hand, sought a platform provision guaranteeing that property rights of slaveholders would be respected in the territories. The difference could not be reconciled, resulting in the splitting of the Democratic Party between North and South, and paving the way for the election of the Republican candidate for president, Abraham Lincoln, who was perceived throughout the South as a threat to the institution of slavery.

Lincoln was elected in November 1860, and the first Southern state to leave the Union, South Carolina, seceded in December. Lincoln was undoubtedly opposed to slavery, and Southerners viewed this opposition as a direct threat to slavery and their way of life. In an effort to defuse Southern fears, Lincoln, in his first inaugural address, made it clear: "I have no purpose, directly or indirectly, to interfere with the institution of slavery in the states where it exists. I believe I have no lawful right to do so, and I have no inclination to do so." Nevertheless, Lincoln was adamant that expansion of slavery into the territories would not be permitted. Despite his efforts at appeasement, the cry for secession rose throughout the South. In a stance far stronger than his views on slavery, Lincoln was unwavering in his conviction that no state had the right to secede, and he vowed to use his power and authority to maintain the Union.

Thus the stage was set, and emotion prevailed over reason. Southern troops under the command of General P.G.T. Beauregard surrounded Fort Sumter in Charleston Harbor, South Carolina, and demanded its surrender. Major Robert Anderson, Beauregard's artillery instructor at West Point and the commander of the garrison, refused and, on April 12, 1861, at 4:30 A.M., the Civil War began when the Confederates bombarded the fort. The battle lasted barely a day and was essentially bloodless, ending when Major Anderson, short on ammunition and supplies and with little hope of reinforcement, surrendered the fort. Lincoln then called for the states to supply troops to put down the rebellion. That request led Virginia, Arkansas, Tennessee and North Carolina to join South Carolina in secession.

Gordon believed strongly that the property rights of Southerners in their slaves must be protected to allow continuation of the institution and its expansion into the territories. He saw a threat to slavery as a threat to Southern liberty. Following the election of Abraham Lincoln, the governments of Alabama and Georgia considered the monumental issue of secession. Gordon spoke to the delegates of both states encouraging Southern independence. As did most Southerners, Gordon perceived that Lincoln's election constituted a direct threat to slavery in the South. Because, for him, this threat undermined Southern liberty, secession was necessary to protect Southern rights.

As far as Gordon was concerned, the union formed under the Constitution was a union of consent, the states retained the right to withdraw from that union, and the federal government had no right to coerce any state into maintaining the union. Alabama seceded on January 11, 1861, and Georgia followed soon thereafter, on January 19. In response to the attack on Fort Sumter, Lincoln called for 75,000 volunteers to put down the rebellion. For Southerners who were reluctant to secede or engage in war with the United States, this call pushed them over the edge. It was now a matter of defending the South.[3] In his *Reminiscences*, Gordon wrote as follows:

> There was at the outbreak of the war a class of men both North and South over whose inconsistencies the thoughtful, self-poised, and determined men who did the fighting made many jokes, as the situation grew more serious. It was that class of men in both sections who were most resolute in words and most prudent in acts; who urged the sections to the conflict and then did little to help them out of it; who, like the impatient war-horse, snuffed the battle from afar — very afar but who, when real war began to roll its crimson tide nearer and nearer to them, came to the conclusion that it was better for the country, as well as for themselves, to labor in other spheres; and that it was their duty, as America's great humorist put it, to sacrifice not themselves but their wives' relations on patriotism's altar.

Gordon was not one of those men. He knew it was his duty to fight for the newly formed Confederate States of America. Yet, he was concerned for the welfare of his wife and young sons. Fanny settled the dilemma for him. Feeling a sense of duty to her husband as strong as Gordon felt to the South, she left their two sons with Gordon's mother and went to war with her husband. Her presence was a joy and inspiration to Gordon throughout the war, and with tender care, she would nurse him back to health from several battle wounds.[4]

In April 1861, Gordon helped raise and organize a volunteer company of mountaineers from Georgia, Alabama and Tennessee. They named themselves the Raccoon Roughs, no doubt because of the coonskin caps most of them wore. As was the custom among volunteers, officers were elected by their men. Gordon was elected captain. As Gordon observed, "Not a man in the company had the slightest military training, and the captain himself knew very little of military tactics." Accustomed to horseback, the Raccoon Roughs wanted to join the cavalry but were told no cavalry was required. So, they reluctantly abandoned their horses and agreed to join the infantry. Nevertheless, on their way to Milledgeville to enlist, the group was told by the Georgia governor that no more volunteers were needed. While Gordon was willing to acquiesce in the order to return home, his men revolted, uncoupling the homebound train cars from the engine. As Gordon recalled, "There was no course left me but to march them through the streets of Atlanta to a camp on the outskirts. The march, or rather struggle, through that city was a sight marvelous to behold and never to be forgotten. Totally undisciplined and undrilled, no two of these men marched abreast; no two kept the same step; no two wore the same colored coats or trousers. The only pretence at uniformity was the rough fur caps made of racoon skins, with long, bushy, streaked racoon tails hanging from behind them."

They then telegraphed the governors of several states, requesting leave to volunteer with a regiment from whomever would have them. Their persistence paid off when Governor A.B. Moore of Alabama agreed to incorporate the Raccoon Roughs into one of his state's volunteer regiments — the 6th Alabama. Gordon was unanimously elected major of the 1400-man regiment on May 14, 1861. In addition to being accompanied by his wife, Gordon was also joined by his brothers, Eugene and Augustus, who enlisted in the 6th Alabama and went to war for the South.[5]

On their way from Atlanta to Montgomery, Alabama, the Raccoon Roughs encountered, as Gordon called it, "one unbroken scene of enthusiasm." Large crowds of Southerners met the soldiers at every train depot, greeting them with cheers and singing verses of "Dixie" and the "Bonnie Blue Flag." At one stop, Gordon was presented with a flag on which were the words "No Retreat." As the captain, he was compelled to respond, in turn, with assurances that his men would live up to those words. Gordon recounted the following:

> My men applauded and sanctioned this outburst of inconsiderate enthusiasm, but we learned better after a while. A little sober experience vastly modified and assuaged our youthful impetuosity. War is a wonderful developer, and destroyer, of men; and our four years of tuition in it equalled in both these particulars at least 40 years of ordinary schooling. The first battle carried us through the rudimentary course of a military education; and several months before the four years' course was ended, the thoughtful ones began to realize that though the expense account had been great, it had at least reasonably well prepared us for final graduation, and for receiving the brief little diploma handed to us at Appomattox.[6]

Gordon and the Raccoon Roughs traveled first to Montgomery, Alabama, then, in late May 1861, to Corinth, Mississippi, for training. It did not last long. On June 4, the regiment was ordered to Richmond. As they traveled through eastern Tennessee and Kentucky, they experienced the division that civil war portended. Some people cheered, while others jeered. Houses on one side of the street flew the flag of the Confederacy, while houses on the other side proudly displayed their loyalty to the United States. In Virginia, Confederate forces were gathering at Manassas Junction in preparation for what would be the Battle of Bull Run, or First Manassas, on July 21, 1861. The 6th Alabama became part of the Second Brigade of the First Corps. The brigade commander was Brigadier General Richard S. Ewell.[7]

The Union army marched out of Washington, D.C. to confront a smaller Confederate force at Manassas Junction, against the wishes of the Union commander, Brigadier General Irvin McDowell. Believing that his men were insufficiently trained to engage in combat, McDowell unsuccessfully sought more time to prepare his army. As Lincoln noted, "You are green, it is true, but they are green also." General Beauregard, the Confederate hero of Fort Sumter and a classmate of McDowell's at West Point, commanded the Confederate forces at Manassas.[8]

With news of the upcoming battle, Washingtonians, dressed in their Sunday best, rode on horses and in carriages west 30 miles to watch, bringing their picnics with them. Although the battle began well for the North, unbeknownst to McDowell, a Confederate force in the Shenandoah Valley escaped the Union force which was intended to hold them at bay. The Confederates arrived at Manassas as the battle began. The Battle of Bull Run, or First Manassas, resulted in a full-scale rout of the Union army back to Washington, D.C., soldiers and civilians competing for space on the road.[9]

While Gordon and his regiment were present for the battle, they saw little of it. They reconnoitered, moved into position to fight, and redeployed, but they were not engaged. The regiment would not "see the elephant"—as soldiers called going into battle for the first time—until the following spring. After First Manassas, Gordon and his men remained in the area of Bull Run, training and preparing a camp for the winter months. Meanwhile, Gordon taught himself the art of war and tactics. After being elected lieutenant colonel by the men of the 6th Alabama, the Alabama governor appointed him to that rank on December 26, 1861.[10]

The views of Chamberlain on slavery were consistent with those of Lincoln. He considered it repugnant but also considered outright abolition an infringement of the property rights of Southern slaveholders. As did Lincoln, he supported limiting the reach of slavery. And as did most Northerners, Chamberlain would probably not have gone to war for the sole purpose of freeing the slaves. He noted, "We would not right the wrong at the cost of Country. Loyalty to freedom was held in abeyance by loyalty to the Union."

At least initially, the men who volunteered to become soldiers of the United States did so primarily, if not almost exclusively, to preserve the Union. While Gordon and Southerners saw Lincoln as a threat to slavery and to the liberty of the South, Chamberlain, along with most Northerners, saw secession as an attempt to destroy the United States: "There was no war between the States. It was a war in the name of certain States to destroy the political existence of the United States." In his view, "the flag of the Nation had been insulted. The honor and authority of the Union had been defiled. The integrity and the existence of the People of the United States had been assailed in open and bitter war."[11]

Whereas Gordon saw no choice but to fight for the South, Chamberlain felt compelled to fight to preserve the Union. He could not tolerate the thought of secession: "There was a boastful pretense that each State held in its hands the death-warrant of the Nation; that any State had a right, without show of justification outside of its own caprice, to violate the covenants of the constitution, to break away from the Union, and set up its own little sovereignty as sufficient for all human purposes and ends; thus leaving it to the mere will or whim of any member of our political system to destroy the body and dissolve the soul of the Great People." Some students at Bowdoin answered Lincoln's call for volunteers before Chamberlain; but as the war entered its second year, and it was apparent that it would not be short, duty called Chamberlain to act.[12]

Early in July 1862, Lincoln requested 300,000 more volunteers to sign up for three years in the Union army. Fearing that the Bowdoin trustees would not give him permission to join, Chamberlain opened the door for himself when he accepted a new position at Bowdoin that included a two-year leave of absence in Europe. With this ace up his sleeve, Chamberlain wrote to Governor Israel Washburn of Maine and offered his services. The governor immediately responded favorably, offering Chamberlain command of a regiment and the rank of colonel.

During the Civil War, men of rank on both sides thought highly of themselves and some often went to great means to achieve positions of power despite being unfit. Unlike others with little or no military background who seized the opportunity for high rank and command responsibility for selfish reasons, Chamberlain acknowledged his own lack of experience and declined the colonelcy. He did agree to accept the lesser rank of lieutenant colonel, a position that would allow him to learn from a more qualified military man.[13]

On August 8, 1862, Governor Washburn offered Chamberlain a commission as the lieutenant colonel of the newly formed 20th Maine, a regiment composed of the excess of volunteers for four regiments — the 16th, 17th, 18th and 19th Maine — which constituted Maine's quota to fulfill Lincoln's call for troops. Chamberlain accepted. Despite the efforts of the Bowdoin administration to prevent Chamberlain from using his leave of absence for military service, he insisted he was joining the army nonetheless. Undoubtedly possessing mixed emotions of sadness and trepidation upon leaving his young family, yet also feeling excitement and satisfaction that he was fulfilling his duty to his country, Chamberlain, at the age of 33, bade goodbye to his children and traveled to Portland.[14]

Lt. Col. Chamberlain arrived in Portland on August 18. With him was his brother, Sergeant Thomas Chamberlain, and approximately 980 officers and men of the 20th Maine. Fortunately for the Chamberlain brothers and the other men of the 20th Maine, command of the regiment was given to Colonel Adelbert Ames, an 1861 graduate of West Point, whose service at the Battle of Bull Run had earned him a minie ball through the thigh and the Medal of Honor. The volunteers were undisciplined, disorganized, and, like Chamberlain, lacked military training. When Ames exclaimed, "This is a hell of a regiment!," he was not being complimentary.[15]

Ames' methods of training and discipline were often considered harsh, and some wondered if he would not die in battle from a misdirected shot from one of his own men. However, once the 20th Maine experienced the fright and confusion of war, they developed an appreciation for Ames' heavy-handed methods, which prepared them as soldiers. Ames was Chamberlain's military mentor, and he spent many evenings instructing his novice lieutenant colonel in military tactics. Despite Chamberlain's lack of military knowledge and experience, Ellis Spear of the 20th Maine noted that he was "a man of such intelligence and urbanity and kindliness of feeling that he exerted a useful influence even in the organization of the regiment."[16]

Fanny went to Portland to say good-bye to Chamberlain. Despite her expressed wish to join him at the front, Fanny Chamberlain, unlike Fanny Gordon, would not accompany her husband during the war. From Portland, the 20th Maine, in uniform but with no arms, traveled by rail to Boston, then by steamer to Alexandria, Virginia, outside Washington, arriving September 7, 1862. In Washington, they marched to the United States Arsenal, where each man was given an Enfield rifle and 40 rounds of ammunition. They camped at Fort Craig on Arlington Heights and were assigned to the Third Brigade of the First Division of the Fifth Corps of the Army of the Potomac. With the 20th Maine in the Third Brigade were the 12th, 17th and 44th New York regiments, the 83rd Pennsylvania Regiment, and the 16th Michigan Regiment. Chamberlain and the 20th Maine would remain in Washington only a few days before receiving orders to march westward, toward an impending battle near Sharpsburg, Maryland, on Antietam Creek.[17]

CHAPTER 4

The Peninsula Campaign

Gordon's men spent the winter in quarters in the dense pine thickets on the rough hills bordering the Occoquan River southeast of Manassas. The Virginia winter was harsh, and the Southerners, accustomed to milder temperatures, "suffered greatly," according to Gordon. Illness, such as measles, was rampant. Supplies had to be gathered from the countryside. The soldiers lacked heavy clothing needed to combat the bitterly cold nights. Gordon noted, "Perhaps the utter lack of preparation for the war on the part of the South is proof that its wisest statesmen anticipated no such stupendous struggle as ensued."

The spring of 1862 brought fairer weather and the movement of the Union army, now designated the Army of the Potomac, under the command of Major General George B. McClellan. Shortly after the disaster at Manassas, the 34-year-old McClellan was appointed by Lincoln to the head of all Union armies. Though McClellan would prove weak as a field commander, his skills in organizing and training the Union army in Washington were exceptional. As McClellan observed, "The defeated army of McDowell was only a collection of undisciplined, ill-officered and uninstructed men, who were, as a rule, demoralized and ready to run at the first shot." He restored order in the ranks and imposed strict discipline, and, in the process, earned the men's respect and admiration. McClellan took a beaten army of 50,000 men and molded them into a proud, battle-ready force of almost 170,000.[1]

The goal of the Union forces would be the Confederate capital at Richmond. Faced with a choice between a direct overland route from Washington and McClellan's preference for an advance to the Virginia Peninsula by water, the Federal government approved the latter approach. In late March 1862, McClellan took an army of 100,000 soldiers — the

4. The Peninsula Campaign

remainder being held back for the protection of the Federal capitol — down the Potomac River through the Chesapeake Bay to Fort Monroe at the tip of the Peninsula. He planned to proceed northeast past Yorktown and Williamsburg to Richmond. Strong Confederate fortifications, and McClellan's propensity to grossly overestimate the number of men he faced, allowed Confederate commander Major General John Magruder and his overmatched force to hold McClellan at Yorktown throughout the month of April. On April 6, Gordon and the 6th Alabama boarded a train for Yorktown and helped improve the Yorktown defenses. The train, which also carried Fanny Gordon, was hit head-on by a train moving in the opposite direction, killing and maiming several Confederate soldiers but sparing the Gordons.[2]

Confederate commander Major General Joe Johnston reinforced Magruder but soon realized he would be unable to withstand the artillery bombardment McClellan had prepared. On May 4, 1862, the Confederates withdrew up the Peninsula toward Richmond. The Confederate army marched slowly due to excessive rain and mud. During the withdrawal, Gordon demonstrated the humility that contributed to his greatness as a soldier and his status as a beloved commander. Gordon's regiment marched at the rear of the Confederate column. Because of their position, Gordon's men were often called upon to move an artillery piece stuck in the Virginia mud. Knowing that Federal troops were following closely behind, slowing their march was unnerving. Coming upon some of his men attempting to unloose a gun, Gordon dismounted his horse, waded through the mud and joined in, to the cheers and increased efforts of his men. As a consequence of Gordon's willingness to do what was expected of a common soldier, there was never, thereafter, any hesitation by his men to jump into the water and mud when such was required. On the same march, Gordon found one of his youngest soldiers lying on the roadside weeping. His feet were in terrible condition, and the young man feared his inability to march would lead to his capture. Determined that the lad would not fall into Union hands, Gordon ordered the boy to mount his horse and ride ahead until he found an ambulance or a wagon, then tell the quartermaster to send the horse back as soon as possible.[3]

As the Union army marched up the Virginia Peninsula and approached the Confederate capitol, McClellan attempted to broaden his front by sending two Federal corps across the Chickahominy River. When a downpour made the river impassable, Johnston realized an opportunity and attacked the isolated Union force at Seven Pines, also known as Fair Oaks, on May 31. In April, Gordon had been unanimously elected colonel of the

6th Alabama, which was now part of the brigade of Brigadier General Robert E. Rodes. At Seven Pines, Colonel Gordon led them into battle for the first time.[4]

Gordon used his oratory skills to prepare his apprehensive troops for battle, reminding them of Union atrocities and the cause for which they fought. Upon his command, Gordon's men deployed as skirmishers for the brigade near the Williamsburg Road. Once the entire brigade was on the field, Rodes ordered Gordon to move to the extreme right of the Confederate line. The first Federal line was forced to retreat. After re-forming, Rodes attacked the second Federal line with greater difficulty. As Gordon rode along his line pressing his men forward, he passed the prostrate figure of his 19-year-old brother, Captain Augustus Gordon, who had been shot through the lungs and was badly bleeding, but Gordon could not stop. Augustus would recover, only to be mortally wounded at the Battle of Chancellorsville in May 1863.[5]

Most of the officers of the 6th Alabama were shot down. As the last officer mounted, Gordon attracted the attention of Union sharpshooters who could be heard exclaiming, "Shoot that damn Colonel!" Gordon himself was not hit but his horse was killed and bullet holes in his uniform evidenced how close death had come. The 6th Alabama encountered heavy musketry on its right and front, then on the rear of its right wing. Faced with fire from several sides, Gordon ordered his men to lie down. The right flank of the regiment was unsupported and suffered terribly from Union troops taking advantage of the weakness.

Using his newly learned knowledge of military tactics, Gordon refused (bent back) the flank to provide some protection, but the Union fire was devastating. Ultimately, the Confederate troops were forced to withdraw, with Gordon being placed in temporary command of the entire brigade due to the wounding of Rodes. Being the most junior regimental commander in the brigade, Gordon found his selection to be "unexpected ... unwelcome and extremely embarrassing." Nevertheless, it demonstrated the high regard in which he was held by his superiors. His humility endeared him to his peers, who took no offense at the choice.[6]

The Battle of Seven Pines was a Confederate defeat. The 6th Alabama lost nearly 60 percent of the men it took into the fight, which Gordon referred to as "one of the bloodiest of my war experience." Gordon's inspection of the field revealed a "sickening and shocking" scene. Soldiers in blue and gray floated side by side in the Chickahominy's flooded swamps. Successive and continuous fighting often led to hasty and imperfect burials. As Gordon relates it, his unit was assigned to camp at a portion of the field where fighting had been intense. He laid down to sleep with his head on a slight mound of dirt and was soon fast asleep. During the night, he frequently brushed away what he thought was a twig or limb. Upon waking, he learned to his horror that the object was the hand of a dead soldier sticking out from the shallow grave that had been Gordon's pillow.[7]

During the fighting, Fanny Gordon was not far away. Accompanied by her uncle, Major John Sutherland Lewis, Fanny could only watch and listen as the Battle of Seven Pines raged. Major Lewis wrote:

> The battle in which Mrs. Gordon's husband was then engaged was raging near the city with great fury. The cannonade was rolling around the horizon like some vast earthquake on huge crashing wheels. Whether the threads of wedded sympathy were twisted more closely as the tremendous perils gathered around him, it was evident that her anxiety became more and more intense with each passing moment. She asked me to accompany her to a hill a short distance away. There she listened in silence. Pale and quiet, with clasped hands, she sat statue-like, with her face toward the field of battle. Her self-control was wonderful; only the quick-drawn sigh from the bottom of the heart revealed the depth of emotion that was struggling there. The news of her husband's safety afterward and the joy of meeting him later produced the inevitable reaction. The intensity of mental strain to which she had been subjected had overtasked her strength, and when the excessive tension was relaxed, she was well-nigh prostrated; but a brief repose enabled her to bear up with a sublime fortitude through the protracted and trying experiences which followed the seven days' battle around Richmond.[8]

Despite the repulse of the Confederate forces at Seven Pines, the battle proved to be a momentous event for the Confederacy. Johnston was seriously wounded, and General Robert E. Lee, up to now an adviser to the Confederate president, Jefferson Davis, replaced Johnston as commander of the Confederate army. Rather than act in an effort to exploit this change, McClellan hesitated, believing, based upon faulty intelligence reports, that the Confederate army of 65,000 to 70,000 men actually numbered close to 200,000, twice that of the Union army. McClellan went on the defensive and sought reinforcements. Meanwhile, audacious Lee planned his attack.[9]

On June 26, 1862, the first day of what came to be known as the Seven Days' Battle, Lee attacked the Union right flank north of the Chickahominy at Mechanicsville, on the outskirts of Richmond. Although the attack was unsuccessful, Lee planned a renewal of fighting the next day. That night, McClellan moved his troops to a new position near Gaines' Mill. Lee attacked on June 27 with more favorable results, though once again Confederates sustained more casualties than the Federals. Gordon and the 6th Alabama, in the center of the Confederate line, advanced through thick woods and swamp only to find themselves isolated from the remainder of their brigade. They received enfilading fire, and, unable to effectively respond, Gordon again ordered his men to lie down. When reinforcements failed to arrive, Gordon knew he must withdraw. As the firing slackened, he calmly led his regiment back to the shelter of the swamp.[10]

After Gaines' Mill, the remainder of the Union forces north of the Chickahominy crossed the river to join with those units to the south. Despite counsel from some subordinates to attack the Richmond defenses, McClellan, fearing a disaster, ordered a retreat. Lee doggedly pursued the Union forces. Confederates attacked at Savage Station on June 29 and at White Oak Swamp on June 30, again with no decisive result. By July 1, McClellan's army had reached Harrison's Landing on the James River where transports could extricate them from the certain defeat McClellan believed awaited if they remained.[11]

Lee made one last try at Malvern Hill, a disastrous decision for the Southern troops. Crowded along the hill were four corps of Union troops with massive numbers of artillery poised wheel to wheel to meet the Confederate assault. Adding to Union firepower were Federal gunboats on the James. An attempt to soften the Union position with Confederate artillery was a dismal failure, as Union guns pounded Rebel batteries into oblivion. Nevertheless, an infantry assault would be attempted. Three days earlier, Rodes again was forced to relinquish command of the brigade to Gordon. In a battle report, he noted that Gordon's conduct was "distinguished for all that a soldier can admire." The brigade was part of the division of General D.H. Hill, which was ordered forward with nothing but open field between them and the powerful Union batteries 700–800 yards away.[12]

The Confederate attack up the hill was met with devastating artillery and rifle fire. In his memoirs, Gordon stated that, within 15–20 minutes, half of the men of the 3rd Alabama, the regiment with which he moved, were either dead or wounded. One shell in his immediate presence killed six or seven men. Of D.H. Hill's division, one brigade retreated in disorder while another was streaming to the rear. Only Gordon and his brigade continued to move forward. They advanced to within two hundred yards of the Union batteries, but grapeshot and canister made it impossible to proceed. He, once again, wisely ordered his men to lie down and open fire. They exchanged fire with two Union infantry regiments under the command of Colonel Francis C. Barlow. (Gordon and Barlow would cross paths again at Antietam, Gettysburg and Spotsylvania.) Gordon, however, remained standing, walking among his men to provide encouragement in the difficult situation. An artillery shell exploded nearby, temporarily blinding him with dirt and sand. The handle of one of Gordon's pistols was shattered, his canteen was pierced, and the front of his coat was torn away. Yet, Gordon himself was not wounded. When expected support failed to arrive, the Confederates withdrew under cover of darkness. At the end of the day, 5000 more Confederate casualties could be counted. Nearly half of Gordon's brigade were killed or wounded.[13]

The Battle of Malvern Hill ended the fighting on the Peninsula. Lee had secured the defense of Richmond. McClellan and the Army of the Potomac remained at Harrison's Landing until August, then boarded transports on the James River and returned to the vicinity of Washington. For most of July and August, the armies remained relatively quiet. On August 29 and 30, the armies met again at Manassas Junction to fight the Second Battle of Bull Run, or Second Manassas. A Union army under Major General John Pope was defeated by combined Confederate forces under Major General Thomas J. "Stonewall" Jackson, Major General A.P. Hill, and Major General James Longstreet, and once again the Northern troops scurried back to Washington. Gordon and his men did not participate in the battle, remaining with D.H. Hill's division in the Richmond vicinity.[14]

CHAPTER 5

Antietam

Recognizing that the Confederate army could not remain inactive after its victory at the Second Battle of Bull Run, Lee chose to advance the army north into Maryland. The Washington defenses were too strong to attack; and retreat, never an option at the front of Lee's mind, brought its own disadvantages. Also, Lee felt that a move into Maryland would be a good opportunity for Jefferson Davis to make a peace proposal to Washington based upon permanent separation of the North and South.

Invasion of Maryland also had several practical advantages. The army needed provisions, and the unspoiled Maryland countryside offered a plentiful supply. Lee also determined that a march into Maryland would require pursuit by the Federal army, minimizing the threat of another advance on Richmond. It was hoped that the presence of Lee's army in Maryland would convince the people of that state to join the Confederate cause. So, on September 4, 1862, less than a week after their victory at Manassas, the Army of Northern Virginia, comprising about 50,000 effectives, began crossing the Potomac River into Maryland. By September 6, the Army of the Potomac, with McClellan at its head, was marching to meet Lee.[1]

Lee's judgment regarding the wisdom of invading Maryland was uncharacteristically flawed. More than a few Confederate soldiers refused to cross into Maryland, having joined the army to defend the South, not to invade the North. The reception by Marylanders was hardly warm. While there were most certainly Southern sympathizers in Maryland, Union sentiment was greater. As Gordon later recounted, "The Confederate graves which were dug in Maryland's soil vastly outnumbered the Confederate soldiers recruited from her citizens." Many Marylanders with no strong allegiance to one side or the other viewed Lee's invasion as an encroachment on their neutrality.[2]

To remove threats to the rear of the army, Lee, against the advice of Longstreet, divided his forces, sending Stonewall Jackson to Harpers Ferry where 11,000 Union soldiers were garrisoned. Meanwhile, Longstreet moved to Boonesboro with four divisions, supported by D.H. Hill's division which had rejoined the Army of Northern Virginia after Second Manassas. Lee, with nine brigades, marched to Hagerstown. While the Confederate army was camped near Frederick, Maryland, Special Orders No. 191, which encompassed Lee's overall plan and detailed the movements of the respective parts of the Confederate army, was distributed to the affected commanders.[3]

On September 7, the Army of Northern Virginia camped at Frederick, Maryland, and remained there for three days. When they marched away, little did Lee know — and horrified he would be to find out — that a copy of Special Orders No. 191 was lying in a field, wrapped around three cigars. On September 12, the Army of the Potomac approached Frederick, settling down in the surrounding fields. On the next morning, the prized tobacco was found by two Indiana soldiers who soon recognized the significance of the paper, entitled "Headquarters, Army of Northern Virginia, Special Orders 191." Within an hour, Lee's entire plan, the most important the fact that he had divided his army into several parts, was known to McClellan. Once he was assured the order was legitimate, McClellan confidently proclaimed, "Here is a paper with which if I cannot whip Bobby Lee I will be willing to go home." The gift order did not result in the destruction of Lee's army and, eventually, Lincoln would indeed send McClellan home.[4]

Unwilling to act rashly, now that he knew exactly what to do, McClellan and the Army of the Potomac slowly moved toward the Confederate forces at Boonesboro. On September 14, a full day after discovering Lee's plan, Union forces marched up the slopes toward Turner's and Crampton's Gap on South Mountain. Guarding Turner's Gap, D.H. Hill and his division of 2300 Confederates, including Gordon and the 6th Alabama in Rodes' brigade, watched Federal columns totaling 70,000 soldiers heading in their direction — the remainder moving toward Crampton's Gap. The numbers grossly favored the Federal army but the terrain favored defense.[5]

Rodes' brigade of 1200 Alabamians, including Gordon and the 6th Alabama, had the weighty responsibility of holding high ground overlooking Turner's Gap. Rodes defended the Confederate left, and Gordon's men held the very end of the Southern flank. Although reinforcements had arrived with Longstreet, they were too exhausted to provide much help. A Union division under Brigadier General George Gordon Meade attacked the Confederate flank but was repeatedly repulsed by Gordon and the 6th Alabama. Eventually, overwhelming numbers of Federal forces penetrated the Confederate ranks and threatened the rear of Rodes' brigade, forcing them to fall back, one-third of the brigade being killed, wounded or captured. Gordon's regiment alone remained intact thanks to his steadfast courage and unwavering leadership. The Battle of South Mountain ended with Confederate forces still in control of the mountain passes. The valiant Confederate defense, for which they suffered dearly, bought valuable time for Lee, who, having learned from a Southern sympathizer at McClellan's headquarters about the discovery of Special Orders No. 191, now acted quickly to consolidate his forces. The place chosen for the army to reunite was Sharpsburg, Maryland, on Antietam Creek.[6]

The Army of the Potomac began arriving at the Antietam on September 15. At the same time, the Union garrison at Harpers Ferry, Virginia, surrendered to Jackson's forces. While Jackson, with three divisions, immediately marched toward Sharpsburg, another Confederate division under A.P. Hill remained in Harpers Ferry to parole the thousands of Federal

Bloody Lane, Battle of Antietam (present day), taken from the approximate location of Gordon's position (author's photograph).

prisoners. Lee deployed his army in a line almost four miles long, with Jackson on the left and Longstreet on the right, in a predominantly north-south direction along the Hagerstown Pike facing east. The cavalry of Major General J.E.B. Stuart was placed at Nicodemus Heights on the northern portion of the field to the west of the pike. The Army of the Potomac gathered on the east side of the Antietam and would cross the creek using the upper, middle and lower bridges.[7]

Lee was in a precarious position. His army, with about 40,000 soldiers, numbered less than half of the 87,000 available to McClellan and had their backs to the Potomac River, a short distance away. Except at certain points, the river was too deep to be crossed by infantry. Defeat and rout of the Confederate army could result in, at the least, temporary disorganization of the army or, at the worst, its total destruction. Lee counted on McClellan's caution, and McClellan did not disappoint him. The advantage gained by discovery of Special Orders No. 191 had been lost, as Lee's forces were given time to rejoin. Despite the numeric disadvantage, Lee and his ragtag Confederate army prepared for battle. Through the 16th, forces of the Army of Northern Virginia and the Army of the Potomac — all Americans — gathered for what would become, and remains, the bloodiest day in American history.[8]

The Battle of Antietam, which Gordon described as leaving a "lasting impress[ion] upon my body as well as my memory," was fought on September 17, 1862, in three distinct parts. McClellan started the battle from the north with the First Corps under Major General Joseph Hooker, while the Twelfth Corps under Major General Joseph K.F. Mansfield remained in reserve. Hooker attacked the Confederate left flank with his three divisions down the Hagerstown Pike through the North Woods and East Woods past the Miller cornfield toward the Dunker Church. The attack began shortly after 6:00 A.M.

As Hooker approached the Miller cornfield, he noticed the bayonets of Confederate soldiers extending above the tall stalks of corn. Artillery was summoned that raked the field with shell and canister. The effect was devastating, as pieces of men and equipment flew into the air. In Gordon's words, "McClellan's compact columns of infantry fell upon the left of Lee's lines with the crushing weight of a landslide." Federal troops then advanced south through the cornfield and saw the Dunker Church ahead, only to be driven back by a charge out of the west woods from the brigades of Brigadier General John Bell Hood at 7:00 A.M. Possession of the cornfield would change hands several times during the morning fighting.[9]

Even with the addition of the Twelfth Corps under Mansfield, who was shot and killed when he mistook Rebel forces for his own, the Union forces could not reach the Dunker Church. The Union Second Corps under Major General Edwin Vose "Bull" Sumner were brought forward. Shortly after 9:00 A.M., he struck from the east woods across the Hagerstown Pike, only to be hit squarely on the flank by Confederates in the west woods under Major General Lafayette McLaws, who had been sent to reinforce Jackson. Because of his weaker forces, Lee spent much of the day pulling units from one part of the field to another wherever the Union pressure was strongest. More than 2,000 men out of 5,000 in the division of Major General John Sedgwick were shot down in 20 minutes. Union troops which had advanced westward toward the Hagerstown Pike and the Dunker Church were forced to fall back.[10]

Withdrawal of Sedgwick's division effectively ended the fighting on the northern side of the field. Both sides were decimated. In less than 4 hours of fighting, three Union corps, totaling 31,000 men, suffered nearly 7,000 casualties, while Confederate casualties on Jackson's part of the field, where his overall numbers were considerably less, exceeded 5,000.

Riding along the rebel lines on the right and center, Lee suspected that the next Federal blow would fall upon the Confederate center. And so it did. The battle now shifted to the center where the division of D.H. Hill occupied a sunken lane near the Samuel Mumma farm, a track forever known thereafter as Bloody Lane. Colonel Alfred Colquitt's brigade was placed on the left, and Brigadier General George B. Anderson's brigade was on the right. In the middle was Rodes' brigade with Gordon and the 6th Alabama. Gordon's troops held the most advanced position with no supporting line behind them.[11]

Confronting the Confederates from the northeast was the division of Brigadier General William H. French, also of Sumner's Second Corps. The approach of French's division to the sunken road required them to march up and over a ridge. The Federal soldiers would be unable to see the Rebels until they crested the ridge, less than 100 yards from the sunken lane. The road ran west to east, then turned southeast. In addition to the protection provided by the road itself, Confederate soldiers stacked the rails of split-rail wooden fences to build breastworks. With Hill's division, four brigades of Major General Richard H. Anderson's division crowded into the sunken road. Approximately 2,500 of Hill's Confederates faced about 5,700 of French's Federals. French began his attack at 9:30 A.M., followed an hour later by another of Sumner's divisions under Major General Israel Richardson. What the Union soldiers would see as they marched in formation, with their flags flying, up and over the ridge, was a mass of Confederate rifles loaded, primed, cocked, and aimed directly at them.[12]

From his position near the salient, where the sunken road turned east to southeast, Gordon could see both armies and the entire field. He realized that, in his advanced position, his force would receive the initial impact of the Federal assault. Prior to French's attack, D.H. Hill and Lee, who believed that the next attack would fall on his center, rode along the line. Using the oratorical skills that served him well throughout the war, Gordon spoke to Lee, but loud enough for his men to hear, intending his words to strengthen the resolve of his men: "These men are going to stay here, General, till the sun goes down or victory is won." Soon after Lee rode away from the front, the battle in the center began. Gordon saw French's troops form an assaulting column four lines deep and, with perfect precision and bayonets gleaming, move to the attack. He thought it a "pity to spoil with bullets such a scene of martial beauty." But that is exactly what he knew he must do.[13]

The actions of the Union commander indicated to Gordon that French intended to rely on a bayonet charge, and his first thought was to fire upon the mass of Federal troops as soon as they came within range. However, aware of the vast number of Federal soldiers advancing on his position, Gordon determined that it would be far more effective to wait until the men were very close. He correctly perceived that the Federal lines would not withstand the sudden shock of withering fire opened at point-blank range. Gordon's men were advised not to fire until they heard the order from him. Gordon described the stillness as "literally oppressive" as Federal soldiers continued their march toward his position, while the tension among his own men made it difficult for them to wait for Gordon's command.[14] As the Federal forces approached within 30 paces of his line, Gordon shouted, "Fire!" He described the effect:

> My rifles flamed and roared in the Federals' faces like a blinding blaze of lightning accompanied by the quick and deadly thunderbolt. The effect was appalling. The entire front line, with few exceptions, went down in the consuming blast. The gallant commander and his horse fell in a heap near where I stood — the horse dead, the rider unhurt. Before his rear lines could recover from the terrific shock, my exultant men were on their feet, devouring them with successive volleys. Even then these stubborn blue lines retreated in fairly good order. My front line had been cleared; Lee's centre had been saved; and yet not a drop of blood had been lost by my men. The result, however, of this first effort to penetrate the Confederate centre did not satisfy the intrepid Union commander. Beyond the range of my rifles he reformed his men into three lines, and on foot led them to the second charge, still

with unloaded guns. This advance was also repulsed; but again and again did he advance in four successive charges in the fruitless effort to break through my lines with the bayonets. Finally his troops were ordered to load. He drew up in close rank and easy range, and opened a galling fire upon my line.[15]

In the first Union volley, a North Carolina colonel with whom Gordon was talking was shot through the head, while Gordon was hit by a ball in the calf of his right leg — the first of five wounds he would sustain that day. Federal troops were now subjecting Confederates in the sunken road to a deadly cross-fire, from the north and the east. Both Union and Confederate soldiers stood in the open firing at one another, without the protection of breastworks. Gordon was next shot higher up in the right leg but remained at his post. He limped along the line, giving encouragement to his men. As he did so, he passed an old man and his son, lying side by side. The son was dead, and the father was dying. He called to Gordon, "Here we are. My boy is dead, and I shall go soon; but it is allright."[16]

The next ball struck Gordon's left arm, mangling tendons and muscle. His men saw blood dripping from Gordon's fingers and pleaded with him to go to the rear. He refused. "I could not consent to leave them in such a crisis," he said later. A fourth shot tore through his left shoulder, leaving its base and a wad of clothing in its path. Incredibly, Gordon was still able to stand and walk but realized that his strength was waning due to loss of blood. At that moment, he recalled his assurance to Lee that he and his men would not abandon that post. Believing that the right of his line was wavering, Gordon struggled toward that position when he was shot in the left cheek. The ball passed through and out of his jaw, just missing his jugular vein. Gordon fell forward, unconscious, with his face in his cap. Blood filled the hat and would have drowned Gordon but for a Federal shot fired earlier in the fight that left a hole in his hat through which the blood drained out.[17]

The loss of Gordon proved disastrous for the Confederates still fighting in the sunken road. Command of the 6th Alabama passed to Lt. Colonel James Lightfoot. To counter a destructive fire from Federals on high ground overlooking the road, Rodes ordered Lightfoot to pull back the right two companies of the 6th Alabama. Lightfoot misunderstood the order and directed his men to face about and march out of their position in the sunken road, toward the Piper farm. The 5th Alabama on the left of the 6th Alabama followed, and soon all of Rodes' five brigades were moving to the rear. Troops from Richardson's division surged into the gap in the Confederate line, and the Southerners' position in the sunken road was lost. They retreated toward the Piper farm. One of the Union commanders who exploited the Southern withdrawal was Colonel Francis C. Barlow, in joint command of two New York regiments. He and Gordon would later meet on the field at Gettysburg with their roles reversed — Gordon advancing as Union soldiers retreated, while Barlow lay, with an apparently mortal wound, on the ground.[18]

Meanwhile, Gordon, alone and lying in the sunken road, regained sufficient consciousness to consider whether he was still alive. Finding that he was able to move his leg, Gordon crawled 100 yards to the new but temporary Confederate line. From there, he was carried from the field by litter. His part in the Battle of Antietam was over. The Federal advance reached as far south as the Piper farm but was stopped with artillery and infantry rallied by Longstreet and D.H. Hill. Neither side could make any further headway. Richardson ordered his men back across Bloody Lane to safety beyond the ridge to be resupplied with ammunition and await reinforcements. The attack would not be renewed. Richardson was mortally wounded by an artillery shell, and orders from Union headquarters ended the fight in the center. It was shortly after 1:00 P.M. Bloody Lane had cost the rebels almost 2,600 killed and wounded, approximately one out of every three soldiers engaged. In the divisions of French and Richardson, 509 were dead and over 2,200 were wounded. According to one of Gordon's officers, he could have walked on the dead bodies of Gordon's men from one end of the line to the other.[19]

Gordon awoke later that evening lying on a pile of a straw in an old barn, which served as a hospital for Confederate wounded. His physician attempted to reassure him that the outlook was hopeful but Gordon knew the doctor did not believe it. Gordon reassured him: "You think I am going to die; but I am going to get well." Despite the reluctance of doctors to permit Fanny Gordon to be with her husband, she was soon at his side. Gordon was concerned about the impact his appearance would have on his wife: "My face was black and shapeless — so swollen that one eye was entirely hidden and the other nearly so. My right leg and left arm and shoulder were bandaged, and propped with pillows." To allay the anticipated shock, Gordon sought to reassure her: "Here's your handsome husband; been to an Irish wedding."[20]

Fanny bravely suppressed a scream. She then went to work, and she worked throughout the time Gordon's condition was critical, remaining at his bedside to provide nourishment, a task made more difficult because Gordon's jaw was rendered immobile. Even Gordon's confidence in his recovery was tested when he developed erysipelas on his left arm. During the Civil War, erysipelas, an infectious skin disease, killed 40 percent of the soldiers afflicted with it. The doctors advised Fanny to paint iodine around the affected area three to four times per day. Gordon recollected that she applied the treatment three to four hundred times each day. Even after his life was no longer in danger, recovery would take months. Fanny was with her husband every step of the way. Gordon said, "Under God's providence, I owe my life to her incessant watchfulness, night and day, and to her tender nursing through weary weeks and anxious months."[21]

In his report after the Battle of South Mountain, D.H. Hill stated, "Colonel [J.B.] Gordon, the Christian hero, excelled his former deeds at Seven Pines and in the battles around Richmond. Our language is not capable of expressing a higher compliment." Hill referred to Gordon as the "Chevalier Bayard" of the army. Rodes, too, cited Gordon as deserving special mention for "admirable conduct" and "customary gallantry" at Antietam. After the battle, Lee recommended that Gordon be promoted to brigadier general and given command of a brigade. However, the Confederate war department did not immediately confirm the promotion in light of the uncertainty of Gordon's recovery and the fact that Colonel Alfred Colquitt had been placed in charge of the brigade to be assigned to Gordon, who would spend the next seven months recuperating.[22]

The Battle of Antietam now entered its third and final phase. On Antietam Creek, south of Sharpsburg, was the narrow, stone Rohrbach Bridge. Major General Ambrose E. Burnside's Ninth Corps, 14,000 strong, was designated to cross the bridge and assault Lee's right flank. It was McClellan's intention that the crossing be accomplished early in the day. However, repeated efforts by Union troops were beaten back by a group of 500 Georgians under the command of Brigadier General Robert Toombs. The Confederates were posted on the wooded bluff directly opposite the approaching Federals in protected positions with an excellent line of sight at anyone attempting to approach and cross the bridge.[23] At about 1:00 P.M., two regiments were called upon to charge the bridge—the 51st New York and the 51st Pennsylvania. Up to that point, Union troops had approached the bridge by following the road next to the creek, making them easy targets for Toombs' rifles. Now, the plan was changed. The 51st New York and the 51st Pennsylvania would attack straight down a hill to the bridge.

The liquor ration of the 51st Pennsylvania had previously been suspended by the brigade commander, Brigadier General Edward Ferrero, for misconduct. When told of its assignment, one soldier asked if the whiskey ration of the regiment would be returned if they took the bridge. "Yes, by

God!," answered Ferrero. And so they did, and so it was. The successful crossing of the bridge — known thereafter as the Burnside Bridge — forced the Confederates to retreat. Soon, the Ninth Corps was across Antietam Creek. But it would be nearly 3:00 P.M. before they advanced toward Sharpsburg.[24]

The right flank of the Army of Northern Virginia was beginning to collapse under the weight of Union advance. Union soldiers were fighting in Sharpsburg and had advanced to within one-half mile of the road that represented Lee's route of escape over the Potomac. At his headquarters, Lee looked to the south and noticed the dust of an approaching column of soldiers. What he saw was the division of A.P. Hill, whose forced march from Harpers Ferry, where they had remained to parole captured Federal prisoners, brought them upon the flank of the Union's Ninth Corps at a critical moment. Burnside's troops, whom McClellan had declined to reinforce, were driven back to the bridge. The delay in effecting a crossing and in advancing upon Sharpsburg had provided A.P. Hill with just enough time to march the 17 miles from Harpers Ferry. As the sun finally went down on September 17, 1862, the Battle of Antietam drew to a close.[25]

On the 18th, the armies did not engage. The Army of Northern Virginia, which probably should have withdrawn, remained in place. McClellan, too concerned about losing despite his continued numerical superiority, chose not to renew the attack. On September 19, Lee withdrew from Maryland back into Virginia, crossing the Potomac at Shepherdstown. The Battle of Antietam became, and remains, the bloodiest day in American history. Of the Army of the Potomac, over 2,100 were dead, 9,500 were wounded, and 750 were missing, a total casualty count of 12,400. Confederate losses, as best as could be determined, were over 1,500 dead, 7,750 wounded and 1,000 missing, a total of 10,300. Combined casualties exceeded 22,700.[26]

Antietam would be the first major battle seen by Chamberlain and the 20th Maine, though they were never in it. Similar to that of Gordon and the 6th Alabama, the initial training of Chamberlain and the 20th Maine had been exceedingly brief. When it was learned that Lee and the Army of Northern Virginia had crossed the Potomac River and entered Maryland, the Union army marched out of Washington on September 12, 1862. The first march of the 20th Maine would not be easy. Ranks were in disorder and files were broken. Soldiers limped and staggered along as the army marched mile after mile day after day. Many strong men dropped out.[27]

Camped near Frederick on the fourteenth, the 20th Maine could hear the battle for the South Mountain passes. As they approached the battle-scarred slopes of South Mountain, they saw Rebels, a group of prisoners, for the first time — "tall, lank, slouchy looking fellows, clad in dirty gray uniforms." Soon they saw their first real signs of war — ground and trees torn by shells and buildings pocked by rifle fire. Then they saw the human toll — wounded soldiers, surgeons at work amputating arms and legs, and fresh graves of Union dead. Confederate bodies remained where they fell. Chamberlain would never forget the sight of one of the dead Confederates — a boy, no more than 16, with his back against a tree and a Bible in his hand. It was difficult for Chamberlain to comprehend that this boy was his enemy, and he prayed for God's forgiveness for those who made it so.[28]

Upon its arrival at Sharpsburg, the 20th Maine with the Fifth Corps was posted in reserve on the east side of the Antietam behind Middle Bridge. According to the recollections of Private Theodore Gerrish, they possessed a clear view of the battle. Chamberlain and the 20th Maine watched as Hooker and Hood's men fought through the Miller cornfield and the fields near the west woods and the Dunker Church. They saw the fight for Bloody Lane and the Burnside Bridge. Chamberlain and the 20th Maine were formed and advanced to reinforce the Union right but were returned to their original position without engaging. Finally, they saw A.P. Hill from Harpers Ferry strike the Federal left and drive them back to Antietam Creek and recognized that but for reinforcements the day could have been a Union victory. But the Fifth Corps was never employed in the battle.[29]

The 20th Maine was, however, engaged as Lee and the Army of Northern Virginia withdrew to Virginia at Shepherdstown. On September 19, a portion of the Fifth Corps was sent to pursue Lee's retreating army. Many Union soldiers, including the 20th Maine, reached the west bank of the Potomac River but were met by intensive Confederate fire from the bluffs above. Even as Chamberlain's men attempted to cross, other Union soldiers were returning to the east side of the Potomac to escape a counterattack by the Rebels. An order finally came for the 20th Maine to recross. As Chamberlain supervised the retreat from the middle of the river, his horse was shot from under him, the first of several times this would happen in Chamberlain's Civil War career. Union artillery supported the withdrawal, and Chamberlain was able to return his men to the Maryland side with only a few wounded. The 20th Maine returned to Sharpsburg. The Battle of Antietam was now officially over.[30]

Before the Army of the Potomac departed Sharpsburg, Lincoln paid a visit to McClellan and was a guest at Fifth Corps headquarters. Chamberlain and his men had the opportunity to see him up close, his rugged features and his deep, sad eyes. Chamberlain recalled, "The men conceived sympathy and an affection for him that was wonderful in its intensity." Lincoln was given a grand review of the army and, Chamberlain observed, "He took in everything with earnest eyes." As Lincoln's party passed in front of Chamberlain and his men, Chamberlain recalled "he checked his mount to draw McClellan's attention to my horse, whose white-dappled color and proud bearing made me almost too conspicuous on some occasions."[31]

Five days after the battle, Lincoln issued the Emancipation Proclamation. Lincoln had contemplated issuing the proclamation for some time but was advised to wait for a military success before doing so. Antietam was certainly not a clear-cut Union victory, but it was close enough. As of January 1, 1863, "all persons held as slaves within any State or designated part of a State the people whereof shall then be in rebellion against the United States, shall be then, thenceforward, and forever free." It was strictly intended as a military measure to lessen the use of slaves in support of the Confederate cause.[32]

As Lincoln himself stated, restoration of the Union, not abolition of slavery, was his primary goal: "If I could save the Union without freeing any slave, I would do it; and if I could save it by freeing all the slaves, I would do it; and if I could save it by freeing some and leaving others alone, I would also do that. What I do about slavery and the colored race, I do because I believe it helps save the Union." Militarily, his action had a more immediate consequence. Issuance of the Emancipation Proclamation foreclosed any possibility that England or France would enter the war on the side of the Confederacy. Despite condemnation of the proclamation, from those in the North who either had no desire to free the slaves or who felt that the proclamation did not go far enough, and those in the South who felt that their reasons for seceding were now fully justified, from September 22, 1862, a Federal victory meant both that the Union would be restored and that slaves would be freed.[33]

Chapter 6

Fredericksburg

The end of the Battle of Antietam meant that the 20th Maine would now get the training Col. Ames knew they needed. Chamberlain worked hard, studying every military work he could find. He spent evenings with Colonel Ames learning the art of war. While military life was a chore and inconvenience to many, for Chamberlain it was an awakening. He readily adapted to military life and found it far more enriching than his life as a professor at Bowdoin. He saw his worth as an officer and appreciated the responsibilities his position carried. Chamberlain felt alive. In a letter to Fanny, he wrote, "I have my care and vexations but let me say no danger and no hardship ever makes me wish to get back to that college life again. I can't breathe when I think of those last two years. Why I would spend my whole life in campaigning, rather than endure that again." He recognized that military service was a sacrifice and might ultimately result in his death or disability, but he felt he was where duty called him.[1]

For its part, the regiment learned how to handle weapons and how to march into battle formation. Ames' harshness, while initially prompting the enmity of his men, eventually transformed the 20th Maine into a battle-ready regiment, instilling pride in themselves as soldiers. The soldiers of the 20th Maine also admired their lieutenant colonel. Corporal William Livermore, no doubt expressing the sentiments of many, referred to Chamberlain as "one of the finest men that ever lived.... He is full of military, brave but considerate and treats the men like men not like dogs.... He don't say go boys but come. Why! would you believe if he had some breastworks to throw up and what did he do but off his coat and into it himself." In late October, they marched from Sharpsburg through Harpers Ferry, Virginia. In November, their path led through Warrenton and then to

Fredericksburg. They camped on Stoneman's Switch near Falmouth across the Rappahannock River from Fredericksburg.[2]

The march to Fredericksburg was ordered by the new commander of the Army of the Potomac, Major General Ambrose Burnside. Lincoln had endured enough of McClellan. On October 1, Lincoln had visited McClellan at Sharpsburg to prompt a movement of the army but the general insisted he needed time to prepare. A telegram from General-in-Chief Henry Halleck, after Lincoln returned to Washington, instructing McClellan to cross the Potomac and fight Lee met with no results. Lincoln also wrote a letter encouraging McClellan to act. Still, McClellan, asking for more horses and for more men to fight the Confederate army he was sure outnumbered him, did not respond until October 27. By the time the Army of the Potomac marched toward Warrenton, Lee had moved the Army of Northern Virginia to Culpepper to block McClellan's previously unobstructed path to Richmond. Nothing remained of the relationship between commander and commander-in-chief. On November 5, 1862, Lincoln issued orders removing McClellan from command of the Army of the Potomac, supplanting him with Burnside.[3]

Burnside had not sought the position and insisted that he was not qualified to hold it. His self-deprecating modesty was not encouraging to Chamberlain and the Union army. Coming events would substantiate Burnside's opinion of his own lack of abilities. But, to Lincoln's satisfaction, Burnside did have a plan and was ready to act. He formed the Army of the Potomac into three Grand Divisions under Hooker, Sumner and Major General William B. Franklin and intended to cross the Rappahannock at Fredericksburg, then move south and threaten Richmond.[4] Despite the soundness of the plan and Lincoln's admonishment that Burnside act quickly, circumstances worked against him. The pontoons needed for the army to cross the river were delayed. By the time they arrived on November 25, Lee and his army had occupied Fredericksburg and established an elevated and formidable defensive position on Marye's Heights, west of town. The Confederate line extended southeast to the Rappahannock. With his path now blocked and Lee's army entrenched, Burnside would have been wise to abandon the Fredericksburg crossing. Instead, he persisted in his plan, resulting in one of the most lopsided and bloody defeats the Union army would suffer in the entire war.[5]

Early on the morning of December 11, 1862, Union engineers began laying the pontoon bridge which would lead directly into the town of Fredericksburg. The effort did not go uncontested. Sixteen hundred Mississippians under Brigadier General William Barksdale were posted in the brick houses on the west bank of the Rappahannock. Before daybreak, when the Confederate riflemen could judge by sound the approximate location of the Union pontoon builders, they opened fire. Time and time again, the Union engineers would drop their tools, retreat, run back, then attempt to resume their work, only to be forced back to the east shore. When Federal artillery fire did nothing to drive the Mississippi soldiers from their posts, three Union regiments used the pontoons to cross the river and eventually drive the Confederates out of the town. But this process took an entire day. Not until December 12 were the pontoon bridges completed and the first wave of Union troops across the river into Fredericksburg.[6]

The battle of Fredericksburg was fought on Saturday, December 13, 1862. Longstreet's divisions on the left of the Confederate position defended 5 miles of Lee's seven-mile line, including Marye's Heights. Jackson's men extended the line southeastward toward the Rappahannock, while the cavalry of Major General J.E.B. Stuart guarded Jackson's right flank. An attack by a Union division under Major General George Gordon Meade made a temporary breakthrough on the Union left in Jackson's line but was forced back. The bulk of the fighting, or slaughter as it is more accurately described, occurred on the Union right and the Confederate left where Longstreet's men held Marye's Heights.[7]

To get to that position, Union forces marched west from the town itself, across a plain which consisted mainly of open ground that provided little protection, either natural or manmade. A swell in the ground partway up the slope offered minimal shelter. At the base of Marye's Heights ran a slightly sunken road bordered by a stone wall four feet high facing the attackers. Confederates standing four to five rows deep were posted behind the wall. To make matters worse, Confederate infantry and artillery were situated to provide crossing lanes of fire. On almost any point on the field, Union soldiers would be subjected to fire from one side or the other, or both. Chamberlain readily recognized that "[t]he ground afforded every advantage for his artillery, both for cover and efficiency, and enabled him to dispose his whole line so as to bring a front and flank fire upon any assault of ours." As Major E. Porter Alexander, the chief of Confederate artillery on this part of the field, noted to Longstreet, "General, we cover that ground now so well that we will comb it as with a fine-tooth comb. A chicken could not live on that field when we open on it." To Lee's satisfaction, Burnside was not deterred.[8]

The Union attack on Marye's Heights began around 11:30 A.M. As the first wave moved toward the stone wall, a Confederate volley rang out.

6. Fredericksburg

As Chamberlain and the 20th Maine, which had been held in reserve with the Fifth Corps, watched from the east side of the Rappahannock, Private Theodore Gerrish of the 20th Maine described what they saw: "Men fell by hundreds, battalions melted away, the line was shattered, it staggered then halted, and the next moment fell back repulsed." Chamberlain stated that the federal line fell "as if swallowed up in the earth, the bright flags, quenched in gloom, and only a writhing mass marking that high-tide halt of uttermost manhood and supreme endeavor." The Union soldiers charged again and were destroyed again. They attacked a third time "as though they were breasting a storm of rain and sleet, their faces and bodies being only half turned to the storm, with their shoulders shrugged." Not a single Union soldier reached within 50 yards of the wall. A fourth and fifth charge later in the afternoon met with similar results.[9]

Preparing to face real combat for the first time, Chamberlain found the waiting carried its own stress:

> Waiting and watching, intent and anxious, stirred by the pulse of manhood and the contagion of comradeship, conscious of strength to help, but forbidden to strike, all this wears sorely on every generous spirit. And that other not unmanly impulse — if the worst is coming, let us meet it — may have its part, too, in the drama. It is really less trying to go in first and deliver your blow in the flush of spirit and strength, with the feeling that if the worst comes you will be reenforced or "relieved," than to be held back till some dire disaster calls, when the life and death grapple clinches and you must recover the lost ground or die trying. Or, on the other hand, to be called to advance in triumph over a field already carried — something then is lacking to the manly sense of service rendered according to strength.

Then came the call for the reserves. As they watched the First and Second brigades of the First Division advance ahead of them, Chamberlain recalled, "Few words were spoken among officers, however endeared to each other by confidences deepened by such pressure of life on the borders of death as war compels; the sense of responsibility silenced all else. Silence in the ranks, too; one little word, perhaps, telling whom to write to."[10]

Across the pontoon bridge, through the town and into the open field they marched, passing crushed bodies and severed limbs. As a Confederate battery opened on the right of the 20th Maine, Col. Ames called to Chamberlain, "God help us now! Colonel take the right wing; I must lead here." They passed the bodies of the dead and the dying as they moved up the slope, made slippery by the blood of those who had gone before. Chamberlain recalled, "We picked our way amid bodies thickly strewn, some stark and cold; some silent with slowly ebbing life; some in sharp agony that must have voice, though unavailing; some prone from sheer exhaustion or by final order of hopeless commander." Many of those who lay on the field warned the passing soldiers not to try it, even grabbing the legs of the advancing men to hold them back. According to Private Gerrish, the impossibility of taking the Confederate position was apparent to every member of the regiment. They reached the final crest near the stone wall and exchanged volleys with the Confederate riflemen. Fortunately for Chamberlain and the 20th Maine, it was nearly dark by the time they reached this position. Unable to advance or retreat, they fell to the ground.[11]

The 20th Maine remained on the wet, muddy ground throughout the bitterly cold night of December 13. Chamberlain lay between two dead soldiers and used a third for a pillow, pulling the flap of the dead man's coat over his face as protection from the wind. The moaning heard from all parts of the field was almost unbearable. At midnight, Chamberlain and an adjutant ventured out to offer help to the wounded. He found "some breathing inarticulate agony; some dear home names; some begging for a drop of water; some for a caring word; some praying God for strength to bear; some for life; some for quick death." The two men took water from the canteens of the dead, made the wounded comfortable, and administered, as best they could, to their medical needs.[12] For many, death was approaching. Chamberlain listened to their words for loved ones back home: "It was something even to let the passing spirit know that its worth was not forgotten here." From the pocket of the dead soldier Chamberlain used as a pillow fell a copy of the New Testament containing the man's name and address. Knowing what it would mean to the soldier's family, Chamberlain later returned the keepsake to the soldier's mother.[13]

Despite the devastating losses of the 13th, Burnside intended to renew the assault on Marye's Heights on Sunday the 14th, still believing he could break Lee's line. All three commanders of Burnside's Grand Divisions, Sumner, Hooker and Franklin, strongly advised against another attack. Such advice from normally aggressive soldiers caused Burnside to call off any further assault. Meanwhile, the Union troops from yesterday's last attack, including Chamberlain and his men, continued to lie on the field, risking a bullet through the brain if they raised their heads above the grisly breastworks of dead Union soldiers. At one point, two to three hundred Confederates left the protection of the stone wall to subject Chamberlain and his men to a flank attack but were forced back by fire from the 16th Michigan, the 20th Maine, and the 83rd Pennsylvania. All day, they could hear bullets thud into the flesh of the dead soldiers that formed their ghoulish barricade. They could do nothing but lie in the mud, cold and hungry.[14]

At 10:30 that night, the 20th Maine was finally ordered to withdraw. Before they departed, shallow graves were dug for the dead with bayonets and fragments of shells. Each dead man's name was crudely carved into broken fence rails or rifle musket butts for later identification. Chamberlain and his men crossed back over the field into Fredericksburg without incident, save for the emotional trauma of passing "men torn and broken and cut to pieces in every indescribable way." They bivouacked on the stone streets of the town during Monday, December 15th.[15] That night, the 20th Maine and two other regiments were ordered to the extreme front to cover the retreat of the army. The men were told to settle in and prepare earthworks. They were close enough to hear the Rebels conversing in their own rifle pits. Believing that one of his men was not digging according to instructions, Chamberlain directed the unseen soldier, "Throw to the other side, my man; that's where the danger is!" The response came in a distinctly Southern drawl: "Golly, don't ye s'pose I know which side them Yanks be? They're right onto us now." Thinking quickly, Chamberlain replied in his best Southern imitation: "Dig away then, but keep a right sharp lookout!" The impersonation worked. It would not be the last time Chamberlain would get out of danger by fooling Southern soldiers into believing he was one of them.[16]

Later that night, a Union staff officer frantically rode up with an urgent message intended for the commander: "Get yourselves out of this quick as God will let you! The whole army is across the river!" Chamberlain had to act quickly to avoid a panic. Certain that the enemy pickets had heard the officer's dire statement, and needing to reassure his men and convince the nearby Confederates that his men were not alone and isolated, Chamberlain exclaimed, "Steady in your places my men! One or two of you arrest this stampeder! This is a ruse of the enemy! We'll give it to them in the morning!" Taking the officer aside, Chamberlain quietly but forcefully rebuked him for his rashness. Realizing the man was simply afraid, Chamberlain told him the indiscretion would not be reported.[17] Ames and Chamberlain knew they needed to retreat quickly but secretively. The order was given for every even-numbered man to resume digging while every odd-numbered man moved out of the line. Half of the regiment withdrew first and re-formed 100 yards in the rear to cover the retreat of the others. The even-numbered men then withdrew past the new line and formed their own line 100 yards farther back. The movement was repeated until the 20th Maine was safely in the rear. At dawn on Tuesday, December 16, the regiment recrossed the Rappahannock.[18]

As Chamberlain looked back toward Fredericksburg at the bodies of blue lying on the field, Hooker came to him with words of comfort: "You've had a hard chance, Colonel; I am glad to see you out of it!" The experience of the past three days led Chamberlain to respond forthrightly: "It was a chance, General; not much intelligent design there." When Hooker stated that it was not his decision to send Chamberlain's men into the battle, Chamberlain responded with uncustomary frankness to an officer of superior rank: "That was the trouble, General. You should have put us in. We were handled in piecemeal, on toasting forks." Hooker let it go. Chamberlain also attributed to Burnside his share of the blame for the disastrous Union defeat. Statistics verified the extent of the loss. Federal casualties totaled 12,653 men, while Confederates lost barely 4,200.[19]

The Federals set up winter camp at Stoneman's Switch. The monotony of drilling was interrupted by Burnside's plan in January to cross the Rappahannock upstream, beyond Lee's left flank, and march southward to threaten the Confederate supply line. As the movement began, so did the rain. The countryside was described as an "ocean of mud." Marching slowed to a crawl, and wagons carrying pontoons for the river crossing bogged down. Movement of artillery became impossible. When Burnside saw the hopelessness of continuing, the army was ordered to return to winter quarters. Soon after completion of the "Mud March," Lincoln relieved Burnside of command and placed Joe Hooker at the head of the Army of the Potomac.[20]

Chapter 7

Chancellorsville

Gordon would not be with the Army of Northern Virginia at Fredericksburg as he convalesced from the multiple wounds he sustained at Antietam. Although present, the 6th Alabama also played no part in the Confederate victory at Fredericksburg. Despite the severity of his wounds, Gordon recovered and reported for duty on March 30, 1863. His accomplishments had earned him the rank of brigadier general, a promotion "richly deserved" for Gordon's heroism on the Peninsula and at Antietam, according to Colonel E. Porter Alexander.[1]

On April 11, 1863, Gordon was assigned by Lee to command a brigade in the division of Major General Jubal A. Early in Jackson's corps. The brigade, one of the largest in the Confederate army, consisted of the 13th, 26th, 31st, 38th, 60th, and 61st Georgia regiments. While Gordon was certainly pleased with his new command, parting from the men with whom he had fought and bled was difficult. Gordon explained that "there are few ties stronger and more sacred than those which bind together in immortal fellowship men who with unfaltering faith in each other have passed through such scenes of terror and blood."[2]

Not long after Gordon's return, the Federal and Confederate armies would once again be engaged in a momentous struggle. Similar to Burnside's ill-fated Mud March of January 1863, Hooker planned to march far west of Fredricksburg, cross the Rappahannock and Rapidan rivers, beyond Lee's left flank, and threaten the rear of the Confederate army. It was necessary to cross both rivers because the Rappahannock turned north above Chancellorsville, while the Rapidan branched off and ran to the west. The ford of the Rappahannock was too well defended by Confederate troops to permit a crossing there. Union forces would need to march farther west before turning south. Arrogant and blusterous, Hooker declared that his plans were perfect and said that God may have mercy on Lee but he would not. Execution of his plan began with the advance of Union cavalry under Brigadier General George Stoneman. Hooker then divided his army, initially leaving 60,000 men in the vicinity of Fredericksburg to keep Lee's attention and sending 60,000 troops to attack the Confederate army from the west. The march began April 27.[3]

Three Federal corps crossed to the south of the rivers and marched through the Wilderness toward the road junction at Chancellorsville, which consisted of a mansion and a few outbuildings. Two more corps were summoned, bringing the strength of the Union force behind Lee's army to almost 78,000. Lee's forces totaled about 60,000. Hooker's plan was a good one and was well-executed. Lee was unaware of the existence of a substantial Union force in his rear until the evening of April 29. He reacted quickly, sending two Confederate divisions. Believing that Hooker's main attack would come from the west, Lee dispatched a total of 45,000 soldiers toward Chancellorsville. Remaining behind at Fredericksburg to hold Marye's Heights were approximately 10,000 Confederates, including Early's division with Gordon's brigade.[4]

Five corps of Hooker's army were marching toward Fredericksburg, far outnumbering the Confederate forces opposing them. Around midday on May 1, 1863, a Union corps under Major General George Sykes ran into the main Confederate body on the turnpike east of Chancellorsville. Sykes sent back word to Hooker that he was in need of help, as the Rebel forces flanked then forced back Sykes' Federals. Help was on the way from Major General Winfield S. Hancock's division, but before it arrived, the fearless Hooker suddenly lost his nerve. He sent orders to Sykes to pull back. Hancock favored advance but Hooker reiterated his order to withdraw. Shortly thereafter, he changed his mind again, but by then it was too late to restart the offensive. Rather than attack Lee's undersized army as originally planned, Hooker began entrenching around Chancellorsville.[5] This was a mistake. It gave Lee the opportunity to take the offensive, and he did not fail to take advantage. In reconnoitering, Confederate cavalry commander J.E.B. Stuart discovered that Hooker's right flank was "in the air." In other words, the right end of the corps of Major General O.O. Howard on that part of the field was unprotected by any natural obstacle, except the Wilderness itself, or by any substantial force of men facing west.

Lee and Jackson met around sundown to discuss the situation. It was decided that Jackson, with his entire corps of 29,000 men and the help of a local 17-year-old boy familiar with back roads in the area, would march south then west until he was astride the Union left flank. Lee remained to the east of Chancellorsville with about 14,000 men to hold off Hooker should he decide to resume his attack.[6] Jackson's men set out shortly after 7:00 A.M. on May 2 on perhaps the most famous flanking movement of the Civil War. After an all day march to get into position, Jackson's attack began about 5:30 P.M. The Union troops, caught completely by surprise, were forced to flee. One Union regiment after another joined the stampede to the east.[7] As darkness fell and the charge lost momentum, Jackson decided to ride forward to evaluate the Union position to determine the feasibility of a night attack. Upon returning to Confederate lines around 9:00 P.M., North Carolina troops, unaware of Jackson's presence in their front and fearful of Union cavalry, fired at the Confederate party. Jackson was seriously wounded, twice in the left arm and once in the right hand. A.P. Hill, who assumed command, was also wounded, and the Confederate attack was halted for the night.[8]

Hooker was forced to consolidate his forces and retreated north toward the rivers. On May 3, despite his numerical inferiority, Lee intended to attack the Army of the Potomac, now with its back against the rivers. Before he could do so, Lee was told that Marye's Heights in Fredericksburg had been overrun, and Sedgwick's corps was moving west to threaten his right flank. The assault on Hooker would have to wait. Lee once again divided his army, leaving 37,000 men to face Hooker's 80,000, while 7,000 soldiers under McLaws marched east to meet Sedgwick.[9]

While Jackson executed his flanking movement around the Union right flank, Sedgwick planned his assault on Marye's Heights. Sedgwick had approximately 28,000 men to confront Jubal Early's five brigades. Gordon's brigade formed part of the right of Early's depleted line, closer to Hamilton's Crossing on the Rappahannock below Fredericksburg. Because the flanks of Marye's Heights were well-defended, Sedgwick was forced to attack the hill head-on, as Burnside had tried to do in December. There was an important difference now. The Confederate force on Marye's Heights was significantly smaller; only about two Confederate regiments protected the sunken road. The lead Union regiments were directed not to waste time reloading during the attack. Instead, they were ordered to charge without stopping until they breached the wall, brandishing their bayonets on the Confederates in the road. By 11:00 A.M. on May 3, the assault was successful, forcing Early to retreat. Following Hooker's orders, Sedgwick then marched west to strike Lee's right flank, leaving one division to guard Marye's Heights.[10]

The Federals reached Salem Church west of Fredericksburg around 4:00 P.M. on May 3, still several miles from Chancellorsville, when they ran into the Confederate force sent to meet them. After a difficult day, Sedgwick determined to put his 22,000 soldiers in camp for the night. On May 4, it became apparent to Lee that Hooker's forces north of Chancellorsville were well-entrenched. Lee decided to leave Stuart with 25,000 men to hold Hooker while he moved east to direct an attack on Sedgwick personally.

Marye's Heights was reoccupied by the Confederates shortly after sunrise, thanks to Gordon, who had forced the Union division holding the hill back into Fredericksburg. He did so despite a misunderstanding of Early's orders. Early had intended that Gordon's brigade be part of the attacking force. However, Gordon interpreted the orders as a directive to commence the attack with his brigade. By the time he was advised to halt and wait for additional forces, it was too late to stop Gordon's men. Thus, Gordon's brigade of Georgians, with belated support from other brigades of Early's, threw a Union division off of Marye's Heights and back into Fredericksburg.[11]

During the retaking of Marye's Heights, Gordon came into possession of perhaps the most remarkable horse he rode throughout the Civil War. He named her "Marye," after the hill where the fight occurred. She belonged to a Union officer who had been shot from the saddle. Ordinarily sluggish, Marye was transformed upon the commencement of battle:

> She seemed at once to catch the ardor and enthusiasm of the men around her.... With head up and nostrils distended, her whole frame seemed to thrill with a delight akin to that of foxhounds when the hunter's horn summons them to a chase. With the ease of an antelope, she would bound across ditches and over fences which no amount of coaxing or spurring could induce her to undertake when not under the excitement of battle. Her courage was equal to her other high qualities. She was afraid of nothing. Neither the shouting of troops, nor the rattle of rifles, nor the roar of artillery, nor their bursting shells, intimidated her in the slightest degree. In addition to all of this, she seemed to have a charmed life, for she bore me through the hottest fires and was never wounded.[12]

With Hooker bottled up, Lee focused on Sedgwick. He intended to attack Sedgwick's corps of 22,000 men with his own 22,000—comprising the divisions of McLaws, attacking from the west, Major General Richard Anderson attacking from the south, and Early with Gordon attacking from the east. Like Hooker, Sedgwick had his back to the Rappahannock River. Difficulties delayed the attack until 6:00 P.M.[13]

Gordon moved rapidly down the Plank Road and drove the extreme left of the Union troops from the vicinity of Bank's Ford. As noted by Col. C.C. Sanders of the 24th Georgia Regiment:

Gordon moved in echelon — that is, one brigade behind another at greater or less distance apart, forming a somewhat lengthened line of battle, each brigade ready by a rapid movement to support one another in case of either one meeting too strong resistance. He in this way struck Sedgwick's left flank and rear like a tornado, and poured such a torrent of shot and shell, grape and canister into his strongly massed legions as had seldom or never been seen before on any field of battle.... This splendid echelon movement made by Gordon, which proved so successful, seemed to have come to him by intuition. He was a born soldier, and did not realize at the time that he was but repeating a movement that Poshua, Hannibal, Charlemagne and other eminent commandants had used ages before.[14]

Fog and darkness made the advance more difficult. By the time Confederate infantry reached Sedgwick's works, they found them empty. The Union forces had escaped and recrossed the Rappahannock.

Lee, still on the offensive, sent McLaws and Anderson back to Chancellorsville for an attack on Hooker. But Hooker had held a council of war among his corps commanders and, despite the fact that more of them preferred to stand and fight, he ordered a withdrawal. Soon, the entire Army of the Potomac was on the north side of the Rappahannock, where they had been since December 1862. Lee then marched the Army of Northern Virginia back to Fredericksburg.

Chancellorsville is considered Lee's greatest feat of the war, dividing his army multiple times in the face of superior numbers contrary to military convention, and defeating Union forces at every point, save the temporary Union victory at Marye's Heights. Confederate casualties totaled less than 13,000, while Union forces were depleted by more than 17,000. However, proportionately, Confederate losses were greater, and Confederate victories bought at such a disproportionate price would ultimately lead to Southern defeat. One of those killed was Gordon's brother Gus. Before the battle, Gus quietly said to Gordon, "My hour has come." Gordon joked and chided him, telling him not to let such thoughts affect his imagination. Gus reaffirmed, "You need not doubt me. I will be at my post. But this is our last meeting." As he rode at the head of the 6th Alabama, commanded by Gordon at the start of the war, Gus was struck by grapeshot and killed.

The Battle of Chancellorsville also cost another life that the Confederacy could never replace. After Jackson's wounding on May 2, his left arm was amputated and buried near the Wilderness, while he himself was transported to Guinea Station to convalesce. Though Jackson's physician was initially optimistic about his recovery, Jackson developed pneumonia and, on Sunday, May 10, 1863, he died after proclaiming, "Let us cross over the river and rest under the shade of the trees."[15]

And where was Chamberlain and his 20th Maine throughout this battle? In quarantine — at least at the beginning. The Army of the Potomac had been inoculated for smallpox. The vaccine given to the 20th Maine was apparently defective, causing numerous men to actually develop the disease. Several died. Shortly before the Battle of Chancellorsville, the regiment was placed in quarantine. Col. Ames had obtained a place on Meade's staff, leaving Chamberlain at the quarantine camp. Seeing the Army of the Potomac march west on April 27 to initiate Hooker's flanking attack, Chamberlain was severely disappointed that he would miss the battle. When his request that the 20th Maine be given some role was denied, Chamberlain in frustration replied, "If we couldn't do anything else, we could give the rebels the small pox!"[16]

On May 3, the day after Jackson's devastating flank attack, Chamberlain and the 20th Maine were summoned to guard telegraph and signal lines running from Hooker's headquarters near the fords over the Rappahannock River. Though the 20th Maine remained north of the river, Chamberlain would not. He crossed the Rappahannock and joined Major General Charles Griffin's division in a fight with J.E.B. Stuart. For the second time, his horse was wounded as Chamberlain rode into battle. Chamberlain was also present to steady Hooker's disgusted forces as they crossed back over the Rappahannock in retreat.

The 20th Maine returned to its old camp on May 6 but remained in quarantine until mid–May. Chamberlain's actions had so impressed General Griffin that when Ames was promoted to brigadier general and brigade command shortly after the Battle of Chancellorsville, Griffin joined Ames in recommending Chamberlain's promotion to colonel. The promotion became effective June 23, 1863. As the time of the greatest battle in American history approached the small town of Gettysburg, Pennsylvania, the Bowdoin professor was now in sole command of the 20th Maine.[17] One of his first command problems would have tried the skill and patience of even the most veteran officer. Shortly after his promotion, Chamberlain was faced with handling 120 mutinous soldiers of the 2nd Maine. Most of the men in that regiment had signed on for two years back in May 1861 and were now being discharged. Unbeknownst to these 120, they had signed 3-year enlistment papers and were extremely upset that many of the men with whom they had joined and fought were being sent home, while they were not. They refused to obey orders and, as a result, were isolated and treated poorly. Then they were sent to Chamberlain, as he and his regiment also came from Maine.[18]

The 2nd Maine mutineers were marched under guard to Chamberlain. They came with orders from General Meade, commander of the Fifth Corps, to "make them do duty, or shoot them down the moment they refused." As did Chamberlain, the men called the area near Bangor and Brewer home. Chamberlain had no intention of shooting them. He requested and was granted leave from Meade's headquarters to handle the situation in his own way. He dismissed the guard and fed the men. He decided to divide them up by placing them into different companies, thus minimizing their ability to act as one body.[19] Chamberlain then spoke to them as a group. Later he explained: "I had called them together and pointed out to them the situation; that they could not be entertained as civilian guests by me; that they were by authority of the United States on my roles as soldiers, and I should treat them as soldiers should be treated; that they should lose no rights by obeying orders, and I would see what could be done for their claim." Chamberlain's honesty and humane treatment caused all but a handful of the 2nd Maine men to serve loyally with the 20th Maine. How critical the addition of these men would be became clear on July 2, 1863, on Little Round Top, south of Gettysburg.[20]

CHAPTER 8

Gettysburg

Gordon was appointed brigadier general on May 11, 1863. On May 20, Lee sent a letter to President Jefferson Davis advising him that Gordon would be placed in command of Rodes' former brigade. But the Georgians would not let him go. The officers in Gordon's new brigade were so impressed by his abilities in the fight around Fredericksburg they unanimously petitioned for him to remain with them. Gordon agreed, as did Lee.[1]

The death of Jackson required Lee to reorganize. Lieutenant General Richard S. Ewell was placed in command of the Second Corps. Early's division with Gordon and his Georgians were assigned to that corps. On June 4, the Second Corps left their camp at Fredericksburg and marched toward the Shenandoah Valley, the first movement of the Army of Northern Virginia according to Lee's newest plan for a northern attack. Due to the uncertainty of exactly where or how far the army was going, Fanny Gordon would remain at Richmond and not accompany her husband on this campaign.[2]

Lee had determined that he would, once again, take the Confederate army north of Virginia. Several considerations prompted this decision. Few provisions remained in the battle-worn fields of Virginia, and a march into Pennsylvania would not only supply Lee's army but would also remove the Federal army from Southern soil during the harvest season. Lee's presence would undoubtedly frighten people in the North, who, for the most part, had escaped the devastation inflicted on those in the South where all major battles, save Antietam, had been fought. He hoped that a victory would create an outcry for Washington to accept a negotiated settlement of the war or, perhaps, prompt England or France to enter on the Confederate side. Though by no means his primary reason, Lee also thought that an invasion of the North might relieve pressure on Confederate forces in Vicksburg, Mississippi, currently under siege by a Union army under

Major General Ulysses S. Grant. As Gordon later noted, "In the logistics of defensive war, offensive movements are often the wisest strategy."[3]

By June 12, the Second Corps had crossed the Blue Ridge Mountains and were in Front Royal, Virginia. From there they marched down the Shenandoah Valley (northward) toward the Federal garrison at Winchester. On the 13th, in accord with Early's instructions, Gordon formed his brigade in line of battle near the Staunton Pike about three miles south of Winchester. They advanced and drove Union skirmishers from behind a stone wall. In his report, corps commander Ewell stated, "The rapid and skillful advance of Gordon's brigade on June 13, near Winchester ... was one of the finest movements I have witnessed during the war, and won for the troops and their gallant commander the highest commendation."

Early then ordered Gordon to attack the main Union works. In his *Reminiscences*, Gordon relates several incidents when his fellow soldiers related presentiments of impending death. Gordon never felt such a presentiment but, seeing the strength of the Union position Early had commanded him to assault, posted on a hill as it was, Gordon was certain he would not survive and wrote a letter to Fanny with directions that it be delivered after his death. Early on June 15, Gordon's brigade started forward, expecting, at any moment, Union rifles and batteries behind the works to open up and pour death and destruction onto Gordon and his men. To their great relief, they found the Federal position abandoned. The Union garrison had fled, but not before 3,350 officers and enlisted men were captured.[4] Gordon then led his command northward, crossing the Potomac River at Shepherdstown on June 22. They marched through Boonesboro, Maryland, and Gettysburg, Pennsylvania, on their way to York, thirty miles to the northeast, and the Susquehanna River. As they marched through Gettysburg, Gordon forewarned his staff that should a battle be fought there, whichever army held the hills south of town would win. A week later the armies would be in Gettysburg with the Union forces holding the southern heights.[5]

Gordon marched into undefended York on Sunday, June 28. He was met by a nervous committee of the mayor and prominent citizens hoping to preempt a destruction of life and property. Gordon assured them that "the troops behind me, though ill-clad and travel-stained, were good men and brave; that beneath their rough exteriors were hearts as loyal to women as ever beat in the breasts of honorable men; that their own experience and the experience of their mothers, wives, and sisters at home had taught them how painful must be the sight of a hostile army in their town; that under the orders of the Confederate commander-in-chief both private property and non-combatants were safe; that the spirit of vengeance and of rapine had no place in the bosoms of these dust-covered but knightly men." He pledged "the head of any soldier under [his] command who destroyed private property, disturbed the repose of a single home, or insulted a woman." Gordon recalled an "insignificant exception" to the Confederate commitment to preserve Union property when, at the request of his men, he granted permission for them to take only the top rail of a fence near their camp. In the morning, with each man assuring Gordon he took only the top rail, the entire fence was gone.[6]

Early had instructed Gordon to march farther northeast to Wrightsville to secure the Columbia bridge over the Susquehanna River. Evidently, not everyone in York was upset by the presence of the Confederate soldiers. As he and his men began their movement, a young girl approached Gordon with a bouquet of flowers in which was concealed a note "in delicate handwriting," according to Gordon, providing the numbers and disposition of Union soldiers in Wrightsville. Upon arriving at that town, the accuracy of the information was verified. Gordon was not, however, able to secure the bridge. The Union forces retreating over the Susquehanna set fire to it behind them, and the efforts of Gordon and his men to extinguish the blaze were unsuccessful. The fire spread to the town. Gordon formed his brigade and with buckets and pails, provided by the citizenry of Wrightsville, that had not been made available when only the bridge was ablaze, the Confederates saved much of the Union town from destruction.[7]

One of the houses saved by Gordon's men belonged to Mrs. L.L. Rewalt. She watched in appreciation as the Confederate soldiers fought the flames around her home, and, on the following morning, insisted upon feeding as many of Gordon's men as would fit into her dining room. In light of her graciousness and generosity, Gordon wondered whether Mrs. Rewalt might be a Southern sympathizer. When he gently broached the subject, Mrs. Rewalt bravely responded in words and tone that left no doubt where she stood: "General Gordon, I fully comprehend you, and it is due to myself that I candidly tell you that I am a Union woman. I cannot afford to be misunderstood, nor to have you misinterpret this simple courtesy. You and your soldiers last night saved my home from burning, and I was unwilling that you should go away without receiving some token of my appreciation. I must tell you, however, that, with assent and approval, my husband is a soldier in the Union army, and my constant prayer to Heaven is that our cause may triumph and the Union be saved." Gordon and every Confederate soldier departed her home with a feeling of great respect and unqualified admiration for this brave and noble woman.[8]

While Ewell harried Pennsylvania, Lee nervously awaited word from his cavalry commander J.E.B. Stuart as to the location of the Federal army. About June 20, Stuart requested permission to move with almost his entire corps of horsemen into the rear of Hooker's army. Lee approved the plan but with strict admonitions that Stuart resume his position on Lee's flank as soon as it was evident that Hooker was on the move. But Stuart failed to adequately heed the limitation on his expedition and allowed his cavalry to become isolated on the east side of the Army of the Potomac — which was marching north to confront Lee — as Stuart could find no gap in the Union line large enough to cross back to the west. Unbelieving, Lee learned through one of Longstreet's scouts, a man named Harrison, that the Union army had crossed the Potomac and was closing in on Lee's divided army. He ordered an immediate concentration. On June 30, Early and Gordon rode back in the direction of Gettysburg. The scout brought one more piece of news. The Army of the Potomac was no longer being led by Joe Hooker.[9]

Hooker had diligently and effectively pursued Lee across the Potomac, but friction between him and Washington was intense, particularly with General-in-Chief Henry Halleck. Hooker's suggestion that he move on Richmond was rebuffed, as was his request for control of Union forces at Harpers Ferry. Frustrated, Hooker tendered his resignation, which Halleck promptly forwarded to Lincoln. On June 27, a courier left Washington with orders removing Hooker from command and appointing George G. Meade, currently leading the Fifth Corps, to command of the Army of the Potomac. A confrontation with Robert E. Lee was imminent and, once again, the Union army would be led by a different commander. Lee's army, numbering approximately 75,000 men, was concentrating near Cashtown, west of Gettysburg, while Meade with about 95,000 men approached from the south.[10]

Because the Confederate army was still separated, Lee advised his commanders to avoid any general engagement with the enemy. Circumstances, however, caused a reconnaissance into Gettysburg to develop into a skirmish and then a full-fledged battle. On June 30, a brigade in the division of Confederate major general Henry W. Heth had marched to Gettysburg to secure a supply of shoes. In accordance with Lee's orders, the brigade, under Brigadier General Johnston Pettigrew, withdrew when they encountered Union cavalry under Colonel John Buford posted to the west of Gettysburg. After consulting with A.P. Hill and obtaining his consent, Heth determined to return to Gettysburg the next day with his division, knowing that dismounted cavalry was no match for his infantry. But

Buford was not so willing to oblige Heth by simply abandoning the field. He deployed his troops along McPherson's Ridge on Willoughby's Run a mile northwest of Gettysburg, on both sides of the Chambersburg Pike. He also sent word to Major General John F. Reynolds, commander of the First Corps but now leading a wing of the army which also included the Third and Eleventh corps, to hurry his men forward.[11]

As Heth approached Gettysburg on July 1, 1863, he formed his division in line of battle along Herr Ridge and marched southeastward toward Buford's cavalry. Buford had only two brigades but they possessed a distinct advantage over Heth's infantry. The cavalrymen were equipped with the new Spencer carbine, which allowed them to load seven rounds at a time and shoot twenty shots per minute, compared to the Confederate's muzzle-loader, which discharged one ball at a time and could be reloaded and fired no more than three to four times per minute.

At about 8:00 A.M., an Alabama brigade under Brigadier General James Archer approached the field and came under artillery fire. Heth also sent a Mississippi brigade under Brigadier General Joseph R. Davis, nephew to Jefferson Davis. Archer proceeded south of Chambersburg Pike, while Davis was on his left, north of the pike. Buford knew he could only hold out for so long. At about 8:30 A.M., to Buford's relief, Reynolds rode up and was advised of the situation. He immediately gave orders for the three infantry corps under his direction to advance on Gettysburg and sent word back to Meade that Confederates were approaching Gettysburg in force.[12]

Reynolds led his First Corps to McPherson's Ridge and directed their deployment. As he turned to give a command, a Confederate sharpshooter's bullet struck him in the back of the head, toppling him from his saddle and killing him almost instantly. Meanwhile, Archer's men advanced up McPherson's Ridge. He soon saw, to his surprise, that he was not facing Union cavalry but infantry — specifically the Iron Brigade, distinguished by their black hats. Archer's men were forced to retreat, but about 75 Confederates were captured, including Archer, the first Confederate general to merit that distinction. North of the Chambersburg Pike, Davis' men fared better until, believing they had found cover from Federal fire, they poured into an unfinished railroad cut. Union troops soon lined the edge of the cut, firing down into the helpless, trapped Confederates, many of whom were captured and others shot as they tried to escape.[13]

Just as matters appeared to be under control from the Union perspective, a Confederate division under Robert Rodes, one of Ewell's, arrived on Oak Hill to the north of the morning's fight. His position on the Union right flank was ideal. Howard, the senior Union commander on the field following Reynolds' death, reacted by bending the northern end of the First Corps line back to the east. By 2:00 P.M., Rodes sent his brigades forward. They hit the Union line hard and forced the Federal soldiers back. Lee, who had arrived on the field, saw the battle, which he did not want, unfolding before him and ordered a general attack. Soon, the Union position on McPherson's Ridge was outflanked north and south, forcing the Iron Brigade and the First Division to retreat. The intensity of the fighting was evident from some of the casualty numbers. The 24th Michigan of the Iron Brigade suffered 80 percent casualties, while the casualties of Pettigrew's 26th North Carolina, which the 24th fought, were proportionately even higher.[14]

When Howard arrived with his Eleventh Corps, two divisions were deployed north of Gettysburg. One of Howard's divisions was commanded by Brigadier General Francis C. Barlow, who commanded infantry that decimated Gordon's brigade at Malvern Hill and who had marched through Bloody Lane at Antietam after Gordon was wounded and the 6th Alabama and other Confederates vacated the sunken road. On July 1, 1863, the tables were turned. At about 3:00 P.M., Early's division, with Gordon's brigade in the lead, arrived and struck the right flank of the Union Eleventh Corps. Although the Union soldiers stubbornly resisted, even fighting hand to hand, they were soon overwhelmed and, like the First Corps, fled back into the town of Gettysburg around 4:30 P.M. Gordon noticed a Union officer, Barlow, attempting to rally his men, when Barlow was shot from his horse. As Gordon rode forward with his advancing line, he stopped to offer aid to Barlow, whom Gordon, and even Barlow himself, presumed was dying.[15]

Gordon asked Barlow if there was anything he could do for him. Barlow asked that, should Gordon survive the battle, he tell Mrs. Barlow, who was now near Meade's headquarters, of their meeting and of his thoughts of her as he died — that his deepest regret was that he must die without looking upon her face once more. Barlow then asked Gordon to remove a packet of letters from the breast pocket of his coat — letters from Mrs. Barlow — and to read him one. Gordon did so. Barlow requested that Gordon then take the letters and destroy them, so they would not be read by others. Gordon gave him water from his canteen and directed stretcher bearers to carry Barlow to a place of shade out of the hot July sun. At the end of the day, Gordon wrote a message to Mrs. Barlow stating that her husband was seriously wounded and informing her where he lay.[16]

Unbeknownst to Gordon, Barlow recovered. Later hearing of the death of a General J.B. Gordon of North Carolina, Barlow presumed it was the man who had been so kind to him on the Gettysburg battlefield. Thus, each soldier thought the other was dead. Nearly 15 years later, at a dinner in Washington, the men were fortuitously reunited. Gordon asked, "General, are you related to the Barlow who was killed at Gettysburg?" Barlow replied, "Why, I am the man, sir. Are you related to the Gordon who killed me?" "I am the man, sir," Gordon responded. The emotional reunion generated a friendship that lasted until Barlow's death in 1896.[17]

After the routing of the Eleventh Corps, Gordon was ordered by Early to halt. Federal troops poured through the streets of Gettysburg to the hills south of town, the hills Gordon had prophetically predicted would provide victory for whichever army held them in its possession. Lee hoped to continue the pursuit, but A.P. Hill could provide no support. Heth's division was in bad condition after the day's fighting and the division of Major General Richard H. Anderson was too far away. So Lee turned to Ewell.

But for the death of Jackson at the hands of his own men at Chancellorsville two months earlier, he would be leading the advance to dislodge the Union soldiers massing south of town. And there is little doubt he would have done so, or at least made the attempt. Ewell was not Jackson. Through a staff officer, Lee gave instructions to Ewell to carry the hills south of Gettysburg if "practicable." For several reasons, including the lack of support from Hill, Ewell did not find an attack to be practicable.[18] As far as Gordon and other Confederate commanders were concerned, the attack should have been made. Gordon deeply regretted the order that halted his Georgia brigade. He believed:

> [N]either General Early nor General Ewell could possibly have been fully cognizant of the situation at the time I was ordered to halt. The whole of that portion of the Union army in my front was in inextricable confusion and in flight. They were necessarily in flight, for my troops were upon the flank and rapidly sweeping down the lines. The firing upon my men had almost ceased. Large bodies of the Union troops were throwing down their arms and surrendering, because in disorganized and confused masses they were wholly powerless either to check the movement or return the fire. As far down the lines as my eye could reach the Union troops were in retreat. Those at a distance were still resisting, but giving ground, and it was only necessary for me to press forward in order to insure the same results which invariably follow such flank movements. In less than half an hour my troops would have swept up and over those hills, the possession of which was of such momentous consequence.

Gordon knew that Jackson would not have let such an opportunity pass. He recalled, "No soldier in a great crisis ever wished more ardently for a deliverer's hand than I wished for one hour of Jackson when I was ordered to halt."

Several efforts by Gordon to gain such permission were rejected. He was unable to sleep that night, knowing that a mistake had been made: "Much of my time after nightfall had been spent on the front picket-line, listening to the busy strokes of the Union picks and shovels on the hills, to the rumble of artillery wheels and the tramp of fresh troops as they were hurried forward by Union commanders and placed in position." Even at 2:00 A.M., he sought permission from Ewell and Early to attack but his suggestion was not followed. For Ewell, it was too late. Gordon was relegated to guarding the York Road due to persistent rumors that a Union force might be approaching the rear of the Confederate army.[19]

Major General Winfield Scott Hancock took full advantage of the precious time the Union army had been given. At Meade's request, Hancock relinquished command of the Second Corps at Taneytown and hurried ahead to Gettysburg to assess the situation. He arrived at Cemetery Hill at about 4:00 P.M. and, after consulting with Howard, determined that the hills south of town were a good place for a fight and sent word to Meade, who ordered a concentration of all Union forces there. Hancock then directed that troops be posted on the northern side of Cemetery Hill to deter a further Confederate advance. He also assigned units to Culp's Hill and the area between Cemetery Hill and Culp's Hill, and then south along Cemetery Ridge toward Little Round Top. The Union defensive position took the shape of a fishhook, extending from Culp's Hill in the northeast around the northern edge of Cemetery Hill, then down Cemetery Ridge to Little Round Top and the somewhat larger hill to the south, Round Top.[20]

On the evening of July 1, seeing the Union army entrenching on the hills south of Gettysburg, Longstreet proposed to Lee that the Confederate army move around Meade's left to a good defensive location between the Army of the Potomac and Washington, which position Meade would be forced to attack. Lee would have nothing of it. His unwavering intent was to strike the Union army at Gettysburg. No amount of persuading by Longstreet, on either the evening of July 1 or the morning of July 2, would deter Lee from his purpose.

Lee's plan for the second day of battle required Longstreet to take the divisions of Major Generals Lafayette McLaws and John Bell Hood south down Seminary Ridge, which ran roughly parallel to and a mile west of Cemetery Ridge, for an attack north up the Emmitsburg Road running between the ridges. When Longstreet began his attack on the Union left,

Ewell would demonstrate against the Union right on Culp's Hill, with authorization to attack if the opportunity presented itself. Longstreet's march to the start-off position was long and difficult because it was necessary to avoid being sighted by the enemy. By the time Lee issued his orders and Longstreet's men moved out and got into position, it was nearly 4:00 P.M. on July 2.[21]

Hood's division was on the right with McLaws on his left and Major General Richard Anderson's brigades of Hill's Corps to the left of McLaws. The attack was to be made in echelon by brigade from right to left. When the position had been scouted earlier in the day, there were no Union troops along the Emmitsburg Road. That was no longer the case. The southern part of Cemetery Ridge just north of Little Round Top was now occupied by the Union Third Corps under Major General Daniel Sickles.[22]

Though he had originally been posted along Cemetery Ridge, Sickles believed that better defensive ground existed to his front. He moved his divisions, 10,000 men, west to a new line running partially down the Emmitsburg Road to a peach orchard, then turning east across a wheatfield to a grouping of large boulders, known as the Devil's Den, located just to the west of Little Round Top. The result was that his corps was now far in advance of the main Union line, with no support at either end, and also directly in the path of the planned Confederate assault. When Meade expressed grave concerns about Sickles' movement, Sickles offered to withdraw to his original position. Just then, Confederate artillery announced the commencement of Longstreet's attack. Now, for Sickles, it was too late.[23]

Noting the difficulty presented by Sickles' Corps and the existence of a better opportunity if Confederate troops moved south and around to the right of the Union flank, both McLaws and Hood repeatedly attempted to convince Longstreet to change the plan of attack in light of the Union disposition. Repeatedly the requests were rejected, with Longstreet insisting that Lee's orders must be followed. Confederate soldiers in the first brigade under Brigadier General Evander Law of Hood's division set off about 4:00 P.M., but if Longstreet would not alter Lee's orders to attack up the Emmitsburg Road Law would do it on his own. Contrary to Lee's orders, Law charged east directly toward the Devil's Den and Little Round Top. Fighting in the Devil's Den was fierce but Confederate troops forced Sickles' men out of the huge boulders. Union sharpshooters fired at Law's brigade from the base of the northwest slope of Round Top, so Law sent Colonel William C. Oates, commander of the 15th Alabama, with his regiment and the 47th Alabama to dislodge them.[24]

As the Confederate regiments advanced, the sharpshooters retreated up the hill. Oates succeeded in getting to the top of Round Top and saw the panorama of the battle before him. He was at the highest elevation on the field, which he believed could be turned into an unassailable position from which the entire Union line could be enfiladed by artillery. But a staff officer from Law delivered the message that Oates must press forward to Little Round Top, which was undefended, and he must do so without delay. He was forced to depart before the return of 22 of his soldiers, sent to fill canteens for his thirsty regiment. Those men, though sorely needed, would not be with him when he arrived at Little Round Top.[25]

Chamberlain and the 20th Maine had engaged in successive forced marches in their pursuit of Lee's army. On June 21, Chamberlain suffered a heat stroke, which forced him to temporarily relinquish command. Even after several days of rest, his health remained poor. The extent of their effort can be seen in the miles Chamberlain and his men marched: June 26, twenty miles; June 27, twenty miles; June 29, eighteen miles; June 30, twenty-three miles; and July 1, twenty-six miles. The regiment camped at Hanover, Pennsylvania, 16 miles from Gettysburg, on the evening of July 1, but their rest was cut short. News of the battle on July 1 at Gettysburg required them to immediately move out in that direction. After a brief stop around midnight, Chamberlain and his men resumed their march, arriving at the heights east of Gettysburg at 7:00 A.M. on July 2. The Fifth Corps was held in reserve for most of the day but was sent forth in support of Sickles when the Confederate assault on the Union left began at 4:00 P.M. The 20th Maine could see the desperate fighting. They saw the peach orchard to their right and the struggle for the Devil's Den. As they reached the wheatfield, their orders suddenly changed.[26]

Brigadier General Gouvernor K. Warren climbed Little Round Top and found it unoccupied. Although Union troops had been assigned there on July 1, they had redeployed and now the hill was empty, a fact known to Confederate commanders. Instantly recognizing the significance of the position and that occupation of it by the Confederates would be disastrous for the Union army, Warren notified Meade, who directed the Fifth Corps commander to send troops to occupy Little Round Top. Col. Strong Vincent, commander of the 3rd Brigade of the First Division of the Fifth Corps, heard of the need and immediately rushed his men to the hill. His regiments were the 16th Michigan, the 44th New York, the 83rd Pennsylvania, and the 20th Maine.[27]

Confederate artillery took aim at the brigade as it approached Little Round Top from the north and began its ascent up the eastern side. At that time, Chamberlain was riding with his brother Tom, a lieutenant in

Company G and adjutant of the 20th Maine, and another brother, John, who, as a member of the United States Christian Commission, would aid with care for the wounded. A solid shot from Longstreet's guns flew closely past them. "Boys," Chamberlain said, "I don't like this. Another such shot might make it hard for mother." He sent Tom to the rear of the regiment, and John up ahead to find a place for the wounded.[28]

Vincent's brigade deployed around the south side of Little Round Top in their order of march: 16th Michigan, 44th New York, 83rd Pennsylvania, and 20th Maine. Once in position, the 16th Michigan faced west and the other regiments curved around the southwestern slope of Little Round Top, with the 20th Maine facing south. Ominously, Vincent said to Chamberlain, "I place you here! This is the left of the Union line. You understand. You are to hold this ground at all costs!" Chamberlain's regiment was at the extreme end of the left flank of the Army of the Potomac. No Union troops were farther south. He knew that if the 20th Maine retreated or was wiped out, the Union flank, regiment after regiment, would be rolled up in the same way as the right flank of Hooker's army at Chancellorsville.[29]

Confronting Vincent's four regiments would be seven Confederate regiments: the 4th Alabama, 15th Alabama, 44th Alabama, 47th Alabama and 48th Alabama, all of Law's brigade, as well as the 4th and 5th Texas regiments of another brigade. At that time, the 20th Maine consisted of 358 men, including most of the 120 members of the 2nd Maine who had decided to fight with the 20th Maine after Chamberlain had treated them so respectfully. Chamberlain sent Company B under Captain Walter G. Morrill into the woods to the left to protect the flank of the 20th Maine.

No more than ten minutes after Vincent's brigade took its place, the Confederates struck. They hit first at the right center of Vincent's brigade. According to Oates, "They poured into us the most destructive fire I ever saw." Although initially repulsed, the Confederates began to overwhelm the 16th Michigan and 44th New York and to climb to the summit of the hill, but they were forced back by timely Union reinforcements, once again provided by Warren. Col. Vincent was mortally wounded defending the western slope. The fighting rolled toward the 20th Maine. Capt. Howard L. Prince saw Chamberlain: "Up and down the line, with a last word of encouragement or caution, walks the quiet man, whose calm exterior concealed the fire of the warrior and heart of steel, whose careful dispositions and ready resource, whose unswerving courage and audacious nerve in the last desperate crisis, are to crown himself and his faithful soldiers with ... fadeless laurels."[30]

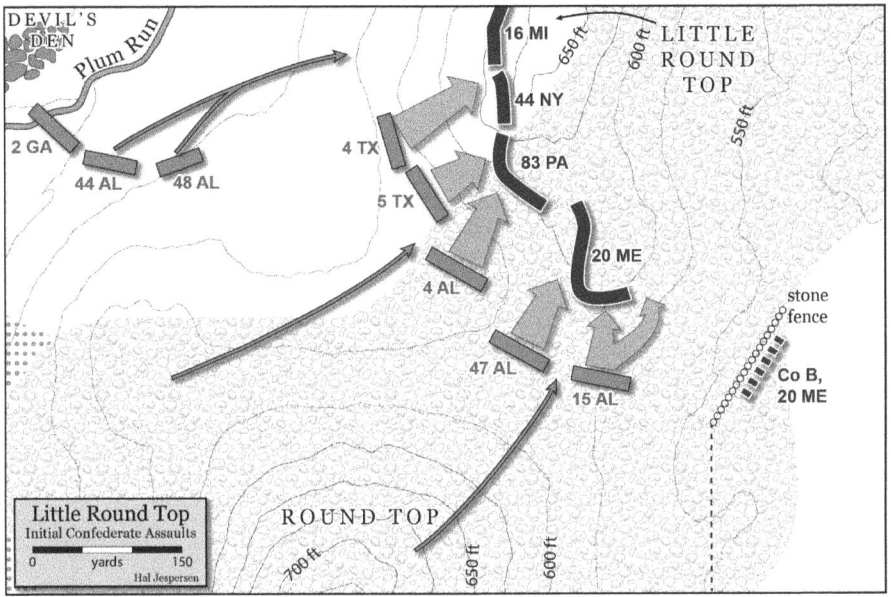

Little Round Top — Confederate assault (map by Hal Jespersen, www.cwmaps.com).

An observant officer under Chamberlain's command noticed "something queer" in the woods beyond the 47th Alabama, with whom the 20th Maine was engaged. It was Oates' 15th Alabama moving along the base of Round Top around to what they believed was Chamberlain's exposed left flank. Now Chamberlain, having learned from the example set by Ames at Fredericksburg, acted coolly and calmly, maintaining the composure necessary to instill confidence in his men. Chamberlain ordered that, while his men maintained their fire, they extend the line by sidestepping to the left, with the second rank filling in the first rank. Chamberlain placed the colors at the extreme left "where a great boulder gave token and support," then he bent his left wing back, almost to a 90 degree angle to his right wing. The monument of the 20th Maine, dedicated October 3, 1889, sits somewhat to the left of the spot where those colors stood.[31]

To the chagrin of Oates and the 15th Alabama, the flank of the Union left was no longer undefended. This time, by only a matter of moments, certain victory was snatched from Oates' grasp. The Maine men delivered a destructive fire which staggered the Alabamians. The trees and boulders behind which the 20th Maine fought provided welcome protection from the Confederates' return fire. The first Confederate attack was repulsed

20th Maine monument, Little Round Top, near position of the colors (author's photograph).

but the scene would be replayed several times, at very close range and sometimes in hand-to-hand combat. The 20th Maine would be forced back at points, then would recover the lost ground.[32] Private Theodore Gerrish of the 20th Maine described the scene:

> I wish that I could picture with my pen the awful details of that hour,— how rapidly the cartridges were torn from the boxes and stuffed in the smoking muzzles of the guns; how the steel rammers clashed and clanged in the heated barrels; how the men's hands and faces grew grim and black with burning powder; how our little line, baptized with fire, reeled to and fro as it advanced or was pressed back; how our officers bravely encouraged the men to hold on and recklessly exposed themselves to the enemy's fire, a terrible medley of cries, shouts, cheers, groans, prayers, curses, bursting shells, whizzing rifle bullets and clanging steel.

Chamberlain also painted an awe-inspiring picture:

> The two lines met and broke and mingled in the shock. The crash of musketry gave way to cuts and thrusts, grappling and wrestlings. The edge of conflict swayed to and fro, with wild whirlpools and eddies. At times

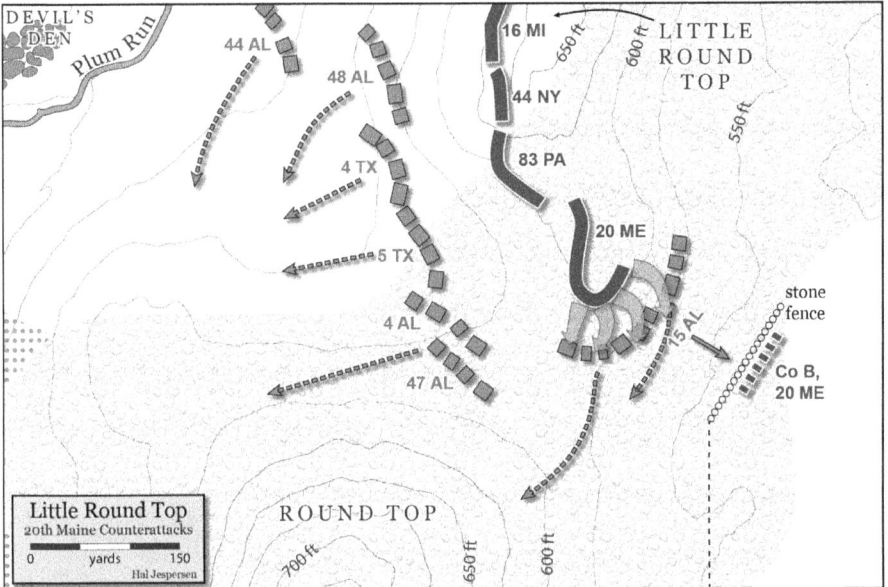

Little Round Top — Union counterattack (map by Hal Jespersen, www.cwmaps.com).

I saw around me more of the enemy than of my own men, gaps opening, swallowing, closing again with sharp convulsive energy; squads of stalwart men who had cut their way through us, disappearing as if translated. All around, strange, mingled roar — shouts of defiance, rally, and desperation; and underneath, murmured entreaty and stifled moans; gasping prayers, snatches of Sabbath song, whispers of loved names; everywhere men torn and broken, staggering creeping, quivering on the earth, and dead faces with strangely fixed eyes staring stark into the sky. Things which cannot be told — nor dreamed.

Even more graphically, Oates described what he saw: "The blood stood in puddles in some places on the rocks; the ground was soaked with the blood of as brave men as ever fell on the red field of battle." One who fell mortally wounded was his beloved brother Lieutenant John A. Oates.[33]

The 20th Maine and 15th Alabama fought back and forth for one and a half hours in repeated attacks and retreats, broken only by intermittent pauses. At one point, Chamberlain looked in shock as the color bearer of the 20th Maine, Sergeant Andrew Tozier, one of the additions from the 2nd Maine, stood almost alone in the center of the line. Chamberlain sent in his brother Tom to fill the gap, closely followed by another soldier because Chamberlain did not expect Tom would get there alive. As the smoke dis-

Breastworks on Little Round Top looking towards Round Top, July 1863 (Civil War Collection, Prints & Photographs Division, Library of Congress, LC-DIG-cwpb-04001).

sipated, Chamberlain and his men could see their comrades lying dead and wounded with the dead and wounded of the 47th Alabama.

During one lull, Chamberlain came upon Private George Washington Buck, who, when the 20th Maine was camped near Fredericksburg, had been demoted from sergeant due to unfair and harsh treatment of a bullying quartermaster. The commander who took Sergeant Buck's stripes had not adequately investigated the matter. Buck was lying mortally wounded with a bullet in his chest. He asked that Chamberlain tell his mother that he did not die a coward. Chamberlain answered, "You die a sergeant. I promote you for faithful service and noble courage on the field of Gettysburg."[34]

Chamberlain did not escape unharmed. One Confederate shot struck a rock by his boot, throwing a shard through the boot and cutting his foot. Another shot hit him in the left leg but was deflected by his sword scabbard, bending the scabbard and bruising his thigh. In one of the strangest and most mysterious incidents of the battle, certainly of the entire war as far as Chamberlain is concerned, his life was spared by the inexplicable inability of a Confederate soldier to shoot him when he had the chance. Several years after the war, Chamberlain received a letter from a person who identified himself only as a member of the 15th Alabama. The letter read:

> Dear Sir: I want to tell you of a little passage in the battle of Round Top, Gettysburg, concerning you and me, which I am now glad of. Twice in that fight I had your life in my hands. I got a safe place between two rocks, and drew bead fair and square on you. You were standing in the open behind the center of your line, full exposed. I knew your rank by your uniform and your actions, and I thought it a mighty good thing to put you out of the way. I rested my gun on the rock and took steady aim. I started to pull the trigger, but some queer notion stopped me. Then I got ashamed of my weakness and went through the same motions again. I had you, perfectly certain. But that same queer something shut right down on me. I couldn't pull the trigger and, gave it up — that is, your life. I am glad of it now, and hope you are. Yours Truly.[35]

Having fought intensely for almost an hour and a half, the men of the 20th Maine were near exhaustion. Chamberlain had sought reinforcements and resupply of ammunition but neither came. Chamberlain's men started with 60 rounds of ammunition each but, even after taking shots from the cartridge boxes of the fallen, Union and Confederate, little remained. Chamberlain looked into the faces of his men as they fired their last rounds, and they looked back for the guidance they expected of their leader. The men prepared to use their muskets as clubs. The battle was in a brief lull, but Chamberlain anticipated another Confederate charge any moment. They could not hold the ground much longer but neither could they retreat. Perhaps he thought back to the words of his father when Chamberlain asked him how to move the immovable rock or how to clear the wheel of the wagon stuck between two large stumps: "Do it!" Just as succinctly, Chamberlain issued a one word command: "BAYONET!"[36]

The men of the 15th Alabama were near the end of their endurance as well. Like the 20th Maine, they had marched far that day, more than 20 miles, before reaching the battlefield. They were tired from their climb up Round Top and, in obedience to Law's directive to move quickly, departed that point before the canteen bearers with badly needed water had returned. They had fought savagely for 90 minutes and needed reinforcements, but they had not come. The Alabamians fought hard, but the Maine men were no less determined. Oates would later say, "There were never harder fighters than the Twentieth Maine and their gallant Colonel." Without reinforcements, and with the perceived threat of Union forces in his rear, Oates realized his position was untenable. He ordered a retreat.[37]

In all likelihood, Chamberlain's decision to charge and Oates' decision to retreat were made almost simultaneously. But the 20th Maine reacted first. The word "BAYONET!" spread from man to man and each knew what it meant. Before a verbal order to charge could be given, the movement forward began when Lieutenant Holman S. Melcher, commander of Company F, stepped out waving his sword, and yelling, "Come on! Come on! Come on, boys!" The colors moved with him. Captain Ellis Spear, commanding the left wing, which was now bent back so far the 20th Maine looked like a "V," saw this and started forward. The line swung to the right and aligned with the right wing under Chamberlain. Then, the entire 20th Maine, or rather what remained of it, swept down the slope of Little Round Top. Chamberlain later recorded the following: "The grating clash of steel in fixing bayonets told its own story; the color rose in front; the whole line quivered for the start; the edge of the left-wing rippled, swung, tossed among the rocks, straightened, changed curve from scimitar to sickle-shape; and the bristling archers swooped down upon the serried host — down, into the face of half a thousand! Two hundred men!"[38]

The exhausted Confederates were caught completely by surprise. Some tried to make a stand among the trees and boulders but were soon overwhelmed. Oates said, "[W]e ran like a herd of wild cattle." Many Confederates threw down their weapons and surrendered. Others were shot, some in the face and others in the back, as they fled toward Round Top. As some members of the 15th Alabama attempted to flee to the east, they ran headlong into Capt. Morrill and Company B of the 20th Maine, positioned behind a low stone wall, who suddenly stood and poured a destructive fire into the unsuspecting Confederates. With Morrill were the Union sharpshooters Oates had forced from the base of Round Top.[39]

Chamberlain approached one Confederate officer brandishing his sword and a pistol. The Rebel pulled the trigger and fired, almost striking Chamberlain in the face. Chamberlain's saber at the officer's neck prompted him to surrender. Chamberlain took the pistol and put it to use against the Confederate officer's comrades. The advance continued into the ranks of the 47th Alabama. Having passed entirely across the front of the 83rd Pennsylvania, Chamberlain finally ordered a halt. Traversing the field back to their original position, the 20th Maine counted 150 Confederate dead and wounded. Approximately 368 Alabamians were taken prisoner. Among the members of the 20th Maine, every single man sustained an injury to his person, his clothes or his belongings, whether it was by rifle, pistol, or bayonet. They entered the battle with almost 358 guns and ended with about 200. Forty members of the 20th Maine were killed or mortally wounded in the battle.[40]

Conclusion of the fighting at Little Round Top did not end the second day of conflict at Gettysburg. At about 5:30 P.M., while Chamberlain's and Oates' men struggled back and forth, McLaws' division was sent forth in the second part of the Confederate echelon attack on the Union left. They headed for the wheatfield, north of the Devil's Den and about halfway between Little Round Top and the peach orchard. Union and Confederate soldiers fought back and forth for possession of the wheatfield as fiercely as they fought on the southern slope of Little Round Top. By 6:30 P.M., the Confederates had gained control of the wheatfield. The Confederates continued to push the Union forces back toward Cemetery Ridge.[41]

Anderson's division of A.P. Hill's corps then began the third and final echelon attack, directly at the Union center on Cemetery Ridge. They headed for a portion of the Union line weakened by the redeployment of troops needed to bolster the defense from the attacks further south. The only Union force available to blunt the charge was the 1st Minnesota, a regiment of 262 men who were being told to charge against a Confederate brigade four times their number. The Minnesotans struck the Confederates and slowed their advance enough to allow other Union troops time to arrive and secure the line on Cemetery Ridge. However, the small regiment was devastated, losing 80 percent of its members as casualties. The Confederate attack continued but faltered without support. The fighting ended on the southern end of the field with the Union still holding Cemetery Ridge.[42]

Union forces had also been taken from Culp's Hill on the northeast portion of the field. In accordance with Lee's plans, Ewell attacked Culp's Hill and east Cemetery Hill. The fighting lasted into dark. Confederate

Joshua L. Chamberlain, Medal of Honor (George J. Mitchell Department of Special Collections & Archives, Bowdoin College Library, Brunswick, Maine).

forces were successful in gaining possession of fortifications abandoned by Union troops sent south but they could not take Culp's Hill itself. Meanwhile, Early, with two of his four brigades, simultaneously attacked and penetrated the Union fishhook defense on east Cemetery Hill with as much success as Brigadier General Ambrose Wright had done previously on Cemetery Ridge. However, the brigades of Gordon and Rodes, which had been kept in reserve, were not sent in to exploit the success. Union troops once again arrived in time to force the Confederates back, ending the major fighting on the second day of the Battle of Gettysburg. Gordon's part in the Battle of Gettysburg was effectively over. In his after-action report, he found nothing even worth mentioning in the events of July 2 and July 3 as they related to his brigade.[43]

Though it probably seemed to Chamberlain and the 20th Maine that they had done enough for one day, they would be called on once again before that day was over. Col. James C. Rice, who replaced the mortally wounded Vincent at the head of the 3rd Brigade, needed Union troops to occupy Round Top. His request to the commander of a brigade of Pennsylvania Reserves was politely declined based upon lack of familiarity with the ground. Without complaint, Chamberlain assented to Rice's request that the 20th Maine take the larger hill. At 9:00 P.M., in full darkness, the 20th Maine left the protection of the boulders on Little Round Top and started up the slope of Round Top. They proceeded without waiting for replenishment of ammunition and with fixed bayonets. Confederates retreated back up the hill until the 20th Maine reached and took the crest. They were later joined by the 83rd Pennsylvania and the 44th New York. Finally, around midnight Chamberlain and the 20th Maine were able to rest. The next morning, they were moved to the left center of the Union line on Cemetery Ridge.[44]

The significance of the successful defense of the left flank of the Union line by Chamberlain and the 20th Maine cannot be underestimated and would not be overlooked. In his report on the battle, Col. Rice stated, "Especially would I call the attention of the general commanding to the distinguished services rendered by Colonel Chamberlain throughout the entire struggle." One of the compliments of which Chamberlain and the 20th Maine could be most proud came from its first commander, Brigadier General Adelbert Ames, who had driven the men so hard in the beginning and been so patient with his military-novice lieutenant colonel. On July 3, Ames wrote:

> My dear Colonel Chamberlain;
> I am very proud of the 20th. Regt. and its present Colonel. I did want to be with you and see your splendid conduct in the field. God Bless you and

the dear old Regiment. My heart yearns for you; and more and more, now that these trying scenes convince me of your superiority.

The pleasure I felt at the intelligence of your conduct yesterday is some recompense for all that I have suffered.

My love to the officers and men.

But, certainly, the words of William C. Oates, the adversary whose men fought and died on the same ground, carry special meaning and express the importance of the achievement of the 20th Maine and Joshua Lawrence Chamberlain: "His skill and persistency and the great bravery of his men saved Little Round Top and the Army of the Potomac from defeat." For his leadership at Little Round Top on July 2, 1863, Chamberlain would be awarded the Medal of Honor.[45]

Neither Chamberlain nor Gordon would participate in the events of July 3, certainly the most well-known engagement of the Civil War and one of the most important in American military history. Though they did not record their personal observations of the fighting on that day, those events undoubtedly impacted them both. Shortly before midnight on July 2, Union corps commanders crowded into the widow Leister's parlor, which served as Meade's headquarters. Meade wanted to know whether the Army of the Potomac should retreat or remain and, if the latter, attack or defend. The vote was unanimous. The army should remain and wait for Lee to make the next move.[46]

Lee would do so. He ordered Ewell to again attack the Union right flank at Culp's Hill. The attack came early in the morning of July 3rd, but after 5 hours of intense fighting, Ewell's men were driven from the hill. Shortly after sunrise on July 3rd, Lee told Longstreet his intention of attacking the Union center with Longstreet's corps of three divisions. Lee believed, correctly, that Meade had weakened the center of his line to defend against the attacks on his right and left flanks. Nevertheless, Longstreet strenuously objected, still believing that the wiser defensive move would be to move around the left flank of Meade's army and place the Army of Northern Virginia between Washington and the Federal army which must defend it. Lee determined that Longstreet would lead the assault with the division of Major General George E. Pickett and two divisions from A.P. Hill's corps, commanded by Brigadier General J. Johnston Pettigrew and Major General Isaac Trimble. The focal point of the attack would be a clump of trees on the right center of the Union line on Cemetery Ridge. The assault would be forever known as Pickett's Charge.[47]

Lee intended to soften the Union center with artillery. That bombardment would be massive. As a prelude to the infantry assault, more than 140 Confederate guns stretched along an arc almost two miles long would fire continuously in an attempt to effect as much damage as possible on the Union artillery and infantry at the point of attack. The Confederate cannonade began at about 1:10 P.M. Before long, Union artillery on Little Round Top, along Cemetery Ridge and on Cemetery Hill responded. Gordon's brigade and Chamberlain's regiment were exposed to the artillery fire, though neither sustained significant damage. The bombardment continued for about 90 minutes before Union fire began to slacken.[48]

Within minutes after the Union artillery stopped firing, the Confederates stopped firing as well. Pickett went to Longstreet and asked if he should advance. Longstreet, despairing that the assault would not succeed, could only nod. Long lines of Confederate infantry poured out of the trees on Seminary Ridge to begin the eastward march of three-quarters of a mile over open ground. A.P. Hill's divisions under Pettigrew and Trimble formed the northern part of the line while Pickett's division, with the brigades of Brigadier Generals James L. Kemper, Richard Garnett, and Lewis Armistead, completed the southern portion. While two Confederate brigades remained ready to join the assault, the primary attack would be made by approximately 11,000 Confederate soldiers. From one end to the other, the Confederate line measured almost a mile.[49]

The Union defense at the point of the Confederate attack consisted of three undermanned divisions under Major General John Gibbon, one of Hancock's Second Corps division commanders, in the middle; Brigadier General Alexander Hays on the right; and Major General Abner Doubleday on the left, a total of 5,700 infantrymen. No other Union troops were posted in close enough proximity to even provide support should an attack be made at the Union center. Throughout most major battles up to this time, Lee had been required to confront the Union army with substantially fewer Confederate forces. Now, at perhaps the most critical of all battles, he possessed a two-to-one numerical advantage.[50] The Confederate infantry attack began at about 3:00 P.M. Within minutes, Union artillery resumed firing. As the men marched in the open shoulder to shoulder, a hit or even a near miss created a gap in the Confederate line, sometimes killing 5–10 men at a time. Soldiers to the left and right closed the gap and continued. Union gunners, on both Little Round Top and lower Cemetery Ridge to the south and on Cemetery Hill to the north, enjoyed the advantage of enfilading fire on the arcing Confederate line.

On the northern side of the field, the enfilading fire and the timely flanking fire from the 8th Ohio sent an entire Confederate brigade running for the rear. Kemper's brigade of Pickett's division, which was positioned at the south end of the Confederate line, suffered substantial losses. Confederate soldiers on the north and south ends of the Confederate line naturally tended to move away from the sound and fury of the Union artillery fire, causing the width of the Confederate front to contract. As Confederate soldiers reached the Emmitsburg Road, Union gunners near the clump of trees less than 200 yards ahead switched to canister (containers of numerous iron balls), tearing large holes in the Confederate line.[51]

Union infantry, feeling the advantage — much like the Confederates on Marye's Heights at Fredericksburg — encouraged Pickett's men on. As they approached within easy musket range, Union soldiers, crouched behind a low stone wall, stood and delivered a galling fire. Confederates returned the fire. Of the brigadiers in Pickett's division, Garnett was shot dead from his horse, and Kemper received a grievous wound. Only Armistead remained. With his black hat on the point of his sword, he led Confederates over the wall and up to the Union guns through a gap left by a retreating Pennsylvania brigade. Lt. Frank A. Haskell of Gibbon's staff saw the danger and helped gather troops to plug the hole. Under Haskell's supervision, one of the Pennsylvania regiments that had withdrawn rushed back into the battle. Armistead was mortally wounded as he placed his hand on the muzzle of one of the Union artillery pieces. The Union line now overlapped the Confederate line on both ends. Ohioans to the north and Vermonters to the south swung out, enclosing Confederates in a three-sided box and shooting the attackers in the front and on the right and left. Hancock himself was seriously wounded but refused to be taken from the field before the contest was decided.[52]

Hancock would not have long to wait. The Confederates who crossed the stone wall were alone. Their only options were to surrender or attempt to retreat over the long open field they had just crossed. Not wanting to be shot in the back, many walked backwards. The two Confederate brigades held in reserve were belatedly sent in but did little more than provide a distraction to Union troops who otherwise could have focused solely on the retreating soldiers. An hour after it began, Pickett's Charge was over. Half of the 11,000 Confederates who made the charge were killed or captured. As one Virginia captain stated, "We gained nothing but glory and lost our bravest men." Union casualties did not exceed 1500. Confederate survivors streamed back to Seminary Ridge and were met by Robert E. Lee, who readily accepted full blame for the failure of the attack. He prepared the men for an anticipated counterattack by Meade that never came. Two inconsequential cavalry engagements on July 3 would end the Battle of Gettysburg.[53]

The numbers of killed, wounded, and captured from the three-day battle were staggering. Union casualties exceeded 23,000, with more than 3,100 listed as killed in action. Confederate casualties, more difficult to determine, topped 28,000, with probably close to 3,000 killed. The Battle of Gettysburg and Pickett's Charge are often described as the high tide of the Confederacy. The Civil War would continue for almost two more years but an objective observer could see little chance after July 1863 for ultimate Confederate victory. However, despite the diminished chance of success, Confederate soldiers would never lose their will to fight. Especially toward the end of the war, it appeared that they fought less for the cause and more for Robert E. Lee.[54]

In retrospect, Gordon blamed Ewell for the failure to secure a Confederate victory on July 1, and he blamed Longstreet for the failure on July 2. He also attributed the failure of Pickett's Charge on July 3 to a failure to promptly execute Lee's orders. Despite Lee's admission as Pickett's men limped back from Cemetery Ridge on July 3, the thought that Lee should share the blame in any part of the defeat never seriously entered Gordon's mind. What Gordon did recognize, however, was that the fate of the Confederacy was decided, for practical purposes, by the outcome of the Battle of Gettysburg.[55]

Despite the overwhelming success of Union forces on the third day of the Battle of Gettysburg, Meade, still very new to command of the Army of the Potomac and content with the decisive victory it had won, chose not to take the offensive. Lee knew it was time to return to Virginia. On July 4, beginning with the withdrawal of the wounded, the Army of Northern Virginia marched south. Gordon's brigade served as the rear guard of the army. When the Confederate army arrived at Williamsport, they were forced to establish a defensive position because the normally fordable Potomac was swollen by recent rains and the pontoons had been destroyed. Though Lee expected Meade to appear at any time, Meade did not send his army in pursuit until July 6, when he was certain that Lee was retreating rather than making a maneuver to draw Meade into a trap. Halleck's persistent efforts from Washington to speed Meade along to crush Lee's army, stuck at Williamsport with its back to the Potomac, had little effect. By the time Meade was prepared to attack the Confederates on July 14, they had crossed the Potomac and were safely back in Virginia.[56]

Before marching out of Gettysburg, Union troops performed the sad and grisly duty of burying the dead of the battle. Chamberlain and his men returned to the Round Tops to see their comrades lying "side by side, with touch of elbow still; brave, bronzed faces where the last thought was written; manly resolution, heroic self-giving, divine reconciliation; or where on some young face the sweet mother look had come out under death's soft whisper." They buried the dead of the 20th Maine there, using ammunition boxes as headboards, "rudely carved under tear-dimmed eyes," to mark the names of their beloved fallen. Fifty dead Confederates were also buried by the Union soldiers. The Maine men would later be reinterred at the national cemetery on Cemetery Hill.[57]

In what spare time Chamberlain found, he wrote to his wife about the historic events of the past few days:

>Field near Gettysburg
>July 4th 1863
>
>Dear Fanny,
> We are fighting gloriously. Our loss is terrible but we are beating the Rebels as they never were beaten before.
> The 20th has immortalized itself. We had the post of honor in the severe fight of the 2d, on the extreme left where the enemy made a fierce attempt to turn the flank. My Regt. was the extreme left and was attacked by a whole Brigade. We not only held our ground but charged on the Rebels & drove them out of all sight & sound, killing & wounding over 100 & taking 200 prisoners including 6 officers, one the inspector Gen. of the Brigade. I received the thanks of my superior officers on the field. After our charge, I was asked if my men could carry a high hill which was a strong hold of the enemy being covered with trees and large rocks.
> I had lost at that time almost half the effective men I took in, but I went in with charged bayonets & line of battle & swept everything before us, taking many prisoners. Col. Vincent is mortally wounded, the greatest loss that could have befallen the Brigade.
> Six officers in the 20th wounded —136 men killed and wounded.
> I am receiving all sorts of praise, but bear it meekly.
> Our army is in fine spirits.
> Many Generals on our side are killed.
> Ames & Brown of the 11th Corps have covered themselves with glory.
> You shall hear from me soon again, if I am spared.
> I shall tell of some little incidents, such as my taking officers prisoners & receiving swords & pistols.
> We captured one whole Rebel Regt.
> Hoping you are all well.
>   Yours,[58]

Four months after the great battle, Lincoln would travel to Gettysburg to help dedicate the national cemetery on November 19, 1863. He was invited as an afterthought; Edward Everett was the keynote speaker. Everett spoke for two hours. Lincoln spoke for barely more than two minutes. Everett later told Lincoln, "I should be glad if I could flatter myself that

I came as near to the central idea of the occasion, in two hours, as you did in two minutes." Lincoln eloquently noted the battle in what became known as the Gettysburg Address, which includes the following:

> But, in a larger sense, we can not dedicate, we can not consecrate, we can not hallow this ground. The brave men, living and dead, who struggled here, have consecrated it, far above our poor power to add or detract. The world will little note, nor long remember what we say here, but it can never forget what they did here. It is for us the living, rather, to be dedicated here to the unfinished work which they who fought here have thus far so nobly advanced. It is rather for us to be here dedicated to the great task remaining before us — that from these honored dead we take increased devotion to that cause for which they gave the last full measure of devotion — that we here highly resolve that these dead shall not have died in vain — that this nation, under God, shall have a new birth of freedom — and that government of the people, by the people, for the people, shall not perish from the earth.

Though Lincoln misjudged that his speech would not be long remembered, he accurately predicted that what the men had done there would not be forgotten.[59]

CHAPTER 9

Interlude of Winter 1863–64

The Army of the Potomac crossed its namesake river back into Virginia, encamping near Beverly Ford on the banks of the Rappahannock River. Several members of the recalcitrant 2nd Maine did not return with them. Of the remaining 6 holdouts, two had picked up rifles and fought at Little Round Top. Four 2nd Mainers died on Little Round Top. On July 10, during the measured pursuit of the Army of Northern Virginia, Chamberlain sent out skirmishers. One of them was Thomas Townsend, formerly of the 2nd Maine, who chose to end his holdout. Townsend was mortally wounded. True to his word that he would do what he could for the 2nd Maine men, Chamberlain recommended to Col. Rice that charges against Townsend be dropped. Townsend died with a clean record.[1]

Chamberlain was sick before the Battle of Gettysburg, and he would fall ill again soon afterwards. In early August, he was sent home to Brunswick on a 15-day leave. His days of commanding the 20th Maine were over, for now. Chamberlain's bravery and skill as a regimental leader were evident to both his superiors and those he commanded. When he returned from Brunswick, Major General Charles Griffin, the new commander of the First Division of the Fifth Corps, placed Chamberlain in command of the Third Brigade and recommended his promotion to brigadier general. Griffin had been impressed by Chamberlain, whom he saw as a "clear-headed and reliable officer." Chamberlain succeeded Rice, who had been made a brigadier general, and replaced Vincent, who had died defending Little Round Top. In describing the tenure of Chamberlain's leadership of the 20th Maine from the winter of 1863 to Gettysburg, Private Theodore Gerrish would state, "In those eventful months, Colonel Chamberlain had, by his uniform kindness and courtesy, his skill and brilliant courage, endeared himself to all his men, and had done much to give his regiment that enviable reputation it has since enjoyed." The men of the other regiments in the Third Brigade, most of whom did not know Chamberlain and some of whom wondered about his abilities, would soon learn the mettle of the Bowdoin professor.[2]

Many of those with whom Chamberlain served, including Generals Ames, Howard and James Barnes, praised Chamberlain and endorsed his promotion. General Rice spoke of his personal knowledge of Chamberlain's "skill and bravery upon the battlefield, his ability in drill and discipline, and his fidelity to duty in camp." Rice credited the men of the 20th Maine with exceptional bravery and fortitude at Little Round Top, and Chamberlain with inspiring their great success with his "moral power and personal heroism." Chamberlain was too humble to actively participate in efforts for his own personal advancement. Perhaps as a result, and despite the magnitude of his achievement at Little Round Top and the accolades of those who knew him best, his promotion would not be soon in coming. Despite frustration of the efforts of many of Chamberlain's superiors to obtain the promotions he deserved, he continued to perform his duty faithfully and diligently without regard to his rank. He would lead his brigade as a colonel.[3]

Late in August 1863, after returning to duty, Chamberlain and the brigade would participate as witnesses to one of the sadder events in a war full of sadness. The end of enlistments and the mounting casualties continually depleted the size of the Union armies. When volunteer enlistments proved insufficient to make up the difference, Congress enacted a draft. One unfair aspect of the draft was a provision which permitted a draftee to pay a sum of money — a bounty, generally about $300 — to a substitute who would go to war in his stead. While many of these substitutes faithfully served, others attempted to take advantage of the arrangement by deserting and, often, seeking another payment under a different name. Five substitutes assigned to the 118th Pennsylvania were caught as they attempted to desert. They were court-martialed and sentenced to be shot.[4]

On August 29, the entire Fifth Corps was formed into an open square, the lines being arranged so that each man would witness the execution. The graves were already dug. Undoubtedly speaking for most loyal soldiers, Private Gerrish of the 20th Maine noted little sympathy for the condemned men. Yet, he acknowledged it was a very solemn event which created an impression that would last a lifetime. The Fifth Corps waited in absolute silence. Music heralded the coming of the deadly procession. Gerrish heard "a measured, slow, and solemn dirge, whose weird, sorrowful notes were poured forth like the moanings of lost spirits." Following the band was the provost guard—fifty soldiers taken from each regiment in the First Division. Ten soldiers were assigned to each of the condemned men.[5]

Behind each set of executioners was a black coffin, followed by one of the condemned men. Gerrish noted that four of the men walked steadily but the fifth staggered weakly, leaning heavily on others for support. Spiritual advisers — two Protestant, two Catholic, and one Jewish — attended to the men. The coffins were set down next to the graves, and each condemned man sat on the end of his coffin. The clergymen withdrew, and the men were blindfolded. Finally, after what seemed an interminable length of time, General Griffin commanded that the men be shot. From the officer of the provost guard came the commands: "Ready!" "Aim!" "Fire!" Gerrish described "a sharp crash like the report of a single rifle." All five men were dead. The regiments marched back to their camps, contemplating what they had witnessed and, according to Gerrish, "feeling more keenly than ever before the solemn responsibilities of his position."[6]

Chamberlain's men spent the first half of September in camp at Beverly Ford, and the second half across the Rappahannock near Culpepper. The remaining confrontations with the Confederate army in 1863 were of small proportions and little military significance. On October 13, Lee crossed the Rapidan, then the Rappahannock, prompting Meade to retreat. On the next day, the Second Corps, now under Warren, fended off A.P. Hill's corps near Manassas Junction. When Lee saw that his effort at an offensive would be unproductive, he returned his army south. On November 7, the Sixth Corps under Sedgwick was sent to dislodge remaining Confederate entrenchments on the north side of the Rappahannock. Though sick with what was described as malarial fever, Chamberlain continued to lead his brigade which was posted on the left of the First Division. For the first time in battle, he rode Charlemagne, a horse captured from the Confederates. The two would ride together into most of the remaining battles of the Civil War. Though Chamberlain would play no major role in the battle, Charlemagne was shot from under him for the first and not the last time.[7]

Meanwhile, men of the 20th Maine once again distinguished themselves. When Captain Morrill, whose Company B at Little Round Top had been sent to guard the regiment's flank and delivered a devastating fire into Oates' retreating Confederates, learned that his old regiment, the 6th Maine, was one of four regiments of the Sixth Corps that would attack the Confederate works, he sought volunteers from the 20th Maine to join in. About 50 did so, as did others from Chamberlain's remaining regiments. They succeeded in scaling the works and overtaking the Confederate position after hand-to-hand combat, capturing 4 guns, eight battle flags, and 1700 prisoners, including two brigade commanders. Gordon's brigade was one of several Confederate units on the south side of the Rappahannock. But there was little he or anyone else on that side of the river could do to mitigate the loss of almost two brigades of Early's division. Morrill would receive the Medal of Honor for his heroics.[8]

Chamberlain's health deteriorated significantly when he was forced to sleep in the snow on November 8 near Kelly's Ford on the Rappahannock. Two days later, he collapsed and was evacuated to Washington, where he recuperated at the Georgetown Seminary General Hospital. Fanny came from Brunswick to help nurse him back to health. Despite his own affliction, Chamberlain extended kindness to others and did not forget those who were kind to him. He befriended a terminally ill officer and received a letter of appreciation from his wife long after the war. Years later, Chamberlain also assisted the army nurse who cared for him in obtaining a widow's pension. In January 1864, Chamberlain was well enough to assume duty on a general court-martial. He remained at that position until the spring campaign began.[9]

Once Meade and the Army of the Potomac recrossed to the southern side of the Rappahannock, Lee moved his army across the Rapidan. From late November into early December, Meade attempted to attack Lee once more but Lee's position at Mine Run was too strong. Gordon's brigade was present and engaged Union cavalry and infantry on the east side of Mine Run on November 27. His troops were withdrawn to the west side of the river during the night. More skirmishing occurred on the 29th. On December 2, the Confederates found that Meade had retreated. With other units, Gordon's men followed in pursuit but the Union forces recrossed the Rapidan. On December 3, Gordon's brigade returned to its camp on the Rapidan. The armies would spend the winter watching each other from opposite sides of the river.[10]

While the winter was harsh, both armies spent the time in relative peace and comfort. Although Lincoln had earlier declared the last Thursday in November as a day of thanksgiving, it is unlikely Union soldiers knew of or celebrated the first Thanksgiving Holiday. Religious revivals, particularly in the Confederate camps, were common. Furloughs were granted to return home to see loved ones, and Meade allowed officers to bring their wives to Camp. At camp, Union soldiers lived in large, comfortable log huts covered with tent cloth. Private Gerrish of the 20th Maine noted that "[g]ood water was plenty, wood was easily obtained, the men were healthy, and this winter's experience was the most pleasant that we enjoyed while in the army."[11]

With no enemy to confront, discipline was relaxed and practical jokes were common. One involved a cook of the 20th Maine. While he was away from his cookhouse, some of the men switched kettles of water with kettles of lard, then set fire to the chimney. When the cook heard the cry that his cookhouse was on fire, he rushed into the structure and threw what he believed was water onto the fire. The lard which he unwittingly used to douse the flames caused the whole cookhouse to erupt. Although the cook could not understand how this had happened, one officer knew that a trick had been played and ordered four men, including Private Gerrish, to rebuild the cookhouse.[12]

Gordon camped near Clark's Mountain south of the Rapidan. From there, Lee could watch the Union camp on the other side of the river. One of the concerns to the Confederate commander was the constant fraternization in which the Union and Confederate soldiers engaged during this relatively peaceful time. Men sometimes declared their own truce so they could bathe in the river, often meeting in the water to shake hands and converse. Soldiers surreptitiously crossed into enemy lines to talk and joke with one another, often trading tobacco, coffee, newspapers and other necessaries. The concern for both sides was that such camaraderie would inadvertently lead to the discovery of militarily significant information.[13] Lee directed Gordon to put a stop to this activity. Gordon made a surprise visit to a Confederate post when he discovered an unusual commotion. He inquired what was going on and doubted the reassurances of the Confederate soldiers that everything was fine. Gordon then saw movement in the weeds on the bank of the river. There he discovered a Union soldier, almost naked.

> GORDON: "Where do you belong?"
> UNION SOLDIER: "Over yonder," pointing to the Union camp on the other side of the river.
> GORDON: "And what are you doing here, sir?"
> UNION SOLDIER: "Well, general, I didn't think it was any harm to come over and see the boys just a little while."
> GORDON: "What boys?"
> UNION SOLDIER: "These Johnnies."
> GORDON: "Don't you know, sir, that there is war going on in this country?"
> UNION SOLDIER: "Yes, general, but we are not fighting now."[14]

Gordon was highly amused by the Union soldier's answers and the paradoxical situation created by the fact that between the times these men fought to kill one another, they desired to visit together as if neighbors back home. Recognizing that he must maintain his dignity and accomplish his purpose, Gordon fought back an impulse to burst out laughing. He ordered the man to stand up and sternly said, "I am going to teach you, sir, that we are at war. You have no rights here except as prisoner of war, and I am going to have you marched to Richmond, and put you in prison."[15]

As disturbing as this was for the Union soldier to hear, his Confederate hosts were horrified. "Wait a minute, general," they exclaimed. "Don't send this man to prison. We invited him over here, and we promised to protect him, and if you send him away it will just ruin our honor." Recognizing that his point had been made, Gordon turned to the Union soldier. "Now, sir, if I permit you to go back to your own side, will you solemnly promise me, on the honor of a soldier, that —." It was unnecessary for Gordon to complete the sentence. The man replied, "Yes, sir," as he jumped "like a bullfrog" into the river and swam back to the Union side.[16]

As Chamberlain's actions had been noticed by his superiors, Gordon, too, was recognized as a preeminent Southern leader. In January 1864, Lee wrote a letter to President Jefferson Davis reflecting his esteem for Gordon. The subject concerned a proper commander for Confederate troops in western Virginia. Lee spoke of great confidence in Early, Rodes, Edward Johnson, and Cadmus Wilcox. But in reference to his brigadiers, Lee thought "Genl Gordon of Alabama one of the best." Several months later, Lee again expressed his thoughts of Gordon as a leader. In discussing the necessity of transferring one of his division commanders, Lee indicated that he could spare Early because Gordon or General Robert F. Hoke could assume his position. Soon into the upcoming spring campaign, Gordon would once again demonstrate why Lee's confidence in him was so well-founded.[17]

Chapter 10

The Wilderness

Despite the past summer's success of the Army of the Potomac at Gettysburg, Congress had not forgotten the frustration of the failures of the numerous Federal commanders that had led the army to that point: McDowell, McClellan, Pope, McClellan again, Burnside, and Hooker. Meade's slow pursuit of Lee after the Gettysburg victory and his inability to deal a damaging blow to the Confederate army in the following months portended similar inconclusive results of the past. In February 1864, Congress responded by passing a bill to revive the rank of lieutenant general in the United States Army with the intent that one commander be chosen who would lead the Federal armies persistently and directly to victory and end the Civil War. The obvious choice for the position was Ulysses S. Grant. With Grant's early successes in the western theatre of the war at Fort Donelson, Tennessee, and Shiloh in Georgia, and later more decisive and significant victories at Vicksburg, Mississippi, and Chattanooga, Tennessee, Lincoln and Congress were convinced he was the man to fill the post. Lincoln signed the bill and immediately appointed Grant as lieutenant general.[1]

The Eleventh and Twelfth corps having been reassigned to Tennessee in the fall of 1863, the remaining portions of the Army of the Potomac were reorganized into three large corps, the Second, the Fifth and the Sixth. After Grant's promotion, he went to visit Meade at his headquarters at Brandy Station, north of the Rapidan. Although Grant initially intended to replace him as commander of the Army of the Potomac, Meade impressed Grant with his humble and unselfish offer to step down in favor of a man better known and more trusted by the new lieutenant general. Grant declined Meade's suggestion. Grant did, however, determine that his own place in the field would be with the army in the east.[2]

Grant's plan for the upcoming campaign was a simultaneous advance by the several Union armies: (1) Meade's Army would attack Lee; (2) the western Federal army, now under the command of Major General William Tecumseh Sherman, would challenge the Confederate Army of the Tennessee under Joseph Johnston camped at Dalton, Georgia, and capture Atlanta; (3) the command under Major General Franz Sigel would move up the Shenandoah Valley, taking possession of valuable Confederate supplies; and (4) Major General Benjamin Butler would advance along the James River toward Richmond and Petersburg. Dissatisfied with the accomplishments of the Federal cavalry, Grant placed Major General Philip Sheridan in command. The latter two suited each other well. Both brought a style of hard-hitting fighting that would cost the Union large numbers of casualties but would ultimately lead to the end of the Civil War and Northern victory.[3]

On May 3, the Confederate signal station on Clark's Mountain saw large clouds of dust signifying the movement of the Union army. Grant had approximately 122,000 battle-ready soldiers, while Lee could count only about half as many. On May 4, the Union army crossed the Rapidan, unopposed, into the Wilderness, an area of dense shrub and trees, difficult to penetrate and almost impossible to see through. The Second Corps under Hancock, the Sixth Corps under Sedgwick, and the Fifth Corps under Warren marched southeast to block each of the major roads from the west on which Lee's army could travel.

Meanwhile, Lee sent Ewell up the Orange Turnpike, while Hill approached on the Orange Plank Road, the roads running roughly parallel to each other. Lee rode with Hill. Longstreet was farther south with a greater distance to go and would not be close enough to participate in the fighting on May 5. The armies camped for the night — both sides remembering the thrashing inflicted on Hooker's army very near this location exactly one year before.[4]

Early on the morning of May 5, Warren's Fifth Corps marched southeast on the Brock Road past the Wilderness Tavern when they spotted Ewell's corps coming toward them on the Orange Turnpike. Ewell was under instructions from Lee not to bring on a general engagement because Longstreet was not yet present. But Ewell could not stop it. Two of his divisions were posted on either side of the turnpike. Gordon, who was in Early's division, trailing the other two, heard the Rebel yell turn to the Union "huzzah." The lead brigade of Major General Edward Johnson's division was hit hard by Griffin and the First Division of the Fifth Corps, including the 20th Maine. Johnson's men broke and fled to the rear, causing other units to panic. Gordon recalled, "These retreating divisions, like broken and receding waves, rolled back against the head of my column while we were still rapidly advancing along the narrow road. The repulse had been so sudden and the confusion so great that practically no resistance was now being made to the Union advance: and the elated Federals were so near me that little time was left to bring my men from column into line in order to resist the movement or repel it by countercharge." Ewell raced back for help from Early's division. Gordon's brigade was in the lead. Ewell exclaimed, "General Gordon! The fate of the day depends on you, sir!" Once again putting his oratory skills to good use, Gordon replied, for the benefit of his own men as well as for Ewell, "These men will save it, sir!" And so they did.[5]

Gordon immediately sent one regiment in a counterattack straight up the turnpike. The remainder of his brigade moved to the right. According to Early, "Gordon's advance, at the time of the confusion in the beginning of the fight, was made with great energy and dispatch, and was just in time to prevent a serious disaster." Gordon noted that, as his men broke through a portion of the Union line, his brigade was in the "remarkably strange position of being on identically the same general line with the enemy, the Confederates facing in one direction, the Federals in the other." From this position, Gordon could not either advance — and risk being cut off in the Union rear — or retreat, and face envelopment by superior Federal forces on both sides.

Recognizing that he must resolve his predicament quickly, Gordon's mind arrived at a solution that no West Point-trained commander had learned himself or taught Gordon. Before the Union troops hit by Gordon's men had time to reorganize, he halted his command and split his brigade into back-to-back lines, facing the flanks of the Union line, newly created by Gordon's breach. He then ordered them to advance. Ironically, in a war full of amazing coincidences, Gordon drove directly between the 20th Maine, still without Chamberlain, and the 44th New York, another of the 3rd Brigade regiments that had defended Little Round Top at Gettysburg. Gordon's move blunted the Union advance, while capturing large numbers of Union troops, and rallying Early's other divisions to join the assault. Fighting on that part of the field came to a close for the day. Gordon's men were then placed on the extreme left of the Confederate line.[6]

Though Warren had promised Griffin he would have support on his flanks, it did not arrive, Warren being unable to find Griffin's flank in the dense thicket of the Wilderness. Griffin's division was outflanked and pushed back. When two Union divisions, sent to provide reinforcements, stumbled unprepared upon the scene, they were hit hard and forced eastward. In obedience to Lee's order, Ewell did not continue the pursuit beyond the point where the battle began. By 3:00 P.M., the fighting on this side of the field was, for the most part, over. Ewell's men entrenched, a mile on each side of the turnpike.[7]

Three miles to the south, the battle was just beginning. Hill hoped to reach the intersection of the Orange Plank Road and the Brock Road and drive a wedge between Hancock to the east and Warren and Sedgwick to the west. However, Hancock raced to the crossroads and arrived first. His men built breastworks along the Brock Road north and south of the intersection. Hancock then sent two of his divisions forward down the Orange Plank Road. Although the Federals vastly outnumbered the Confederates in their front, the Wilderness prevented them from seeing their enemy with any degree of accuracy. Several assaults were made giving Hancock's men the advantage but not a decisive one. Darkness finally brought the fighting to an end on May 5.[8]

Fighting on May 6 began where it had ended the day before, near the intersection of the Orange Plank Road and Brock Road. An assault led by Hancock's Second Corps and reinforced by units from the Fifth and Sixth corps southwest down the Orange Plank Road met with initial success. However, at the Tapp farm, Longstreet appeared on the scene in advance of his First Corps with 10,000 fresh Southern troops. They successfully thwarted further advance by the now tired and disorganized Union force. By 10:00 A.M., the ground that had been lost that morning by the Confederates had been regained. Additionally, an attack by Longstreet's chief of staff, Colonel G. Moxley Sorrel, on Hancock's unsuspecting left flank, sent unit after unit of Federal troops scampering in retreat. The Union troops sought shelter behind the breastworks they had built the previous day, thanks to Hancock's foresight.

With his staff, Longstreet rode forward intending to continue the assault. As he did so, a volley from Virginia troops in the woods killed the three members of his staff and critically injured Longstreet. As Jackson had been mortally wounded almost precisely one year before only a few miles from the present location, Confederate troops once again mistakenly fired into a Confederate command party. The shot, which lifted Longstreet up out of his saddle, entered near his throat and lodged in his right shoulder. He was eased to the ground, laid on a stretcher and taken from the field. The incident put a sudden stop to the Confederate advance against Hancock's men. Not before 4:00 P.M. would the Confederates be ready to resume the offensive. By then, Hancock had strengthened his fortifications, added reinforcements, and protected his flank. An hour of fighting convinced Lee that nothing more could be gained on this end of the field.[9]

On the northwestern side of the field, where Ewell's Second Corps faced Sedgwick's Sixth Corps and Warren's Fifth Corps, fighting had been minimal. Throughout the day, Lee had urged Ewell to either send reinforcements to him or take the offensive to relieve pressure on the Confederate right flank. In accordance with Grant's orders, Sedgwick and Warren had engaged the Confederates, including Gordon's brigade, early in the morning to prevent the reinforcement of the Confederate right where Hancock's assault was being made. Thus, the first option was foreclosed.

On the morning of May 6, Confederate scouts were sent to reconnoiter the Union right flank. They reported to Gordon that the Union flank was unprotected and that the present Confederate line extended well beyond and to the northwest of the Union line. Other scouts were sent by Gordon to assure that Union troops were not lurking in the rear of the present Federal line. To his astonishment, Gordon learned that no Union troops were within miles of the thin, vulnerable Union right flank. Excitedly, Gordon himself rode out to examine the ground. All of the information he had been provided was confirmed.[10]

As Gordon would later recount, "such an opportunity as was here presented for the overthrow of a great army has rarely occurred in the conduct of a war." There were no Union troops directly in front of him. All he need do, with the information he had gained about the vulnerability of Grant's left flank, was to march his command forward, form at right angles to his present line and roll up the Union position. Gordon reported the situation to Early, who took the information to Ewell. Early advised against an assault, believing that Burnside's Ninth Corps might be behind the Union line. As Ewell's caution stopped exploitation of the Confederate victory on the first day at Gettysburg, he once again refused to take the bold move. Supporting Early, Ewell would not authorize the attack.[11]

At 5:30 P.M., after fighting on the southeast side of the field subsided, Lee rode to the Confederate left. When he asked if something could not be done on that end, both Ewell and Early reiterated their objection to an attack on the Union position in their front. Gordon, convinced that his plan would succeed, spoke directly to Lee, advising him of his findings concerning the vulnerability of the Union flank, and requested permission to make the attack. Lee knew that Burnside was not in a position to aid Sedgwick and overruled the continued objections of Ewell and Early. Lee ordered an immediate attack, "his silence and grim looks" displaying his dissatisfaction with the 9-hour delay caused by Ewell's and Early's hesitation.[12]

At 6:00 P.M., Gordon's Georgia brigade and the North Carolina brigade of Robert Johnston marched into position, deployed facing south, and charged. As Gordon predicted, the attack was enormously successful. Union regiments and brigades broke and fled in confusion, offering little resistance. Gordon recounted the following: "There was nothing for the brave Federals to do but fly. There was no time given them to file out from their works and form a new line of resistance. This was attempted again and again; but in every instance the swiftly moving Confederates were upon them, pouring a consuming fire into their half-formed ranks and shivering one command after another in quick succession." Two Union generals and hundreds of Union soldiers were taken prisoner. Gordon reported that nearly all of Sedgwick's corps was disorganized. But the lateness of the attack precluded full exploitation of the advantage. As darkness fell, the attack ground to a halt. It was impossible to tell friend from foe. Gordon had suffered less than 60 casualties and succeeded in pushing the Union flank a mile to the southeast. On May 7, Gordon's exploit was the subject of a letter written by Lee to the Confederate secretary of war. Even Ewell sent a letter to Lee praising Gordon for his "brilliant services" that day. After dark, Union reinforcements were moved to the damaged right flank and posted at a right angle to prevent another such attack.[13]

Gordon was exasperated by the decision of Ewell and Early not to permit the morning attack. Initially, he chose not to dispute the version of events recorded by Early in his postwar autobiography regarding the presence of Burnside. However, upon writing his own memoirs, Gordon felt compelled to set the record straight. He cites Union sources corroborating his information that Burnside was not present on the northwest side of the field. Gordon knew that, had Lee been present on the Confederate left flank in the morning, he would have authorized the attack then. He also concluded that Jackson, too, would have promptly orchestrated the proposed attack. Gordon would say that the failure to take advantage of the weakness of the Union right flank was "even a greater blunder" than Ewell's decision on the first day of Gettysburg not to pursue Union troops onto Cemetery Hill. He was convinced that a concerted Confederate attack, launched early on May 6 as he had proposed, would have swept the Union forces from the field. In Gordon's opinion, "the greatest opportunity ever presented to Lee's army was permitted to pass."[14]

On the night of May 6, reminiscent of Chamberlain's brush with capture at Fredericksburg, Gordon narrowly escaped becoming a prisoner. He and a courier, William Beasley, rode forward to check on a line of pickets Gordon had deployed for protection. They rode toward a body of men Gordon supposed were his pickets but darkness precluded him from ascertaining the color of their uniforms. Suddenly, Beasley anxiously whispered, "General, these are not our men; they are Yankees." Gordon did not believe him until Beasley grabbed Gordon by the arm and emphatically stated that the men were Yankees and they needed to get away immediately. They heard calls by Union officers rallying their men, but no one suspected Gordon and Beasley were Confederates. A Union officer asked to what unit they belonged. When they ignored his request and began to ride away, the Union officer became suspicious and cried out, "Halt those men!"

The orders were immediately obeyed, and Federal soldiers rushed around Gordon and Beasley shouting, "Halt, halt!" Not wishing to spend the rest of the war in a Northern prison, Gordon instantaneously determined that they must try to escape.

> Instantly throwing my body as far down on my horse's side as possible, my right foot firmly fixed in the stirrup, my left leg gripping the saddle like an iron elbow, I seized the bridle-rein under my horse's neck, planted my spur in his flank, and called, "Follow me Beasley!" ... It seems probable that the Union men were in almost as much danger from the hoofs of our horses as we were from the Union rifles.
>
> Strange as our escape may seem, it will be readily understood when it is remembered that the whole affair, like a sudden flash in the darkness, was so unexpected and so startling as completely to bewilder these men, and that they were crowded so closely together that it was difficult to shoot at us without shooting each other.

Gordon, Beasley and their horses escaped unharmed.[15]

No man who spent the night of May 6 near the sites of the day's fighting would forget the horrors. Despite the efforts of stretcher bearers to retrieve the injured, many wounded soldiers of both sides remained between the lines. The moans and cries for help filled the air, as they often do after a battle. But that night would be worse. The firing left glowing embers which were blown into flames by a night wind. The thick, dry brush burned easily, and the fire spread. As it reached the dead, their remaining rifle rounds exploded. Wounded soldiers of both sides gathered together. Those who were unable to crawl away screamed in terror as the flames approached, which engulfed many a poor soldier.[16]

Little fighting occurred on May 7. Neither Lee nor Grant was prepared for further offensive operations. Casualties for the two-day battle in the Wilderness were staggering. Union killed, wounded and captured exceeded 17,600, while Confederate casualties totaled about 11,000. It appeared to be another useless Union effort, after which, in accord with prior experiences, Union soldiers fully expected to retreat back over the Rapidan toward Washington. But Grant was not like his predecessors, and Lee knew it. Though Grant was hit hard emotionally by the events in the Wilderness, he was not intimidated by Lee.[17]

During Gordon's belated attack on the Union right flank on the evening of May 6, a Union officer at headquarters expressed his belief, based upon past experience, that Lee would now interpose his army between the Rapidan and the Army of the Potomac and cut off Union communications. Angrily, Grant responded, "Oh, I am heartily tired of hearing about what Lee is going to do.... Go back to your command and try to think what we are going to do ourselves, instead of what Lee is going to do." On the evening of May 7, sullen Union soldiers marching east suddenly cheered when the army turned south instead of north. They knew this meant Grant would continue his advance. The Army of the Potomac was headed for Spotsylvania Courthouse. Before Grant's movement made the plan apparent, Lee, the consummate military strategist, told Gordon that Spotsylvania Courthouse would be Grant's next objective.[18]

Since January 1864, Chamberlain, having recovered from his summer and fall illnesses, had served on a general court-martial in Washington, D.C. In the spring, he was anxious to return to the front. He made multiple requests regarding his status but he remained in Washington during the Battle of the Wilderness. Absence from his command during this time was extremely distressful for him. The first week in May, he wrote another letter requesting reassignment. Finally, he was allowed to return to the Army of the Potomac at Spotsylvania but did not participate in the battle. In Chamberlain's absence, Brigadier General Joseph J. Bartlett was given command of the Third Brigade, requiring Chamberlain to again lead the 20th Maine. Chamberlain would shuttle back and forth several times in the next few weeks between brigade command and regimental command when Bartlett was ill. Indicative of his character, Chamberlain took his reduction to regimental command without complaint.[19]

Chapter 11

Spotsylvania Courthouse

Unlike the progression of the war previously, with major battles separated by several months, the Army of the Potomac and the Army of Northern Virginia engaged in almost constant fighting and maneuvering from early May until mid–June 1864. Warren began Grant's redeployment from the Wilderness by marching southeast down the Brock Road around the back of Hancock's corps. Hancock followed him, while Sedgwick and Burnside marched east on the Orange Turnpike to Chancellorsville before turning south. Spotsylvania Courthouse was 12 miles away. Lee was prepared to respond and understood the importance of reaching that strategic location before Grant. He directed Confederate engineers to cut a path between the Brock Road and Catharpin Road to shorten the distance Rebel soldiers would need to travel. Command of Longstreet's First Corps was given to Major General Richard H. Anderson, who was ordered to march to Spotsylvania without delay.[1]

Lee was running thin on corps commanders. In addition to Longstreet's wounding, A.P. Hill had become too ill to continue in his command of the Third Corps. Jubal Early was brought in to replace Hill, which created an opening for a division commander in Ewell's Second Corps. Even before the Wilderness, Lee had considered promoting Gordon to division command, as he said in his letter of late April to Jefferson Davis. Gordon's actions on both days of that battle solidified the impression of him as a bold and skillful leader. On May 5, Gordon was called upon by Ewell to save the day and successfully blunted the Union assault down the Orange Turnpike. The next day, he discovered the opportunity to strike the unprotected Union right flank. Ewell and Early believed reason existed not to immediately act, but Lee, once apprised of the situation late in the day, knew that Gordon's plan was sound and decisive, and he ordered the attack.

When Early was moved to the head of the Third Corps, Lee promoted Gordon to command of Early's division.²

By May 9, Hancock and Burnside had arrived at Spotsylvania for the Union and Early for the Confederates. Lee formed a defensive position, three miles long, which roughly resembled an upside down "V" and would be called the Mule Shoe. For the Confederates, Anderson occupied the western part of the line and Early the eastern part, with Ewell in the middle. Warren's Fifth Corps was opposite Anderson, and the Sixth Corps, now commanded by Major General Horatio G. Wright, was to Warren's left. Most of Hancock's Second Corps was initially placed on Warren's right, while Burnside's Ninth Corps faced Early on the eastern side of the Mule Shoe. Wright was now in charge of the Sixth Corps because Sedgwick, beloved by Grant and by his own men, was dead. On the morning of the 9th, Sedgwick was riding among his men, berating them for hiding from a Confederate sharpshooter 500 yards away. No sooner had Sedgwick exclaimed, "They couldn't hit an elephant at this distance!" than he was struck below the left eye by the sharpshooter's deadly aim.³

Grant planned to assault Lee's line on May 10. Two of his efforts that day came to nought. He sent Hancock across the Po River west of the field to maneuver for an attack on Lee's left and rear. However, as Hancock's men prepared to recross the Po, they saw fortified Confederate entrenchments blocking their move. Hancock returned to his original position. Warren attempted to assault Lee's line around 4:00 P.M., only to have his men devastated by artillery fire. But Col. Emory Upton of New York in Wright's Corps came up with a viable idea. He proposed an attack on the Confederate works over a narrow front, with no stopping to fire until the line had been breached. Once into the Confederate works, the Union troops would move to the left and right to widen the gap and also penetrate deeper into the Confederate rear. Wright approved the idea and provided Upton with 12 regiments for the attack.⁴

The attack began at 6:10 P.M. and, for a while, worked precisely as Upton had planned it. The Union men broke through an abatis in front of the Confederate works and within five minutes, the lead regiments were in the Confederate position. The Confederates fought briefly but were overwhelmed by superior numbers and fell back. As planned, Upton's troops spread to the right, left and forward. But miscommunication caused Upton's attack not to be fully supported as planned. The lack of support gave the Confederates the chance they needed to re-form and repulse the attack.⁵

Gordon's division was rushed to the breach and saw Federal troops

100 yards in the rear of the Confederate works. His lead brigade of Johnston's North Carolinians was ordered to charge and drove the unsupported Federals back, forcing Upton to withdraw. Grant, however, was pleased by Upton's initiative and his idea. He immediately promoted Upton to brigadier general and intended to use his plan again on May 12, not with 12 regiments of 5,000 men but with a corps of 20,000. The battle to be fought that day would defy attempts at description and would, by consensus of the participants on both sides, be more intense, more horrific, and more violent than any other fight in the entire Civil War.[6]

In preparation for the attack, Hancock's Second Corps was moved to the apex of the Mule Shoe on the north. At 4:30 A.M. on May 12, Hancock's corps was ordered forward. Because of one of Lee's rare errors of judgment, their approach was much easier than expected. Twenty-two Confederate cannon which had been facing the apex were no longer there. Believing that Grant was preparing to leave Spotsylvania, Lee had ordered that the guns be withdrawn. When Confederates in the apex reported sounds across the line suggestive of a Federal attack, Lee's order was countermanded and the guns were being returned. They got back just in time to be captured. Hancock's men were within 300 yards when the Confederates realized they were under attack. Confederate volleys did little to slow the assault. The Union soldiers rushed on and over the Confederate works, capturing 20 of the 22 guns, 3100 Confederate troops, and Major General Edward Johnson, one of Ewell's division commanders. As had Upton's force two days earlier, Hancock's men spread to the right and left attempting to widen the gap in the Confederate line. Francis C. Barlow, now commanding one of Hancock's divisions, would once again cross Gordon's path.[7]

As Lee rode toward the sound of the fighting, fleeing Rebels passed him going south. Rodes' division on the western side of the salient stemmed the breach in that direction, as did Wilcox on the eastern side. However, a real danger existed that a deeper penetration by Hancock's corps would split the Mule Shoe and Lee's army in two. Gordon's division had been posted in the middle of the Mule Shoe, enabling him to support either Rodes or Johnson as needed. Lee rode to Gordon, who had reacted to the Union attack even before Lee arrived. Gordon sent a North Carolina brigade under General Johnson charging toward Hancock's men: "So rapidly and silently had the enemy moved inside of our works ... that before we had moved one half the distance to the salient the head of my column butted squarely against Hancock's line of battle." Johnson was shot down, throwing his brigade into confusion. Gordon directed the next ranking officer to take command. He ordered the new commander to deploy his whole force as skirmishers, so as to reach across the length of Hancock's line, then charge. Gordon hoped that the fog and mist would conceal Confederate numbers, and that the sheer audacity of the movement would confuse the advancing Union force. The desperate act had its intended effect, slowing the Federal attack while Gordon's remaining brigades were placed into position.[8]

Known to sit straight in the saddle, Gordon relates that as he and a staff officer, whose posture was not so good, rode forward to reconnoiter the situation, a bullet passed through Gordon's coat from one side to the other, grazing his back. The officer asked Gordon if the ball had not struck him. Despite the exigency of Confederate circumstances at the time, Gordon replied in a calm, common sense and almost comical way, "No, but suppose my back had been in a bow like yours? Don't you see that the bullet would have gone straight through my spine? Sit up or you'll be killed." Impressed by Gordon's point, the young officer jerked to attention.[9]

Lee arrived just as Gordon completed aligning his brigades for a countercharge. When Gordon asked Lee for orders, Lee responded that Gordon should continue doing precisely what he was doing. As Gordon prepared to give the order to go forward, Lee became caught up in the emotion of the moment. Lee rode forward to join in the attack. No doubt shocked that Lee, the beloved commander of the Confederate army, would subject himself to grave danger by doing so, Gordon blocked him, stating, "General Lee, you shall not lead my men in a charge. No man can do that, sir. Another is here for that purpose. These men behind you are Georgians, Virginians, and Carolinians." Once again using the excitement of the situation and his powers of speech to inspire his men to exceed the feats of ordinary soldiers, while at the same time accomplishing his immediate objective of stopping Lee's impetuous and unwise advance, Gordon loudly exclaimed, "They have never failed you on any field. They will not fail you here. Will you, boys?" Gordon's men responded, "No, no, no; we'll not fail him!" Even though Gordon and his men shouted for Lee to go to the rear, it took the strong arm of a Confederate sergeant on Traveller's reins to redirect Lee away from the advance.[10] Lee's attempt to lead the Confederate soldiers into battle and Gordon's words to deter him inspired those men for the difficult task ahead. Gordon later described the situation:

> [The scene] had lifted these soldiers to the very highest plane of martial enthusiasm. The presence of their idolized commander-in-chief, his purpose to lead them in person, his magnetic and majestic presence, and the spontaneous pledges which they had just made to him, all conspired to fill them with an ardor and intensity of emotion such as have rarely possessed a body

of troops in any war. The most commonplace soldier was uplifted and transformed into a veritable Ajax. To say that every man in those brigades was prepared for the most heroic work or to meet a heroic death would be but a lame description of the impulse which seemed to bear them forward in wildest transport.

As Lee moved to the rear, Gordon ordered his men forward. His brigades were far outnumbered by Hancock's divisions but Gordon received support from what remained of Johnson's division, as well as the divisions of Rodes and Wilcox on the flanks. He hit the Federal troops while they were disorganized after breaching the Confederate works and were massed tightly together. Grant intended that Burnside's corps on the eastern side of the salient would join the attack but Burnside provided little help to Hancock. As Gordon had hoped, the scene with Lee which preceded the counterattack filled his men with "an ardor and intensity of emotion such as have rarely possessed a body of troops in any war":

> I ordered, "Forward!" With the fury of a cyclone, and almost with its resistless power, they rushed upon Hancock's advancing column. With their first terrific onset, the impetuosity of which was indescribable, his leading lines were shivered and hurled back upon their stalwart supports. In the inextricable confusion that followed, and before Hancock's lines could be reformed, every officer on horseback in my division, the brigade and regimental commanders, and my own superb staff, were riding among the troops, shouting in unison: "Forward men, forward!" But the brave line officers on foot and the enthused privates needed no additional spur to their already rapt spirits. Onward they swept, pouring their rapid volleys into Hancock's confused ranks, and swelling the deafening din of battle with their piercing shouts. Like the debris in the track of a storm, the dead and dying of both armies were left in the wake of this Confederate charge.

Gordon's men stopped the Federal advance, which included Barlow's division, and drove them back to the entrenchments.[11]

At 6:00 A.M., Wright's corps, to the right of Hancock, struck the western side of the Mule Shoe. Rodes, who opposed him on that side of the line, called to Lee for reinforcements. Three brigades of Brigadier General William Mahone's division were rushed to the point of attack. Near the point where Upton had broken through two days earlier, Union and Confederate soldiers fought continuously for the next 20 hours. The place would forever be known as the Bloody Angle. Back and forth they struck at each other over the Confederate breastworks. Rifles with bayonets were thrust through gaps in the logs, piercing men on the other side. Sometimes, they were thrown over the works like javelins. A man would climb onto the works and fire down into the soldiers on the other side, while his comrades passed him loaded rifles. When he was shot down, another soldier would take his place. They fought in the rain, stepping on the bodies of dead and wounded soldiers and mashing them down into the mud. The gunfire was so intense that a 22-inch tree on the Confederate side of the breastworks was entirely severed.[12]

At 9:00 A.M., Warren's infantry attacked Anderson's line farther south but was repulsed before reaching the breastworks. Confederates at the apex of the Mule Shoe and at the Bloody Angle continued their desperate fight as a new line of entrenchments was being prepared 800 yards in the rear to which the Southern soldiers could fall back. They fought throughout the morning, afternoon, and evening of May 12, then into the night. In the early morning hours of May 13, after more than 20 hours of fighting, Confederate units received word that the new position was ready and began to pull back. The Federals made no attempt at pursuit. The horrendous battle was finally over. Gordon described this battle as "having furnished an unexampled muzzle-to-muzzle fire; the longest roll of incessant, unbroken musketry; the most splendid exhibition of individual heroism and personal daring by large numbers, who, standing in the freshly spilt blood of their fellows, faced for so long a period and at so short a range the flaming rifles as they heralded the decrees of death." Casualties on each side exceeded 6,000 and may have been considerably higher.[13]

The remainder of May 13 saw no fighting. On that day, Lee wrote to Richmond, recommending Gordon's promotion. Effective May 14, Gordon became a major general. While both sides pondered the extent of their losses, Lee received further bad news. J.E.B. Stuart, his trusted cavalry commander, had been mortally wounded May 10 north of Richmond at Yellow Tavern. The next few days saw some maneuvering at Spotsylvania but little fighting. On May 18, Grant struck again in the now-decapitated Mule Shoe with Hancock and Wright. Confederate artillery fire was devastating, inflicting heavy losses on the Federal troops. By 10:00 A.M., the attack was over.

Grant then decided that no more could be gained at Spotsylvania and ordered another movement of the Army of the Potomac around the right of the Army of Northern Virginia toward Richmond. The march began May 20. Also on that day, A.P. Hill, having sufficiently recovered, retook command of the Second Corps, so Early returned to his division. Gordon was given command of another division composed of his former brigade and the remnants of Johnson's division, which had been devastated by the attack of May 12. Losses for the Union since the spring campaign began exceeded 36,000, while Lee had lost about half that many.[14]

CHAPTER 12

North Anna to Petersburg

Grant's initial plan for the spring campaign met with limited success. The Federal force under Sigel in the Shenandoah Valley was defeated at New Market by Confederates which included a group of cadets from Virginia Military Institute in Lexington. Meanwhile, Butler became mired near the James River in Bermuda Hundred between Richmond and Petersburg. Farther south, Sherman was pressing the Confederate army under Joseph Johnston. Similar to Grant, Sherman engaged in a series of sidling maneuvers around the flank of Johnston's army, each time moving farther south and closer to Atlanta. The Army of the Potomac, ostensibly under Meade's command but effectively led by Grant, had suffered huge numbers of casualties in the month of May 1864 with little to show for it. Nevertheless, the spirits of his men did not flag. So long as they continued to engage Lee's army, they knew that it would only be a matter of time before victory would be achieved.[1]

The Army of the Potomac marched southeast away from Spotsylvania Courthouse, passing through Guinea Station, where Stonewall Jackson had died one year before. They then turned south toward Hanover Junction, just south of the North Anna River. Lee was obligated to follow Grant and he set out on May 21. On May 22, Chamberlain, once again a brigade commander, attempted to engage Confederates headed south at Pole Cat Creek. Griffin's division was forced to halt its march in response to firing from a Confederate cannon. Chamberlain sent the 16th Michigan and 83rd Pennsylvania in one direction as a diversion, Then, with the 20th Maine and the 118th Pennsylvania, he sought to flank and capture the gun. Their way was blocked by Pole Cat Creek. Spying a plank fence, Chamberlain directed his men to throw the planks into the creek, which they then used to cross. However, their movement was detected by the Confederates, who withdrew the battery before Chamberlain could spring his trap. Though he had not captured the gun, the threat to Griffin's men was eliminated and the division marched on.[2]

The Confederates, who had the more direct route, arrived first. Lee established a defensive position on the south side of the North Anna, once again in the shape of an upside down "V." A.P. Hill's corps formed the western side of the position, while Ewell's corps was on the right and Anderson's corps in the middle. Reinforcements arrived from the Shenandoah Valley, a division under Major General John C. Breckinridge, who had defeated Sigel at New Market, and from Richmond, George Pickett's division, where Butler was bottled up at Bermuda Hundred and unable to provide a direct threat to Richmond. Hancock crossed the North Anna from the south and Warren from the north at Jericho Mill, while Burnside remained on the north side of the river. Wright came up on Warren's right. On May 23, Hill attacked Warren but with insufficient troops to gain a success. During the fighting on the North Anna, Chamberlain conspicuously exposed himself to enemy fire as he stood in front of his men, whom he had ordered to remain prone. He refused the requests of his officers to take cover, explaining that he needed to be where he could see what was going on.[3]

Meanwhile, to the south, Hancock drove Confederates from a bridgehead. Grant planned a major attack for May 24 but Burnside found that Ox Ford, the point at which he was to cross the North Anna, was protected by a significant number of Confederate batteries. Hancock, Warren and Wright also found that the entrenchments Lee's army had prepared were formidable. Grant wisely canceled the assault. On May 26, Hancock, Warren and Wright were directed to recross the North Anna as the Army of the Potomac continued to move southeast around Lee's right flank.[4]

The armies continued to engage in relatively minor affairs at various sites over the next several days. On May 28, Ewell, too ill to continue in command, was replaced by Early, who attacked at Bethesda Church and was repulsed. Chamberlain once again exposed himself to immediate danger from Confederate artillery fire. This time, two sergeants took matters into their own hands. After an explosion of case shot rained iron fragments on Chamberlain and his men, they grabbed Chamberlain and pulled him into their shelter. His good fortune would not last through the month of June.

Grant and Lee headed toward Cold Harbor. Lee came to a realization that the confrontations which began May 5 in the Wilderness and led to this point, though tactically either Confederate victories or stalemates, strategically would lead to the end of the Army of Northern Virginia. As

Lee told Early, "We must destroy this army of Grant's before he gets to James River. If he gets there it will become a siege, and then it will be a mere question of time."[5]

Cold Harbor began as a fight between Union and Confederate cavalry. Lee's cavalry, under his nephew Fitz Lee, occupied the Cold Harbor crossroads, but they were forced out by Sheridan. Infantry began to arrive. The north-south Union line extended 6 miles and consisted of Burnside to the far north, bordered by Warren, Major General William F. "Baldy" Smith with his XVIII Corps of 15,000 men previously assigned to Butler, followed by Wright, and then Hancock at the southern end of the line. Facing east to oppose the Army of the Potomac were, from north to south, Early, Anderson, Major General Robert F. Hoke, a division recently detached from Beauregard's command, and A.P. Hill. Gordon, with Early's corps, was involved in heavy skirmishing with Burnside's and Warren's corps but otherwise saw little action.[6]

Grant planned an assault by at least three of his five corps. Though not evident to Grant and other officers at headquarters, Lee's army had, once again, built formidable, zigzagging breastworks which provided interlocking fields of fire. On the evening of June 2, Union soldiers who would make Grant's assault knew the fate they faced. They could be seen sewing their names and addresses inside their clothing so their bodies could be identified if they were killed the next day. The diary of one Federal soldier left no doubt in his mind of the fate that awaited him. It simply read, "June 3. Cold Harbor. I was killed." His blood-stained diary was found on the field after the battle.[7]

The assault on the Confederate works began at 4:30 A.M. and was a bloody and devastating Union defeat. Sixty thousand soldiers went forward into concentrated firepower. Flanks received enfilading fire. Union troops were struck from different directions by Confederate crossfire, resulting in the distinctive sight of dust fogging from the uniform of a Union soldier in two or three places at the same time. The attack lasted less than 30 minutes, and the gains were minimal. Some Confederates along the line were unaware that an attack had even taken place. Grant intended to resume the attack but his troops could not or would not go forward.[8]

Finally, around 1:30 P.M., Grant called it off. Casualties for the Army of the Potomac reached 7,000, most having fallen in the first assault. Lee lost only 1,500. Grant delayed for two days before requesting that litter bearers be allowed onto the field. When he did make the request, he and Lee engaged in merciless gamesmanship, as Lee would not acquiesce in Grant's informal request and Grant refused to seek a formal truce. When

Grant finally acceded on June 7, four days after the battle, only two live Union soldiers were found. In his memoirs, Grant stated, "I have always regretted that the last assault at Cold Harbor was ever made."[9]

Once again, Grant saw that his offensive was being unproductive, not to mention extremely bloody. Since the spring campaign began a month earlier, the Army of the Potomac had lost half as many men as it had lost in the previous three years. Lee's army had been bled down also, to a proportionately similar degree. The result was that, while the Army of Northern Virginia could build and fight behind breastworks as methodically as ever, it was no longer in a position to engage in effective offensive operations. Rather than play into Lee's hands with another frontal assault, Grant decided upon another sidling maneuver.[10] Now, Grant would move the entire army south of the James River to threaten Petersburg, 30 miles south of Richmond. Petersburg was a vital railroad center that connected the Confederate capital to the north with the rest of the Confederacy. Meanwhile, Lee was forced to deploy Early's corps with Gordon's division to the Shenandoah Valley, on June 13, where Major General David Hunter, who had replaced Sigel, was wreaking havoc on Confederate supplies and civilian property. Grant had already sent Sheridan to join Hunter. As Early and Gordon left for the Valley, the Army of the Potomac stealthily withdrew from Cold Harbor. It crossed the James River, 115,000 soldiers strong, on June 14 and 15.[11]

Grant succeeded in moving his army south of the James before Lee discerned the plan and responded to it. Had Grant pushed his commanders to immediately attack the Petersburg defenses or if those commanders had exercised independent judgment to press the Confederates, it is highly likely that Petersburg would have fallen before Lee reacted. However, neither Grant nor his commanders acted expeditiously, and the war would go on for another nine months. After crossing the James at Bermuda Hundred, Major General Baldy Smith's corps of 16,000 men forded the Appomattox River, within 6 miles of the Petersburg defenses. Hancock's corps of 22,000 crossed the James farther east and was only hours behind Smith.[12]

To man the Petersburg defenses, Beauregard could count only about 3,100 Confederates. They manned the Dimmock Line, ten miles of works covering Petersburg from the south, with one end anchored on the Appomattox River northeast of Petersburg and the other resting on the Appomattox River west of town. Despite the overwhelming numerical odds, Smith stopped when he saw the formidable earthworks which had been in the making for two years. No doubt, the recent bloody repulses suffered by Union soldiers in attacking Confederate works caused him to hesitate.

Smith ordered an evening assault that succeeded in occupying a mile of Confederate trenches but he refused to go farther, fearing that Lee's reinforcements would be arriving at any time.[13]

Hancock arrived later on the night of June 15. Confederate troops from Bermuda Hundred arrived to reinforce Beauregard, raising his number to about 8,000. Yet, he was still massively outnumbered. Meanwhile, Lee, finally recognizing that the Confederacy was in dire danger of losing Petersburg, sent George Pickett's division and a division of Anderson's corps to Beauregard. Union attacks on the Dimmock Line on June 16 were not concentrated and were slow in execution. Although more of the Dimmock Line fell into Union hands, the Confederate defense was not broken. By June 17, the corps of Smith, Hancock, Burnside and Warren, 80,000 men, faced about 15,000 Confederate defenders at Petersburg. Still, no decisive blow was struck. Finally, Meade ordered a large-scale assault for the morning of June 18.[14]

When the advancing units reached the Confederate entrenchments, they found them empty, abandoned the previous night in favor of a new defensive line closer to town. Also, that line was now occupied by more than 15,000 defenders. Anderson's divisions had arrived. Brigadier General David B. Birney, who took command of Hancock's corps after Hancock's Gettysburg wound became aggravated, attacked with a brigade at 4:00 P.M. and was decisively repulsed. The First Maine Heavy Artillery Regiment lost 632 of the 850 men in its ranks. Chamberlain, again leading a brigade in Griffin's division, was also sent in to attack the Confederate defensive line. This time, there would be no benevolent Confederate marksman withholding his shot, no scabbard to deflect the minie ball, nor would there be watchful sergeants to pull him out of the line of fire. The Civil War would come to Joshua Lawrence Chamberlain, as it had to Gordon at Antietam, in a personally painful, crippling and nigh deadly way.[15]

As of June 6, Chamberlain had been given command of the First Brigade of Griffin's First Division in Warren's Fifth Corps. His new brigade was composed of the 121st, 142nd, 143rd, 149th, 150th, and 187th Pennsylvania regiments. Once again, his superior officers sought Chamberlain's promotion to brigadier general. Warren directed Griffin, who was more than willing, to recommend Chamberlain's promotion. Generals Warren, James Barnes, and Joseph J. Bartlett heartily endorsed the recommendation, Warren frankly stating that Chamberlain's promotion to brigadier general would "add to my strength even more than the reinforcement of a thousand men." Meade also endorsed the promotion request and sent it to Washington. However, it would not be the repeated endorsements of his superiors, but the well-aimed shot of a Confederate infantryman that would bring Chamberlain his long overdue promotion.[16]

Warren's Fifth Corps occupied the southernmost position of the Union forces on June 18. Southeast of Petersburg was Rives' Salient, which covered the approaches of the Norfolk Railroad and the Jerusalem Plank Road, both running southeast out of Petersburg. As Griffin's division prepared for an assault on the works in their front, the Confederates opened a strong artillery fire on the division. The guns had to be silenced, and Warren asked if Chamberlain would handle the job. Chamberlain's brigade crossed the railroad into a clump of trees where they succeeded in silencing the Confederate batteries. In the process, a Confederate shell wounded Charlemagne and knocked Chamberlain to the ground. He picked up the division flag with its red Maltese cross from a wounded color-bearer and led his men on foot until the Confederate battery and its supporting infantry fled to avoid capture. Then, however, fire from the main works at Rives' Salient made Chamberlain's position untenable. He ordered his men back to gain the shelter of a crest.[17]

Chamberlain knew he could not hold his position for long. He was closer to the Confederates than he was to the rest of the Union army. He could see, three to four hundred yards in front of his brigade, strong Confederate earthworks with 12–15 guns covering the ground between his men and the Confederates. Also, a large fort across the Jerusalem Plank Road could use its heavy guns to strike Chamberlain and his men on the crest they now occupied. Between these two Confederate strongholds was a solid line of entrenched infantry, containing, in Chamberlain's estimation, at least 3,000 Rebel soldiers. Chamberlain could also see Confederate reinforcements arriving. He did what he could to protect his vulnerable position; he called up three batteries for support.[18]

Perhaps the lost opportunities of the past few days were sinking in at Union headquarters, prompting Grant and Meade to urge their corps commanders to action. As Chamberlain hung on with no Union infantry support in sight, a staff officer approached him with a verbal order from the commanding general to attack the Confederate works in his front with his brigade. When Chamberlain asked, in disbelief and half-sarcastically, whether headquarters intended for him to attack alone, the officer replied that Chamberlain was on his own. Not being a person prone to overreaction, and certainly not lacking the courage to face a dangerous and difficult predicament, Chamberlain's expression of astonishment was itself astonishing. Recognizing the impossibility of successfully achieving the desired result and believing that a mistake had been made in ordering his brigade forward on its own, Chamberlain did what he had never done before and would never do again. He wrote a note questioning the order.[19] Chamberlain's note read:

> I have just received a verbal order not through the usual channels, but by a staff officer unknown to me, purporting to come from the General commanding the army, directing me to assault the main works of the enemy in my front.
>
> Circumstances lead me to believe the General cannot be perfectly aware of my situation, which has greatly changed within the last hour. I have just carried a crest, an advanced post occupied by the enemy's artillery, supported by infantry. I am advanced a mile beyond our own lines, and in an isolated position. On my right a deep railroad cut; my left flank in the air, with no support whatever. In my front at close range is a strongly entrenched line of infantry and artillery with projecting salients right and left, such that my advance would be swept by a cross fire, while a large fort to my left enfilades my entire advance. (as I experienced in carrying this position.) In the hollow along my front, close up to the enemy's works, appears to be bad ground, swampy, boggy, where my men would be held at a great disadvantage under a destructive fire.
>
> I have got up three batteries and am placing them on the reserve slope of this crest, to enable me to hold against expected attack. To leave these guns behind me unsupported, their retreat cut off by the railroad cut — would expose them to loss in case of our repulse. Fully aware of the responsibility that I take, I beg to be assured that the order to attack with my single brigade is with the General's full understanding. I have here a veteran brigade of six regiments, and my responsibility for these men warrants me in wishing the assurances that no mistake in communicating orders compels me to sacrifice them. From what I can see of the enemy's lines, it is my opinion that if an assault is to be made, it should be by nothing less than the whole army.
> Very respectfully
> Joshua L. Chamberlain
> Colonel Commanding 1st Brigade
> 1st Div. 5th Corps[20]

The staff officer took the message to headquarters and returned with a response reflecting little more thought than the original order to attack. It again directed Chamberlain to make the assault with his brigade. As if it would allay his concerns, the note indicated that the whole army would join the advance on his right. At Gettysburg, Hood repeatedly questioned Lee's order to advance up the Emmitsburg Road. Not so Chamberlain. He received his answer, and he would immediately comply. The Union batteries opened on the Confederate guns, and Chamberlain ordered his men to make the advance in a rush with rifles at the shoulder. They could not delay the advance by stopping to fire.

Letter from General Ulysses S. Grant, June 20, 1864, appointing Chamberlain as brigadier general (National Archives and Records Administration).

General Griffin noted that Chamberlain possessed an "absolute indifference to danger" and that his mind worked as quietly and deliberately on the battlefield as in his own study. Chamberlain had commanded the six Pennsylvania regiments for less than two weeks but, as one of their number later reflected, he treated them like equals and was not afraid to lead them. They trusted his judgment and ability as a commander and willingly followed him wherever he ordered them to go. Before the attack, Chamberlain addressed his men:

> Comrades, we have now before us a great duty for our country to perform, and who knows but the way in which we acquit ourselves in this perilous undertaking may depend the ultimate success of the preservation of our grand republic. We know that some must fall, it may be any of you or I; but I feel that all of you will go in manfully and make such a record as will make all our loyal American people grateful. I can but feel that our action in this crisis is momentous, and who can know but in the providence of god our action today may be the one thing needful to break and destroy this unholy rebellion.[21]

The bugler sounded the charge, and the men went forward. Under the intense fire, Chamberlain noted "the earth flew into the air, men went down like scythe-swept grain." Chamberlain led the charge but, within minutes, his horse had been shot from under him. The flag-bearer was shot down, so Chamberlain grabbed the red Maltese cross flag and continued on foot, knowing that his voice could not be heard but the sight of the flag would encourage his men forward. As he neared the Confederate works, Chamberlain turned back toward his men to order them to oblique to the left to avoid the marshy ground. As he did so, a Confederate minie ball struck him in the right hip. The colors fell to the ground, but Chamberlain would not permit himself to go down. He knew that if his men saw their commander shot down, their bravery and the attack might falter. He thrust his saber into the ground and leaned on the hilt, continuing to encourage his men forward. After his men passed him, the trauma of the blow and the loss of blood forced him first to his knees, then he crumpled to the ground.[22]

As Chamberlain anticipated it would, the attack failed. He lay on the ground and watched his men approach the works, get torn to pieces by the Confederate fire, and then retreat. He recalled lying half-buried by clods of torn-up earth for an hour. Men came forward with a stretcher to bear him from the field but Chamberlain, believing that he was mortally wounded, directed them to help others first. But the soldiers were ordered to retrieve Chamberlain, and they complied with those orders. He was carried to a safe position behind the Union lines. Meanwhile, Grant and Meade suspended further attacks, once again experiencing futility in attacking strong Confederate fortifications.[23]

On June 19, Warren sent a letter to Meade, advising him that Chamberlain had been wounded, presumably mortally. He reminded Meade that

Chamberlain had previously been recommended for promotion as a brigadier general and implored him to award the promotion before Chamberlain died. On June 20, Grant appointed Chamberlain to be a brigadier general of volunteers effective June 18 "for gallant conduct in leading his Brigade against the enemy at Petersburg, Va., on the 18th." Chamberlain's on-field promotion was one of only a handful issued by Grant during the Civil War. Warren's letter and Grant's order were forwarded to Secretary of State Edwin M. Stanton for Lincoln's approval. In his memoirs, Grant made special mention of Chamberlain's valor:

> Colonel J.L. Chamberlain, of the 20th Maine, was wounded on the 18th. He was gallantly leading his brigade at the time, as he had been in the habit of doing in all the engagements in which he had previously been engaged. He had several times been recommended for a brigadier-generalcy for gallant and meritorious conduct. On this occasion, however, I promoted him on the spot, and forwarded a copy of my order to the War Department, asking that my act might be confirmed and Chamberlain's name sent to the Senate for confirmation without any delay. This was done, and at last a gallant and meritorious officer received partial justice at the hands of his government, which he had served so faithfully and so well.

Warren would later add that Chamberlain was an officer of the "highest reputation."[24]

When Tom Chamberlain, a captain in the 20th Maine, learned that his brother had been wounded in the attack on Rives' Salient, he took the surgeons of the 20th Maine and 44th New York and looked for Chamberlain. They found him in a division hospital three miles in the rear and were told that his wound was mortal. After entering his right hip, the minie ball severed arteries, nicked his bladder and urethra, fractured the left pelvic bones, and lodged behind the left hip joint. The surgeons operated on Chamberlain during the night of the 18th. Despite the surgeons' belief that the operation might only be inflicting pain, Chamberlain encouraged them to continue. They removed the bullet and patched him up the best they could, believing in the end that he had a chance to survive.[25] On June 19, Chamberlain penciled the following blood-stained note to Fanny:

> My darling wife
> I am lying mortally wounded the doctors think, but my mind & heart are at peace. Jesus Christ is my all-sufficient savior. I go to him. God bless & keep & comfort you, precious one, you have been a precious wife to me. To know & love you makes life & death beautiful. Cherish the darlings & give my love to all the dear ones. Do not grieve too much for me. We shall all soon meet. Live for the children. Give my dearest love to Father & mother

& Sallie & John. Oh how happy to feel yourself forgiven. God bless you evermore precious, precious one.

       Ever yours,
       Lawrence

Chamberlain was carried to City Point, then placed on a ship for transportation to the naval hospital at Annapolis, Maryland. Accompanied by friends, Fanny arrived at the hospital to care for her grievously wounded husband.[26]

Grant unsuccessfully attacked farther west two days later with Birney's and Wright's corps. But the attack on Rives' Salient signaled the end, for the most part, of offensive operations against the Confederate entrenchments and the beginning of the 9-month siege of Petersburg. Both sides dug in. Grant did attempt one major breakthrough, though he knew nothing about it until the action was about to commence. At one point where the Union and Confederate lines were particularly close to each other, Union soldiers with prewar experience as Pennsylvania coal miners dug a tunnel 511 feet in length to a point directly beneath the Confederate line. Digging started on June 25 and was completed a month later. The end of the tunnel was filled with 4,000 pounds of gunpowder. On July 28, Grant learned of the plan to explode the mine. Following the explosion, a division of black troops was to move around the crater into the Confederate lines. Fearing repercussions if the attack failed and the black troops suffered heavy losses, Meade determined that another division, which was untrained in how to approach the crater, would make the assault.[27]

The fuse was lit at 3:30 A.M. on July 30. When nothing happened, two brave volunteers entered the mine and found the fuse had gone out. It was relit and, at 4:40 A.M., earth, Confederate soldiers and equipment were blown high into the air, creating a crater 170 feet long, 30 feet deep and 60 feet wide. The untrained Union division incorrectly crowded into the crater and were unable to climb back out. As the Confederates recovered from the shock of the explosion, reinforcements were rushed forward and decimated the Union soldiers in the crater with rifle fire. In an attempt to salvage the action, the black division was finally sent in but the reorganized Confederates inflicted the heavy casualties Meade had feared. The Union troops were forced to retreat, suffering more than 4,000 casualties in the abortive effort. Although the Army of the Potomac would occasionally engage Lee's army thereafter, Grant did not order another major assault on Confederate works until March 1865.[28]

Chapter 13

Monocacy River and the Shenandoah Valley

Early's corps, which had departed Cold Harbor on June 13 for the Shenandoah Valley, arrived as Hunter prepared for an attack on Major General John C. Breckinridge at Lynchburg. Suddenly, the more than two-to-one numerical advantage the Union enjoyed disappeared, and so did Hunter. He retreated beyond the Blue Ridge into West Virginia, leaving no Union army between Early and Washington. Gordon, still commanding one of Early's divisions, was surprised by Hunter's precipitous withdrawal and, angered by Hunter's wanton destruction of property, such as Virginia Military Institute and the home of Virginia governor Letcher, would have preferred to meet him on the battlefield. Without a fight, Early had accomplished the first of Lee's objectives. Now he would pursue the second — a march eastward to threaten the Federal capital. Such a move, Lee hoped, would force Grant to send reinforcements from Washington, weakening the Union hold on Petersburg.[1]

While still in the Valley, Early placed Gordon's division under the ostensible command of Breckinridge, though Gordon still answered to Early. On July 4, Early's army marched to Harpers Ferry and, on July 6, crossed the Potomac. They passed near the Antietam battlefield at Sharpsburg and continued eastward into Frederick, Maryland. Not until they reached the Monocacy River did they face an opposing Union force — 7,000 soldiers under Major General Lew Wallace.[2]

At about 2:30 P.M. on July 9, Gordon was ordered to cross the Monocacy below the bridge held by Wallace. He formed his division, sending one brigade to overlap and flank the Union left. Gordon could see that his advance would be hampered by strong farm fences and huge grain stacks. The other two brigades then advanced, overcoming the problems these obstacles created, driving back the first Union line against heavy fire, then the second. Gordon came upon a third battle line. His horse, which had not before been wounded, was shot from under him at a critical time. Soon, however, another horse was provided by an officer and Gordon again led his men into the battle. Although he sent for an additional brigade to flank the line, the exigency of the situation required him to direct one of his own brigades in the fight. By 4:00 P.M., the Union troops were forced to retreat, leaving the bridge over the Monocacy in the hands of the Confederates. The road to Washington, less than 40 miles away, was open.[3]

Gordon received high praise from Breckinridge, who told him that this battle would immortalize Gordon. But Gordon's division suffered terribly. Nearly 700 of his men, one-third of the division, including his brother Eugene, were casualties. On this rare occasion, Gordon allowed himself the freedom to reflect upon his mortality and the losses among his men. In a letter to Fanny, two days after the battle, Gordon wondered "why am I spared & so many & so good are taken around me."

Meanwhile, Early's army continued its march toward the Federal capital, camping near Rockville on July 10. The head of the Confederate force reached the outer Washington defenses around 1:00 P.M. on July 11. Although the Union defenses were not heavily manned, Early's army, still suffering from battle losses and hard marching, was not in a condition to immediately continue the advance. Early decided, after consultation with his division commanders, that the assault would be made at dawn. The delay was enough for Grant, who sent two Union corps to Washington's defense.[4]

On the morning of July 12, the Confederates could see that the Union fortifications, weakly defended the day before, were now fully manned. Early cancelled the assault and decided that the time had come for his army to withdraw. Wright, commanding one of the two Union corps sent to Washington, planned an attack before Early could get away. It caught the Confederates off guard but was made late in the day and amounted to little. The Confederates had hoped to free Southern prisoners of war at Point Lookout near the capital but the necessity of immediate withdrawal made achievement of that goal impossible. Gordon's division was placed at the rear of the Confederate column, followed only by a guard of 200 men under Major Henry Kyd Douglas, formerly of Jackson's staff. There would be no more fighting; Early was allowed to leave without being further molested. South of Rockville, the Confederates recrossed the Potomac, then headed west for the Shenandoah Valley.[5]

For the remainder of the summer and into September, Early's Army maneuvered back and forth in the Valley, fighting Union forces in relatively minor engagements. A major development was Grant's appointment of a new commander for all infantry units in the Shenandoah Valley. Grant felt that incompetent leadership in that theatre, as well as interference from authorities in Washington, permitted Confederate forces to roam freely, taking provisions as needed and supplying Lee's army. On August 1, Grant directed that Phil Sheridan, previously commanding Union cavalry forces, take command of Union forces in the Valley. He provided Sheridan with written instructions that, as he progressed up the Valley (south) against Early's army, he should take whatever provisions, forage and stock he could use and destroy the rest.[6]

In his memoirs, Gordon, who bore no hatred toward the Union or Union soldiers and who, after the war, focused his efforts on reconciliation and reintegrating the South into the United States, felt obliged to condemn the destruction inflicted by Hunter and Sheridan. He did not, however, distinguish between Hunter, who took retribution for the acts of Confederate partisans and Southern sympathizers, and Sheridan, who sought to destroy the means by which Lee's army could be sustained. Gordon condemned both men equally based upon the harsh effects their actions imposed upon noncombatants.[7]

In destroying barns and mills with provisions, as Sheridan claimed he did, he had indeed exceeded Grant's directive, which did not extend to buildings and, in fact, called for their protection. However, it was no less condemnable, as Gordon recognized, than the decision of Confederate brigadier general John McCausland to order that the town of Chambersburg, Pennsylvania, be burned on July 30, 1864, when it refused to pay him a $500,000 ransom. More than half of the four hundred buildings that burned that day were homes. Gordon failed to acknowledge that in the destruction of their own supplies upon evacuating Atlanta in September 1864 and later Richmond, Confederates inflicted a great deal of damage upon the personal property of Southern civilians. However, indicative of Gordon's character, he never participated in any such activity and honored, as knightly and chivalrous, Colonel William E. Peters of the 21st Virginia Cavalry, who refused to obey McCausland's order to burn Chambersburg.[8]

The first of three major engagements between Early and Sheridan was fought at Winchester, Virginia, on September 19, 1864. At that time, Sheridan maintained a significant advantage of 38,000 soldiers to Early's 14,000. Early's corps was posted east and north of Winchester along the Valley Turnpike. From Harpers Ferry, Sheridan marched westward past

Berryville and struck the Confederate division under Major General S. Dodson Ramseur east of Winchester. Although Early was aware of Sheridan's approach, he did not seek to consolidate his forces until the battle began. Ramseur held on long enough for Early to summon his three other divisions north of town, including Gordon's, which, with Robert Rodes' division, counterattacked in the hope of slowing Sheridan and permitting the inevitable Confederate withdrawal.

In her attempt to escape, Fanny Gordon, in her carriage, rode on the Valley Turnpike toward Winchester and overtook Rodes' troops. To protect her from pursuing Union cavalry, Rodes halted some of his men and formed a line across the pike. In crossing a wide stream, the tongue of the carriage broke away from the axle, leaving Fanny and the driver in the carriage in the middle of the stream. Fortunately, several Confederate soldiers jumped into the stream and pulled the carriage out. They quickly repaired the carriage, allowing Fanny to make her escape.

As Rodes and Gordon finished discussing the charge of their divisions, Rodes fell mortally wounded next to Gordon. It deeply troubled Gordon that the exigencies of the situation required him to ride away without speaking to his dear friend one more time. The counterattack temporarily slowed Sheridan's men but the Union troops outflanked the Confederates on the left and the right, making it impossible to retreat in an orderly manner. Early's corps was overwhelmed by Sheridan's numbers, and he fell back through Winchester and up the Valley Turnpike (south) around 5:00 P.M. Early suffered almost 4,000 casualties, almost one-fourth of his entire force.[9]

Fanny Gordon had been with her husband for so long that Southern soldiers knew a battle was near when they saw her riding to the rear. Today, however, she had not gone. As Gordon rode through Winchester, he was horrified to see Fanny, whom he believed had already departed. Being a bachelor, Early had little patience with the wives, such as Fanny Gordon, who followed the army to be near their husbands. Perturbed by her constant presence, Early once stated, "I wish the Yankees would capture Mrs. Gordon and hold her till the war is over!" Aware of Early's feelings, Fanny Gordon chose to sit next to him during a dinner and tease him. As Gordon later noted, "[Early] was momentarily embarrassed, but rose to the occasion and replied, 'Mrs. Gordon, General Gordon is a better soldier when you are close by him than when you are away, and so hereafter, when I issue orders that officers' wives must go to the rear, you may know that you are excepted.'"[10]

On September 19, Early may have been even more humbled had he known that Fanny Gordon was attempting to stem the Confederate retreat by imploring the Southern soldiers to stand and fight. One of the Confederates was heard to say, "Come, boys, let's go back. We might not obey the general, but we can't resist Mrs. Gordon." When she encountered some of Gordon's own men, Fanny ran into the street and urged them to go back to the front. That is how Gordon found her: "I saw Mrs. Gordon on the streets of Winchester, under fire, her soul aflame with patriotic ardor, appealing to retreating Confederates to halt and form a new line to resist the Union advance. She was so transported by her patriotic passion that she took no notice of the whizzing shot and shell, and seemed wholly unconscious of her great peril. And yet she will precipitately fly from a bat, and a big black bug would fill her with panic." Although Gordon believed escape at that point was too late for her, she received the help of some of his men, including Major Henry Kyd Douglas, and she fled in her carriage with their son Frank away from Sheridan's advancing army.[11]

On September 22, Sheridan and Early fought their second engagement at Fisher's Hill near Strasburg. Sheridan's movements convinced Early that he intended to attack the Confederate front. Five Union divisions, in fact, faced the front of Early's line but two other divisions under Brigadier General George Crook moved around undetected to the Confederate left, held only by dismounted cavalry. At 4:00 A.M., Crook attacked. The Confederate cavalrymen were overwhelmed and fled eastward. Early's corps suffered the domino effect of a successful flanking attack, division after division being routed and retreating farther south up the Valley Turnpike. Sheridan, not one to be satisfied with minor victories, urged his men not to stop. Two cavalry divisions deployed by Sheridan to cut off a Confederate retreat failed to accomplish their objective. Had they done so, Early's corps may have been completely dismantled that day. As it was, he suffered 1,400 more casualties and continued to retreat.[12]

Believing that Early's corps was no longer a force to be reckoned with, Sheridan's pursuit slowed and finally stopped. On October 6, Sheridan turned his force around to march north. Along the way, he destroyed crops, livestock, farming implements and any other means by which the Confederate armies could be sustained in the Shenandoah Valley. On October 10, Sheridan marched through Strasburg and camped north of Cedar Creek. Reinforced by a cavalry brigade and an infantry division under Joseph B. Kershaw, Early's corps cautiously followed Sheridan's army north, the move necessitated by a lack of food and forage. They arrived at Fisher's Hill on October 13. Sheridan was called to Washington for a conference on the 15th but was back in Winchester by the 18th, as Early, more potent

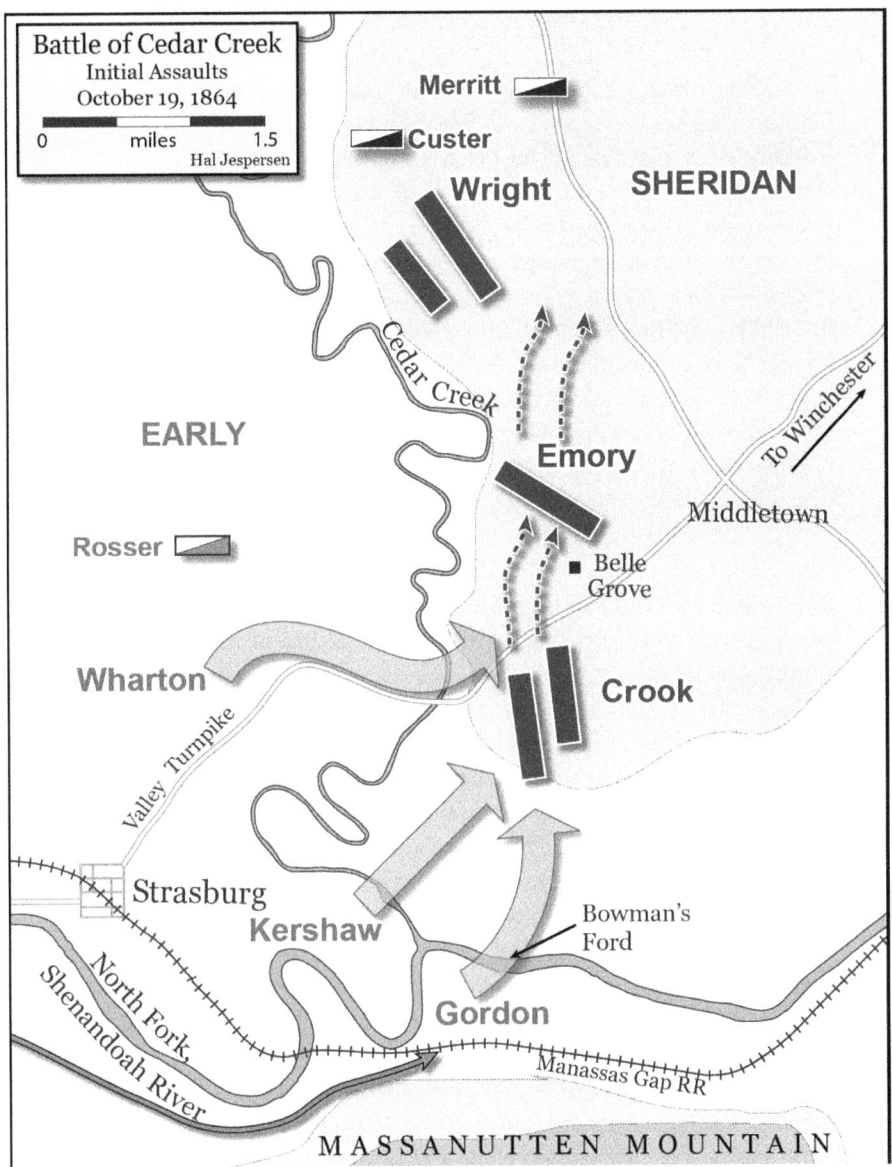

Battle of Cedar Creek — Confederate assault (map by Hal Jespersen, www.cwmaps.com).

than Sheridan had believed, prepared to launch the third and final battle of the Valley campaign.[13]

On October 18, the Union position faced southwest and consisted of the Eighth Corps, Crook's divisions, east of the Valley Turnpike, the Nineteenth Corps, the divisions of Brigadier General William H. Emory to his north across the road, and Wright's Sixth Corps to the northwest of Emory. Union cavalry were posted on Wright's flank. Because of the death of Robert Rodes, Gordon was now Early's senior division commander. After consulting with his commanders, General Early decided to attack the Union right. Dissatisfied with this plan, Gordon took Captain Jedediah Hotchkiss, a staff cartographer, and climbed Massanutten Mountain, south of Crook's location, to examine the Union position. They clearly saw the entire Union line. Gordon concluded that Sheridan expected that any attack Early would make would be on the right side of the Union line, where his cavalry was posted and that the steep north face of Massanutten Mountain would form a natural barrier to an assault on the Union left. Gordon decided that the Confederate attack should be made at that point, where it was least expected.[14]

Gordon proposed a flank attack against the southern end of Crook's corps. The Confederates would cross the Shenandoah River, march around the north face of Massanutten Mountain, then recross the river where they would directly face the Union left flank. This end of the Union line was almost completely unprotected, save for the natural barriers which Sheridan undoubtedly believed would deter a Confederate attack from that direction. Gordon and Hotchkiss reported the situation to Early, who readily approved the plan. Firmly convinced of the plan's success, Gordon volunteered to accept full responsibility should it fail. As darkness approached, the divisions of Gordon, Ramseur and Rodes, the latter now led by Brigadier General John Pegram, prepared for the assault. The men removed canteens, cooking utensils and any other object that might make noise and disclose their approach to Crook's force. Led by Gordon, the three divisions marched over a narrow path along the base of Massanutten Mountain and, at the appointed time, were in position to launch the attack. Gordon recalled, "With every man, from the commanders of divisions to the brave privates under them, impressed with the gravity of our enterprise, speaking only when necessary and then in whispers, and striving to suppress every sound, the long gray line like a great serpent glided noiselessly along the dim pathway above the precipice."[15]

In his memoirs, Gordon spoke of several presentiments or premonitions of death by soldiers before they entered into battle, including his own brother Augustus, who told Gordon, moments before sustaining a deadly shot at Chancellorsville, "My hour has come." At Cedar Creek, as the Confederate soldiers filed into position, Gordon visited with Major General Ramseur, who talked tenderly about his wife and the young son he had never seen. As General Ramseur prepared to ride into battle, he remarked, "Well, general, I shall get my furlough today." Gordon did not initially know what he meant. He understood Ramseur's meaning only when Ramseur was killed by a Union bullet while trying to rally his men as the tide of the battle turned against the South.[16]

Gordon described the atmosphere as the Confederates waited for the designated time to arrive:

> For nearly an hour we waited for the appointed time, resting near the bank of the river in the middle of which the Union vedettes sat upon their horses, wholly unconscious of the presence of the gray-jacketed foe, who from the ambush of night, like crouching lions from the jungle, were ready to spring upon them.... The men were resting, lying in long lines on the thickly matted grass or reclining in groups, their hearts thumping, their ears eagerly listening for the orders: "Attention, men!" "Fall in!" "Forward!" At brief intervals members of the staff withdrew to a point where they could safely strike a match and examine watches in order to keep me advised of the time. In the still starlit night, the only sounds heard were the gentle rustle of leaves by the October wind, the low murmur of the Shenandoah flowing swiftly along its rocky bed and dashing against the limestone cliffs that bordered it, the churning of the water by the feet of horses on which sat Sheridan's faithful pickets, and the subdued tones or half-whispers of my men as they thoughtfully communed with each other as to the fate which might befall each in the next hour.[17]

At 4:30 A.M. on October 19, the Battle of Cedar Creek, the third engagement between Early and Sheridan, commenced. Gordon, Ramseur and Pegram crossed the Shenandoah River and struck the completely surprised Union left flank, many of the men still asleep in their tents. In accordance with the battle plan, Kershaw attacked Crook from a position closer to the Valley Turnpike, while Brigadier General Gabriel Wharton led his division along the west side of the road. Meanwhile, Confederate cavalry under Crook's men were routed northward across the Valley Turnpike into Emory's division, and all four Union divisions fled toward Wright's corps. Gordon noted: "Large numbers were captured. Many hundreds were shot down as they attempted to escape. Two entire corps, the Eighth and Nineteenth, constituting more than two thirds of Sheridan's Army, broke and fled, leaving the ground covered with arms, accoutrements, knapsacks, and the dead bodies of their comrades.... Sheridan's magnificent cavalry was in full retreat before [Brigadier General Thomas L.] Rosser's bold troopers, who were in position to sweep down upon the other Union flank and rear." By 9:00 A.M., seven Union infantry divisions had been routed, and Early believed the battle was over. This was a mistake.[18]

Wright's Sixth Corps, which had been held in reserve, remained a viable force. Colonel Thomas H. Carter told Gordon that his artillery could dislodge them without use of the infantry. Then, however, Early met Gordon on the field and, seeing Sheridan's men fleeing into the distance, commented, "Well, Gordon, this is glory enough for one day." Referring to the Union Sixth Corps, Gordon responded, "It is very well so far, general; but we have one more blow to strike, and then there will not be left an organized company of infantry in Sheridan's army." Early replied that there was no use in attacking the Sixth Corps because they would retreat with the rest of Sheridan's men. Gordon answered, "That is the Sixth Corps, general. It will not go unless we drive it from the field." Early disagreed, again stating, "Yes, it will go too directly."[19]

With Early's refusal to permit a Confederate assault on the remaining Union corps, Gordon's heart sank into his boots. As that attack progressed, he believed that, like the other Union corps, the Sixth Corps would also be forced from the field in the absence of a "truly marvellous intervention." He did not expect that the intervention would come from the Confederate commander. Once again, Gordon was reminded of the fatal failure to pursue the retreating Union forces on the first day at Gettysburg, and the refusal of Early and Ewell to permit him to execute the attack against the exposed Union right flank on May 6 in the Wilderness. Gordon was convinced that had he been permitted to deliver this one last blow with the combined power of artillery and infantry "the battle would have ended in one of the most complete and inexpensive victories ever won in the war." It was not to be.[20]

Sheridan, still in Winchester, heard the firing in the distance and rode toward the field. He put his head on the pommel of his saddle and listened intently to ascertain the location and intensity of the sound. He realized the increased sound meant his army was falling back. As he came upon his retreating men, he announced, "About face, boys! We are going back to our camps. We are going to lick them out of their boots!" The routed corps of Emory and Crook were reorganized. The Confederate failure to pursue the attack provided Sheridan with the time necessary to regroup north of Middletown for a counterattack. At about 3:00 P.M., Early finally permitted Gordon to go forward but he was repulsed. At 4:00 P.M., Sheridan took the offensive. The Confederates initially held their ground. Gordon's division began the day on the right of the Confederate line but, by the time of the Union counterattack, it was repositioned on the Confederate left through its pursuit of the routed Union forces. Alignment of Confederate troops left a large gap between Gordon's men and the remainder of the Confederate line. Gordon rode to Early to request reinforcements to fill the gap.[21]

Early instructed Gordon to stretch his line. By the time Gordon returned, nothing could be done. Emory's corps exploited the gap, surrounding one of Gordon's brigades, then moving eastward against the remainder of the Confederate line. Despite Gordon's efforts to rally his men, they began to flee. Fearful of being flanked, Ramseur's and Kershaw's divisions also retreated in confusion. At that time, Ramseur, just as he had foreseen, was mortally wounded. Even as the sun began to set, Sheridan pushed his men forward. Gordon noted that "resistance ended as the last organized regiment of Early's literally overwhelmed army broke and fled into the darkness." Sheridan's cavalry captured many Confederates as they attempted to cross Cedar Creek. According to Gordon, "The only possibility of saving the rear regiments was in unrestrained flight — every man for himself."[22]

After crossing Cedar Creek, Gordon gathered a small force hoping to check or slow Sheridan's pursuit of the routed Confederate army. It was no use. Sheridan's men crossed the creek higher up and surrounded Gordon's men on three sides, leaving them no alternative but to flee individually or be captured. Gordon was forced to plunge with his horse down a steep slope: "Wheeling my horse to the dismal brink, I drove my spurs into his flanks, and he plunged downward and tumbled headlong in one direction, sending me in another. How I reached the bottom of that abyss I shall never know; for I was rendered temporarily unconscious. Strangely enough, I was only stunned, and in no way seriously hurt. My horse, too, though bruised, was not disabled.... [H]e promptly responded to my call and rose to his feet." Although a great number of Union soldiers were now between Gordon and the fleeing Confederate army, he was able to ride around them and rejoin his command.[23]

Early claimed that the victory was lost because of the "bad conduct" of Confederate soldiers who stopped to plunder the Union camp. He blamed the officers for not imposing discipline to prevent such behavior, going so far as to say "we have very few field or company officers worth anything." Gordon spent an entire chapter of his autobiography defending the honor of his men and placing the blame for the Confederate defeat squarely on Early's shoulders. He attributed the disaster to the fatal mistake of hesitating and halting the Confederate advance as Union troops fled from the field.[24] While acknowledging that many men straggled and plundered the Union camp, Gordon noted that these men were disabled, and not men with guns. Remarks of Sgt. S.A. Dunning of the Confederate Signal Corps reflect how the ordinary soldier saw Early and Gordon. After noting that Gordon planned the attack at Cedar Creek, Dunning stated,

"Early is very unpopular. Gordon is the favorite of the troops." Early would later take some responsibility for the debacle at Cedar Creek: "The Yankees got whipped; we got scared." Gordon stated that the Battle of Cedar Creek was "a most brilliant victory converted into one of the most complete and ruinous routs of the entire war." Henry Kyd Douglas, who also narrowly escaped being captured, described the Battle of Cedar Creek in even more ominous terms than did Gordon: "One thing is certain; it was to us an irreparable disaster, the beginning of the end."[25]

The disorganized remnants of Early's corps retreated to Fisher's Hill, then farther south to New Market, where they remained for several weeks. Hearing that Sheridan was preparing to send troops to Grant, Early again advanced north, on November 10. Finding that Sheridan occupied a fortified position north of Cedar Creek, and lacking supplies and the ability, if not the will, to attack the Union works, Early returned to New Market. The Valley campaign of 1864 came to a close. Before the winter ended, so had the career of Jubal Early, the man under whom Gordon had served since April 1863. In early March 1865, Sheridan destroyed what remained of Early's forces at Waynesboro, Virginia. Early returned to his home, never again called to duty in the Confederate service.[26]

After Sheridan successfully eliminated the Confederate army in the Valley as an effective fighting force at Cedar Creek, Grant recalled Wright's corps from the Shenandoah Valley to Petersburg and, in response, Lee summoned the divisions of Gordon and Pegram. Sheridan, too, would move to Petersburg for the final confrontation with Lee. The Confederate Second Corps was now back in Petersburg and was placed by Lee under the command of the only nonprofessional soldier to occupy such a position, John Brown Gordon. Lee already had a high opinion of Gordon as a commander and now, with A.P. Hill in poor health and Longstreet closer to Richmond, Gordon became one of Lee's closest confidants.[27]

Chapter 14

Winter 1865 to Fort Stedman

Chamberlain remained hospitalized for three months after he was wounded on June 18 at Rives' Salient. Initially, recovery was uncertain. Chills and high fever kept him in serious condition. Finally, about one month after his hospitalization began, his surgeon felt that Chamberlain was out of danger. Even as he recuperated and would have been justified in focusing upon himself, Chamberlain sought promotions and honors for his men. He received an offer from the president of Bowdoin College to return to his old school, but he had no intention of leaving the army. He was anxious to return to the field.

On September 20, Chamberlain was released to go home to Brunswick, where he continued to gain back his strength. On November 18, despite an inability to walk more than a short distance or to mount a horse without help, he reported back to duty at Petersburg and was reassigned to command of the newly reorganized, and smaller, First Brigade, still in the First Division of the Fifth Corps of the Army of the Potomac. His brigade consisted of the 185th New York and the 198th Pennsylvania.[1]

Shortly before Chamberlain returned to his brigade, Abraham Lincoln was reelected president of the United States. Until the fall, his reelection had been anything but a certainty. Opposing Lincoln for the Democrats was George B. McClellan, the former commander of the Army of the Potomac, who campaigned on a platform of peace with the South. Lincoln himself foresaw the likelihood that the country — tired of war and suffering — would abandon the war effort. The stalemate between the Army of the Potomac and the Army of Northern Virginia at Petersburg did not make victory look likely. Then, in the fall, Sherman succeeded in capturing Atlanta, and Sheridan, transferred to the Shenandoah Valley, inflicted a significant defeat on Confederate forces there.[2]

Spirits in the North rose. Union soldiers, who had loved McClellan as a commander, voted for Lincoln in overwhelming numbers. They realized that stopping the war before victory was achieved meant that all of their suffering would have been in vain. They also knew that a vote for Lincoln meant that the fighting would continue and that some of them would never return home. Yet, they voted for him anyway. Chamberlain, inspired by the soldiers' choice to vote for Lincoln, observed:

> The result of this vote showed how much stronger was their allegiance to principle than even their attachment to McClellan, whose personal popularity in the army was something marvelous. The men voted overwhelmingly for Lincoln. They were unwilling that their long fight should be set down as a failure, even though thus far it seemed so. The fact that this war was in its reach of meaning and consequent effect so much more than what are commonly called "civil wars"— this being a war to test and finally determine the character of the interior constitution and real organic life of this great people — brought into the field an amount of thoughtfulness and moral reflection not usual in armies.[3]

During the Petersburg siege, Grant continued to extend his lines westward in an effort to outflank Lee and to cut off the remaining railroads that connected Petersburg and Richmond to the remainder of the Confederacy. The armies engaged in several actions which lengthened the lines around Petersburg southwest and west across the Boydton Plank Road and Hatcher's Run. In December, the Fifth Corps, still under Warren, headed out to finish off the Weldon Railroad. Union forces had previously cut the railroad but supplies still got through when Confederates unloaded them south of the Union line and moved them by wagon to Lee's army in Petersburg. Chamberlain's brigade participated in tearing up 40 miles of track, afterward heating the rails in large bonfires which, when cooled, turned the rails into useless metal.

The men returned to the Union lines around Petersburg six days later, Lee having chosen not to, or being unable to, mount a challenge to the rail destruction. Grant now controlled the Norfolk Railroad, the Jerusalem Plank Road, and the Weldon Railroad. Remaining to the west were the Boydton Plank Road and the Southside Railroad.[4]

In mid–January 1865, Chamberlain went to Philadelphia for more surgery, then back to Brunswick. The third child of Joshua and Fanny Chamberlain, Gertrude Loraine, was born January 16, 1865. Once again, Chamberlain was offered positions in civilian life and, once again, he chose to rejoin the army. His sense of duty to his country continued to outweigh all other considerations. He returned to Petersburg and the First Brigade in late February, though he missed the latest westward movement to cut off the Boydton Plank Road near Hatcher's Run.

The Fifth Corps under Warren and the Second Corps, now under Major General Andrew A. Humphreys—since Hancock, at his request, had been reassigned—struck out on February 4. Gordon, whose Confederate Second Corps was posted on the extreme right of Lee's line, was present and enjoyed initial success defending against the Union advance, but, eventually, they pushed Gordon's men back toward the Boydton Plank Road and succeeded in eliminating that avenue as a means of supply for the Confederate army at Petersburg. Pegram, one of Gordon's division commanders and a newlywed of three-weeks, was shot and killed. Once again, Lee was forced to farther lengthen his defensive perimeter, using fewer and fewer men to cover more and more line.[5]

The condition of the soldiers in Lee's army was pitiable, with no hope of improvement. By the end of the year, Lee could count about 57,000 soldiers, while Grant's force numbered over 124,000. With less than half as many troops as Grant, Lee was attempting to protect about 37 miles of entrenchments. The Southerners who were in the trenches were required to derive their strength from smaller portions of poor quality food. The daily ration was a pint of cornmeal and an ounce or two of bacon. The bacon was rancid, and the soldiers competed with weevils for possession of the cornmeal. At one prayer meeting, a one-legged Confederate private, unable to kneel, sat with his head bowed as Brother Jonas prayed for more manhood, more strength, and more courage. Dissatisfied with the prayer, the private called out, "Hold on there, Brother Jonas. Don't you know you are praying all wrong? Why don't you pray for more provisions? We've got more courage now than we have any use for."

Gordon recalled the Christmas of 1864 as being "joyless." The men lacked necessary supplies, and their families at home had little to send them. Soldiers could sometimes be seen gathering wasted corn from under the feet of half-fed horses, which often made the men sick. Adequate clothing for the cold Virginia winter was also scarce. Gordon directed his commands to send wagons into the countryside to buy anything that could be obtained to sustain the life of the army. He recalled, "Starvation, literal starvation, was doing its deadly work." Desertions rose as men received pitiful pleas from home to return to their families where wives and children suffered many of the same deprivations as their soldiers. Lee wrote to Richmond pleading for reinforcements, but none existed. As Lee had accurately predicted, if the contest became a siege, it would only be a matter of time.[6]

In response to the need for more troops, some in the Confederacy proposed the unthinkable. In late 1863, Confederate major general Pat Cleburne suggested that the South free its slaves and use them as soldiers. Little came of his "outrageous" suggestion until early 1865, when the pressure on Lee's army in defending Petersburg and Richmond was becoming overwhelming and the struggle for the Southern cause had become most desperate. Opinions for and against the proposal were strong. Gordon sent a letter to Adjutant General Walter Taylor on February 18, 1865, advising him that officers and men were decidedly in favor of the voluntary enlistment of Negroes as soldiers. He suggested that his report be conveyed to the authorities in Richmond. Another letter from Gordon dated February 26 noted the high number of desertions, and the disappointment in the ranks because of the apparent defeat of the Negro bill.[7]

Lee also favored the proposal — a highly respected voice in support — but many recognized that freeing slaves and sanctioning their service in the Confederate army contravened the basis for establishment of the Confederacy to begin with — to protect the property rights of Southerners. As Howell Cobb, a leading secessionist, stated succinctly, "If slaves will make good soldiers our whole theory of slavery is wrong." Another opponent to the use of Negro soldiers, Confederate senator Robert Hunter, stated, in language similar to that of Cobb, "If we are right in passing this measure, we were wrong in denying the old government the right to interfere with the institution of slavery and to emancipate slaves."

Nevertheless, in mid–March 1865, the Confederate congress and Jefferson Davis authorized the use of Negro soldiers, though their reward for fighting for Southern independence and, hence, preserving the South's right to maintain the institution of slavery, would be pay, not their freedom. Slaveholders, who had to approve the use of their slaves, provided almost no support. In any case, it was too late. The events which would lead to the collapse of the Petersburg defenses and to the surrender of the Army of Northern Virginia at Appomattox were about to begin.[8]

The most recent proposal for peace had already failed. Lincoln had approved the request of Francis P. Blair to approach his old friend Jefferson Davis to discuss possible resolution of the war. Davis agreed to send a Confederate commission, consisting of Vice-President Alexander H. Stephens, former Supreme Court Justice John A. Campbell, and Senator Hunter. The outcome of the effort was foretold by Davis' communication to Lincoln discussing peace between "the two countries" and Lincoln's response referring to "our one common country." Nevertheless, at Grant's suggestion, Lincoln traveled from Washington and met personally with the peace commissioners aboard his steamer behind Union lines at Petersburg on February 3, 1865.[9]

Stephens asked Lincoln whether there was any way of putting an end to the war. Lincoln bluntly replied, "There is but one way, and that is for those who are resisting the laws of the Union to cease that resistance." The Confederate commissioners were shocked to learn that, only days before, the United States Congress had passed the Thirteenth Amendment prohibiting slavery. As Lincoln disclosed what seemed rather stringent terms for the South's reentry into the Union, Hunter, disheartened, finally asked, "Mr. President, if we understand you correctly, you think that we of the Confederacy have committed treason; that we are traitors to your government; that we have forfeited our rights, and are proper subjects for the hangman. Is that not about what your words imply?" Honest Abe responded directly and forthrightly, "Yes. You have stated the proposition better than I did. That is about the size of it."[10]

In Lincoln's mind, peace had never been and would never be possible if it did not include restoration of the Union, while Davis would never forego his demand for Southern independence. In early March, the last peace proposal was made — this time between the military commanders themselves. At the suggestion of Union major general Edward Ord, Longstreet, who had recovered from his Wilderness wound and returned to command, intimated to Lee that Lee and Grant might be able to resolve the issue themselves. On March 2, Lee sent a letter to Grant proposing to discuss a military settlement. Wisely reluctant to act on his own, Grant promptly forwarded the request to Washington. Submitted through secretary of state Edwin M. Stanton, Lincoln's response was immediate and even more direct than his reply to Hunter: "The President directs me to say to you that he wishes you to have no conference with General Lee unless it be for the capitulation of Gen. Lee's army, or on some minor and purely military matter.... Meantime you are to press to the utmost your military advantages." The war must end on the battlefield.[11]

Despite Lee's many military successes and the belief by many in the South that Lee was their supreme military leader, his command until this time had been limited to the Army of Northern Virginia. In mid–January 1865, the Confederate congress, in the hope of salvaging the deteriorating military situation, authorized creation of the position of general-in-chief. Davis approved the measure and appointed Lee to fill the post, which the Confederate congress readily approved. Lee's first proposal as general-in-chief was directed toward restoration of his ever diminishing army. He sought Davis' consent to pardon all deserters and absentees who returned to their units. Davis agreed. Nevertheless, Confederate desertions continued in alarming numbers.[12]

Lee knew that the days of the Army of Northern Virginia in its present position were numbered. Sherman's successful march through the South meant that it was only a matter of time before he would join forces with Grant and crush what remained of Lee's army. Lee considered abandonment of the Petersburg and Richmond defenses and a movement south to join with the Army of Tennessee, under the command of Joseph Johnston. However, he suspected that Jefferson Davis would oppose the idea, because it would mean the surrender of the Confederate capital; it was also conceivable that Grant would strike him first and make escape impossible. In his dilemma, Lee could have chosen to consult with his veteran corps commanders, A.P. Hill, Longstreet or Ewell. Instead, during February 1865, Lee summoned Gordon to his headquarters.[13]

Upon entering the room, Gordon recalled, "For the first time in all my intercourse with him, I saw a look of painful depression on [Lee's] face." Gordon was presented with a table covered with recent reports from every part of the Confederate army. Lee wanted Gordon to read them. Gordon did so and was shocked by what he learned. The condition of the army was even worse than he had imagined. The reports reflected "depleted strength, emaciation, and decreased power of endurance among those who appeared on the rolls as fit for duty." More than a few cases were reported of "good men, faithful, tried, and devoted" who exhibited "temporary insanity and indifference to orders or to the consequences of disobedience—the natural and inevitable effect of their mental and bodily sufferings." Lee's estimate that Grant possessed three times as many soldiers was frighteningly accurate. After painting the obviously desperate picture, Lee asked Gordon what he thought they should do. Hardly could Gordon have imagined, four years earlier when he joined the Confederate army as captain of the Raccoon Roughs, that now, near the end, he would be one of Robert E. Lee's ablest and most trusted generals, and the one to whom he would turn to avert disaster.[14]

Gordon responded: "General, it seems to me there are but three courses, and I name them in the order in which I think they should be tried: First, make terms with the enemy, the best we can get. Second, if that is not practicable, the best thing to do is to retreat—abandon Richmond and Petersburg, unite by rapid marches with General Johnston in North Carolina, and strike Sherman before Grant can join him; or, lastly, we must fight, and without delay." Lee agreed with Gordon fully. He indicated that he was reluctant to suggest to Davis and the Richmond government that they seek a political solution. Lee doubted that Davis would agree to allow the Confederate army to withdraw, leaving Richmond open to Grant's force. He then discussed the difficulties associated with abandonment of the Richmond/Petersburg defenses and a march to join with Johnston, including the fact that the Army of Northern Virginia consisted of starving men and horses who could hardly be expected to accomplish such a feat.

Lee traveled to Richmond, where Davis confirmed that Gordon's first two proposals were not viable.[15] Upon his return, Lee advised Gordon of the result of his meeting with Davis. In response to Gordon's query regarding what could be done, Lee stated that they must fight. He directed that Gordon's corps switch places with the corps around Petersburg and that Gordon study the Union works to determine where a blow could be struck. After spending a week investigating all possibilities, Gordon recommended a strike at Fort Stedman, on the Union works east of Petersburg. The fort was only about 150 yards from Colquitt's Salient, in the Confederate works from where the attack could be launched. Gordon meticulously planned the attack, then presented his proposal to Lee.[16]

Gordon planned a night assault with his entire corps. First, the Confederates must quietly remove the chevaux-de-frise (a defensive structure consisting of a movable obstacle composed of barbed wire or spikes attached to a wooden frame) in front of their own works. This would begin shortly after dark on the evening before the attack. Gordon advised Lee that the attack would be made at 4:00 A.M., led by 50 men with axes whose job was to cut a passage through the abatis (a defensive obstacle formed by felled trees with sharpened branches facing the enemy) in front of the Union line at Fort Stedman. Gordon's infantry, close behind, would rush into the fort, then take the breastworks to the right and left. To deepen the penetration, Gordon would then move through an open space behind Fort Stedman to three forts in the rear. Through his investigation, Gordon learned the names of Union officers posted in the Union front. Three Confederate soldiers would assume the identity of those officers, and lead a group of 100 men each. They would yell that Fort Stedman had fallen and that they had been directed to defend the three forts in the rear.[17]

Lee approved the plan but, trusting Gordon as he had previously trusted Stonewall Jackson, he left the details to Gordon. Concerned that Gordon's men would have difficulty finding the rear forts in the darkness, Lee found three men, to serve as guides, who were familiar with the area where the forts stood. Additionally, he added the weight of four brigades from A.P. Hill, two brigades from Richard Anderson, and a cavalry division, bringing the assaulting column under Gordon's command to almost half of the Confederate force at Petersburg.

Fanny Gordon, still near her husband, tore strips of white cloth in her room at Petersburg to tie to the uniforms of the leading units so they could recognize each other in the dark and ensuing battle. By 4:00 A.M. on Saturday, March 25, the Confederate obstacles had been removed, the 50 axemen received their axes, and the three men chosen to pose as Union officers and their 100-man detachments were ready. Twelve thousand Southern soldiers in all were prepared for battle. A soldier at Gordon's side was designated, upon command, to fire a single shot to signal the beginning of the attack.[18] Gordon could not help but be amazed at the spirit of the debilitated Confederate soldiers as they awaited the beginning of the assault. Despite their hunger and despair, they "welcomed with a readiness intensely pathetic the order to break camp and move into the trenches at Petersburg." Gordon observed, "Like fires that consume the dross and make pure the metal, Confederate distress and extremity seemed to strengthen and ennoble rather than weaken Confederate manhood." Finding it easy to "comprehend the enthusiasm of these same Confederates during the long period when recurring battles meant recurring victories," Gordon wondered what accounted for their continuing emotional fortitude "in the presence of apparently inevitable and overwhelming disaster … when [e]verything was exhausted except devotion and valor." He attributed their continuing resolve to "a defense of State, of home, and of liberty," for which each soldier was willing to die.[19]

Commencement of the attack on Fort Stedman was preceded by a minor, somewhat humorous event, the type of incident that was perhaps unique to the American Civil War. As Confederates removed the last of the obstructions, a Union picket was alerted by the noise. Because the pickets of the two armies were so close together at this point, an understanding existed between them that they would only shoot if necessary. The Union soldier called out, "What are you doing over there, Johnny? What is that noise? Answer quick or I'll shoot." Thinking quickly, the signalman standing with Gordon responded, "Never mind, Yank. Lie down and go to sleep. We are just gathering a little corn. You know rations are mighty short over here." Satisfied, the Union soldier replied, "All right, Johnny; go ahead and get your corn. I'll not shoot at you while you are drawing your rations."[20]

The last obstruction was removed, and surprise had been preserved. Gordon ordered the private to fire the signal shot. He pointed his rifle into the air, then hesitated, feeling guilt at having misled the Union picket. As Gordon recalled, "He was going into the fearful charge, and he evidently did not feel disposed to go into eternity with the lie on his lips.... He evidently felt that it was hardly fair to take advantage of the generosity and soldierly sympathy of his foe, who had so magnanimously assured him that he would not be shot while drawing his rations from the little field of corn." Gordon again ordered the private to fire. The signalman called out, "Hello, Yank. Wake up; we are going to shell the woods. Look out; we are coming." Satisfied, he fired the shot commencing the attack.[21]

Confederate pickets rushed forward and seized the Union pickets before an alarm could be given. The axemen followed and quickly opened a gap for the Southern infantry. They rushed into Fort Stedman, quickly capturing its defenders before they could use their artillery pieces against the onrushing Confederates. The guns, which had been pointing west, were turned north and south to clear out the Union breastworks above and below the fort, which the Confederate attackers then occupied. Battery 10 to the immediate north and Battery 11 to the immediate south were captured. Gordon, who was now in Fort Stedman, sent a progress report to Lee, who was watching from a hill behind the Confederate lines. The attack, which had been very successful to this point, was about to turn against them.[22]

Near dawn, the three Union officer impostors and their 300 men moved toward the rear. Before long, all three reported to Gordon that the guides were unable to find the rear forts the three 100-man detachments were designated to capture. In fact, there were no Union forts in the rear, only the unoccupied remains of works which had formed part of the old Confederate Dimmock line. The inability of Gordon's force to occupy these forts was disastrous for the assault. The Union defense at Battery 9 to the north and Battery 12 to the south stiffened, precluding a widening of the breach. Union artillery fire pounded the Confederates in Fort Stedman and in the adjoining breastworks that had been captured. Union infantry reinforcements added to the pressure on Gordon's men. At about 8:00 A.M., Lee instructed Gordon to withdraw. The intense Union fire made this extremely difficult. Gordon, slightly wounded, was able to reach the Confederate lines but approximately 1900 Confederates were captured. Total Confederate casualties, which were irreplaceable, reached 3500, while Union losses reached slightly above 1000.[23]

In his memoirs, Grant stated, "The plan was well conceived and the execution of it very well done indeed, up to the point of carrying a portion of our line." However, at the time, he recognized that the Confederate attack on Fort Stedman was a sign of Lee's desperation. Grant immediately ordered an assault on the Confederate right flank, which he believed, correctly, had been weakened to provide troops for the Fort Stedman attack. Hill's entrenched picket line near Hatcher's Run was successfully attacked, inflicting another 1300 casualties on Lee's army. Gordon described the failure at Fort Stedman as "the expiring struggle of the Confederate giant." Lee, too, recognized its significance. On March 26, he wrote Jefferson Davis and advised him that the Army of Northern Virginia could no longer either maintain its present position or prevent Sherman from joining with Grant. Events were now moving rapidly toward a conclusion.[24]

Chapter 15

Quaker Road to Five Forks

At the same time that Gordon prepared to launch his attack on Fort Stedman, Grant sent orders to his commanders for the movement that he believed would flank Lee's army out of its Petersburg defense. Sheridan and his cavalry were now on hand. The Second Corps under Humphreys and the Fifth Corps under Warren would move westward toward Five Forks, where they would assist Sheridan in cutting off the last two remaining railroads out of Petersburg and Richmond to the south, the Southside Railroad and the Danville Railroad. Major General Edward Ord would cross the James River to occupy that portion of the line those corps had been manning. The movement began March 29. Lee immediately responded by reinforcing the Confederate right flank with infantry and cavalry divisions.[1]

Grant's order was exciting to Chamberlain and the Union soldiers who saw the westward shift as the final advance and prelude to victory. On the night before it began, many wrote a final message home. For each man, Chamberlain stated, "there was in his heart a strange mingling of emotion, the vision of great joy, in which, perhaps, he was to lie silent and apart, a little shadow on the earth, but overhead a great light filling the sky. This lifted him to the surpassing joy that, however it should be with him, his work and worth had entered into the country's life and honor." Many men, North and South, who had fought so bravely over part or all of the past four years, who had survived so many deadly battles, and who had experienced the death of so many beloved comrades, would not live to see the peace that was only days away.[2]

The area where the Union and Confederate armies would fight over the next few days was approximately 10 to 15 miles southwest of Petersburg. The Boydton Plank Road ran predominantly southwest from Petersburg through Dinwiddie Courthouse. The Southside Railroad, one of the initial objects of Grant's movement, ran westerly from Petersburg. From a point just south of the crossing of Hatcher's Run and the Boydton Plank Road, about eight miles from Petersburg, the White Oak Road ran westerly through Five Forks. Gravelly Run, which ran northwesterly and parallel to Hatcher's Run, intersected the Boydton Plank Road approximately two miles south of the White Oak Road. The Quaker Road, running north and south, terminated on the Boydton Plank Road about midway between Hatcher's Run and Gravelly Run.[3]

Warren's Fifth Corps moved out early on March 29. Major General Charles Griffin still commanded the First Division, while Brigadier General Romeyn Ayres led the Second Division, and Brigadier General Samuel W. Crawford the Third. Chamberlain's First Brigade in Griffin's Division consisted of about 1750 men of the 198th Pennsylvania led by Colonel Horatio G. Sickel, and the 185th New York, commanded by Colonel Gustave Sniper. Griffin's division marched out first with Chamberlain's brigade in the lead. Around noon, Griffin directed Chamberlain to take his brigade up the Quaker Road to discover the location of the Confederate position. They reached Gravelly Run. The bridge over the run had been destroyed, and Confederates were posted in a defensive position on the north bank, waiting for the Union advance.[4]

Chamberlain proposed a plan which Griffin readily approved. He placed Sickel with eight companies on the right side of the ruined bridge to occupy the Confederates with a heavy fire while Chamberlain led other troops wading over Gravelly Run from the other side of the bridge to strike the Confederate line obliquely. After hand-to-hand combat, the movement succeeded, dislodging the Confederates and pushing them nearly a mile north up the Quaker Road to the Lewis farm, located about 200 yards to the right of the road. Though reinforced at that point, the Confederates fell back farther under the pressure of Chamberlain's advance. At the edge of a thick woods, the retreat stopped where a large body of Confederates waited behind substantial breastworks.[5]

The protected Confederates poured a deadly fire into the oncoming Federals, stopping Chamberlain's brigade, which had been broken into groups, and forcing them backward. Attempting to seize the initiative, Confederates left their defensive position and attacked. Again, the fighting was hand-to-hand. Both sides dragged prisoners back to their lines. Finally, the Confederates were forced back to the woods, and Chamberlain regrouped around the buildings of the Lewis farm.[6] Griffin was eager to resume the attack. Chamberlain placed Sickel on the right of the Quaker

Road and Sniper on the left. With six companies, Chamberlain attacked straight up the road. The object of the assault was a sawdust pile at an old sawmill, which was now the center of the Confederate line, about two to three hundred yards beyond the Lewis farmhouse. The fighting was fierce. As Chamberlain approached the sawdust pile, he gave a check to Charlemagne, who had gotten too far ahead of the troops. At that moment, as the horse reared in defiance, a minie ball aimed for Chamberlain's chest passed through the muscles of Charlemagne's neck, striking and badly bruising Chamberlain's left arm and hitting him in the left breast just below his heart before moving around two ribs and out the back seam of his coat. The shot also smashed through a leather case of field orders and a brass mirror in Chamberlain's pocket. Before finally being spent, the ball knocked Chamberlain's aide out of his saddle.[7]

Chamberlain was knocked unconscious and fell forward onto Charlemagne's neck. The horse stopped and was bleeding badly. Chamberlain regained consciousness to find the arm of General Griffin around his waist. Believing Chamberlain was mortally wounded, Griffin softly stated, "My dear General, you are gone." General Griffin was not the only one who believed that Chamberlain was dead; a telegram was sent to the New York morning papers reporting that he had been killed. Chamberlain also heard a louder, more unfriendly sound, the shrill Rebel yell coming from Confederates breaking through the right of Chamberlain's line. In reply to General Griffin, but in a different sense, as he saw the immediate danger posed by the retreating 198th Pennsylvania, Chamberlain exclaimed, "Yes, General, I am." He spurred Charlemagne and rode, "tattered and battered, bare-headed and blood smeared," to help rally the men on the right. Sickel was wounded but, inspired by Chamberlain's unearthly appearance, the regiment re-formed and forced the Confederates back to their works.[8]

With the right stabilized, Chamberlain rode back to the sawdust pile in the center. Both Union and Confederate soldiers cheered his brave and gallant effort. Due to loss of blood, Charlemagne could go no farther, and Chamberlain continued on foot. As he moved forward in the confusion, Chamberlain suddenly found himself surrounded by the points of Confederate bayonets. In his dingy old coat, hatless, covered in blood, his left arm hanging useless, he hardly presented the appearance of a Union officer. He had successfully employed his Southern drawl at Fredericksburg, and he would try it again. "Surrender? What's the matter with you? What do you take me for? Don't you see these Yanks right onto us? Come along with me and let us break 'em." He pointed with his sword toward his own men, and was followed too far by many of the Confederates he led into capture.⁹

On the left, Sniper's 185th New York had been badly cut up attempting to storm the enemy works, and were now falling back with the Confederates in pursuit. Chamberlain, now astride another horse, rode to where the New Yorkers had been forced back perpendicular to its original line. Griffin came up and assured Chamberlain, "If you can hold on there ten minutes, I will give you a battery." He shouted the news to Sniper, hoping the message would be heard by his men: "Once more! Try the steel! Hell for ten minutes and we are out of it!" Chamberlain planned to smash the Confederates with artillery fire, then charge their works.¹⁰

The New Yorkers held their ground, and, as promised, up rode Lieutenant John Mitchell with Battery B of the 4th United States Artillery. As Chamberlain rode to meet him, Mitchell could not restrain a smile prompted by Chamberlain's remarkable appearance. "Mitchell," Chamberlain said, "do you think you can put solid shot or percussion into those woods close over the rebels' heads, without hurting my men?" Mitchell replied that he could. Satisfied, Chamberlain told him to proceed but to be prepared to stop firing on Chamberlain's signal.¹¹ Chamberlain recalled the scene as Mitchell's guns fired into the woods:

> It was splendid and terrible: the swift-served, bellowing, leaping big guns; the thrashing of the solid shot into the woods; the flying splinters and branches and tree-tops coming down upon the astonished heads; shouts changing into shrieks at the savage work of these unaccustomed missiles; then answering back the burst of fire oblique upon the left front of the battery, where there was a desperate attempt to carry it by flank attack; repulsed by Sniper drawing to the left, and thus also leaving clear range for closer cutting projectiles, when now case shot and shell, now a blast of canister, poured into the swarming, swirling foe.

Griffin rode up looking anxious and troubled. "General," Griffin stated to Chamberlain, "you must not leave us. We cannot spare you now." Somewhat perplexed by the statement, Chamberlain responded, "I had no thought of it, General."

With Griffin came four regiments of reinforcements. Chamberlain's left had been bending under Confederate pressure but Mitchell's artillery fire and the weight of the new units turned the tide. Soon, the Confederates in the woods were routed and forced back up the Quaker Road to their main entrenchments on the White Oak Road. In his post-action report, Chamberlain expressed understandable pride in the conduct of his men and the gallantry of his regimental commanders. Chamberlain's brigade of 1,700, reinforced near the end by 1,000 men from other brigades in the First Division, had been fighting 6,200 Confederates under the command of General Richard Anderson.[12]

After the battle, Chamberlain, his clothes riddled with bullets, rode over the field, which was covered with the dead and dying of both sides. Nearly two hundred Confederate prisoners had been taken. His compassion was not reserved for Union casualties: "Seeking also the wounded of the enemy, led mostly by moans and supplications — souls left so lonely, forlorn, and far away from all the caring; caring for these too, and partly for that very reason; gathering them out of the cold and rain when possible — for 'blood is thicker than water,' — we treated them as our own. 'How far that little candle throws its beams!' Indeed, in the hour of sorrow and disaster do we not all belong to each other?" The death of Union Major Charles I. McEuen particularly touched Chamberlain. With his hand laid on Chamberlain's shoulder, Doctor McEuen of Philadelphia, Major McEuen's father, had commended the care of his only son to Chamberlain. Now, it was Chamberlain's sad and difficult task to write Doctor McEuen "to tell him how, in the forefront of battle and in act of heroic devotion, his noble boy had been lifted to his like, and his own cherished hope merged with immortal things."

Also lying on the field, severely wounded, was Colonel Sickel. As Chamberlain sat beside him to comfort and cheer him, Sickel told him, "General, you have the soul of the lion and the heart of the woman." General Warren was, once again, impressed by Chamberlain's actions. He promised that Washington would hear of Chamberlain's "splendid work." Soon after, Chamberlain was recommended for promotion to brevet major general for "conspicuous gallantry in action on the Quaker Road, March 29, 1865." The promotion was approved in July 1865.[13]

March 30 was a day of relative quiet for the Fifth Corps. Relieved by Humphreys' Second Corps, they moved down the Boydton Plank Road as far as Gravelly Run. The Union success of the 29th on the Quaker Road prompted Grant to redirect Sheridan, away from his original purpose of cutting the railroads, to a movement from Dinwiddie Courthouse to Five Forks. Grant hoped that Sheridan would be able to get around Lee's right flank and into the rear of the Confederate army. Meanwhile, Warren was ordered to support Sheridan by advancing against the White Oak Road. Early on March 31, the Fifth Corps moved about one-half mile north of the Boydton Plank Road. The White Oak Road was a mile and half farther north. Ayres' Second Division was in the lead, with Crawford's Third Division to his right and rear in echelon, and Griffin's First Division in the rear and to the left of Crawford. Chamberlain's brigade was positioned on the extreme left of the First Division and, thus, served as the vulnerable left flank of both the Fifth and Second Corps.[14]

Lee had no intention of merely waiting for Grant to attack him. He had been aggressive in the past when he was outnumbered, and now that matters were even more desperate for the Army of Northern Virginia, Lee sent his undermanned force forward again. Sheridan was at Dinwiddie Courthouse with his cavalry, which he sent toward Five Forks, a critical road junction on the White Oak Road and only three miles from the Southside Railroad. George Pickett, whose division had been devastated on the third day at Gettysburg, was summoned from Longstreet on the James. With his 6,400 infantry and 5,400 cavalry soldiers under Major General Fitzhugh Lee, Pickett was sent against the advancing Union cavalry on March 31. They drove Sheridan's cavalry back all the way to Dinwiddie. Sheridan was not, in the least, discouraged by this setback. Instead, he requested that Grant send him the Sixth Corps so that he could attack Pickett's isolated force. Grant advised Sheridan that the Sixth Corps could not be moved from its present position but sent word on the evening of March 31 for the Fifth Corps to march to Dinwiddie and report to Sheridan, who was given overall command of the field.[15]

The Fifth Corps had also been hard-pressed on March 31. As Ayres began his advance on the White Oak Road, four brigades of Confederate infantry in General Bushrod Johnson's division, under direct command of Lee, poured out of their works and attacked. Ayres' entire front was enveloped. Despite Ayres' best efforts to steady his men, brigade after brigade of his Second Division broke in panic and ran for the rear. They passed through the men of Crawford's division, many of whom joined in the retreat, with the Confederates in pursuit. As they reached the First Division, Griffin ordered his own men to let them through to prevent his line from being broken.[16]

Back on May 5, 1864, as Griffin and the First Division drove General Johnson's division down the Orange Turnpike, it was Ewell who raced to Early's division and exclaimed to Gordon, "General Gordon! The day depends on you!" Now, in the midst of the rout of the Fifth Corps, Warren, the corps commander, and Griffin, the division commander, turned to the man who they believed could save the day for the Union—Chamberlain. They rode to him at full speed with Griffin proclaiming, "General Chamberlain, the Fifth Corps is eternally damned." "Not till you are in heaven," Chamberlain replied. Griffin then stated, "I tell Warren you will wipe out this disgrace, and that's what we're here for." Warren then added a desperate plea: "General Chamberlain, will you save the honor of the Fifth Corps? That's all there is about it." Chamberlain, in defense of his own brigade, which had suffered terribly two days before on the Quaker Road, suggested Bartlett's larger brigade, which had been only minimally engaged on the previous day. Griffin and Warren would not hear of it: "We have come to you; you know what that means." Ready as ever, Chamberlain stated, "I'll try it, General; only don't let anybody stop me except the enemy."[17]

The 198th Pennsylvania, now under the command of Major Edwin A. Glenn, was the first to move across Gravelly Run, followed by the 185th New York. Chamberlain's brigade stopped the Confederate advance and forced them back until they found their support. Brigadier General Edgar M. Gregory's Second Brigade joined in the counterattack with Bartlett's Third Brigade, and the 20th Maine, in reserve. Ayres' and Crawford's divisions also regained their organization and helped push the Confederates back.

After Chamberlain succeeded in regaining all of the ground lost by the Second and Third Divisions, and directly contrary to his request when he commenced his advance, Warren ordered a halt. Chamberlain rode back and persuaded him that his brigade was in a precarious position and that with a further advance, he could take the White Oak Road. With the help of Gregory's Second Brigade, Chamberlain's men struck the right and left of the Confederate position, forcing them out of their entrenchments. Chamberlain described the action:

> What we had to do could not be done by firing. This was foot-and-hand business. We went with a rush, not minding ranks nor alignments, but with open front to lessen loss from the long-range rifles. Within effective range, about three hundred yards, the sharp, cutting fire made us reel and shiver. Now, quick or never! On and over! The impetuous 185th New York rolls over the enemy's right, and seems to swallow it up; the 198th Pennsylvania, with its fourteen companies, half veterans, half soldiers "born so," swing in upon their left, striking Hunton's brigade in front, and for a few minutes, there is a seething wave of countercurrents, then rolling back, leaving a fringe of wrecks — and all is over. We pour over the works, swing to the right and drive the enemy into their entrenchments along the Claiborne Road, and then establish ourselves across the White Oak Road facing northeast and take breath.

According to Griffin, Chamberlain "pushed boldly forward, carrying [the enemy] in a handsome manner, taking one flag and about 135 prisoners, and gaining possession of the White Oak road." Mounting one of the parapets, Private Augustus Ziever of the 198th Pennsylvania captured the flag of the 46th Virginia and handed it to Chamberlain. Such prizes were usually rewarded with a medal of honor. Chamberlain immediately gave the flag back to Ziever and told him to take the credit that belonged to him.[18]

Although the Fifth Corps had accomplished one of Grant's major objectives, it would not be allowed to remain long on the field it had fought so hard to take. Firing could be heard to the southwest and seemed to be receding. This could only mean that Sheridan's cavalry was being beaten back from Five Forks, as, in fact, it was. Before being ordered to do so by headquarters, Warren determined to send troops to Sheridan's support. When he asked Chamberlain if he would go, Chamberlain expressed his willingness but questioned the wisdom of abandoning the position they now held across the White Oak Road. Warren then directed Griffin to send Bartlett's brigade to threaten the rear of the Confederates opposing Sheridan.[19]

At about 6:30 P.M., an hour after sending Bartlett, Warren received orders from Meade directing him to send a brigade to Sheridan's aid. Two hours later, Warren was ordered to withdraw the Fifth Corps to the Boydton Plank Road and send Griffin's division to Dinwiddie five miles away. Grant had determined to abandon the Union hold on the White Oak Road. The night was filled with confusing communications concerning the movement of Warren's divisions and the routes they should take. It would be nearly daylight before Chamberlain's brigade pulled away from the White Oak Road. The entire Fifth Corps would soon follow.[20]

At about 7:00 A.M. on April 1, Chamberlain arrived at the J. Boisseau house near the road between Five Forks and the Dinwiddie Courthouse where he had the misfortune of running into Sheridan himself. Sheridan was angry, having expected the Fifth Corps to arrive during the night for a daybreak attack on Pickett's infantry and Fitzhugh Lee's cavalry. As it turned out, the approach of Bartlett's brigade scared the Confederates back to Five Forks without a shot being fired. Chamberlain saluted and politely addressed Sheridan: "I report to you, General, with the head of Griffin's Division." Sheridan, more interested in results than in ceremony, sternly responded, "Why did you not come before? Where is Warren?" Chamberlain answered that he was at the rear of the column. Sheridan shot back, "That is where I expected to find him. What is he doing there?" As Chamberlain explained that Warren was supervising the disengagement of the Fifth Corps from the White Oak Road, Griffin rode up. Chamberlain thankfully left the two men and returned to his brigade.[21]

Warren arrived around 11:00 A.M. but the remainder of the Fifth Corps would not be present before noon. It would not be Warren's Fifth Corps much longer. Dissatisfied with what he perceived as Warren's dilatory movements in the battle at White Oak Road and in moving to Dinwiddie Courthouse, Grant sent word to Sheridan authorizing him to remove Warren from command if he felt it was necessary. For now, though, Sheridan planned his attack. The Confederate breastworks, manned by Pickett's men, ran for a mile or so along the White Oak Road, blocking the Five Forks intersection. Three-quarters of a mile east of that point, the line bent northward for 150 to 200 yards. Between that flank and the Confederate position near the intersection of the Quaker Road and the White Oak Road was a distance of four miles. While Union cavalry kept the front of the Confederate line occupied, Sheridan intended to hit this gap with 16,000 infantry soldiers.[22]

To Sheridan's extreme disappointment, it was 4:30 P.M. before the advance began. Unbeknownst to Sheridan and the Union field commanders, and even to Confederate subordinates, the Confederate commanders were nowhere near. Convinced that no attack would be made that day, Pickett and Fitzhugh Lee rode to the rear to attend a shad bake, and they failed to tell anyone where they were going. The plan was for Ayres' Second Division to march on the west side of the Gravelly Run Church Road and strike the Confederate line at the "angle"—the point it turned north near the intersection of the Gravelly Run Church Road with the White Oak Road. Crawford's Third Division was to march up the east side of the road, with Griffin's First Division behind. These latter divisions would move to the right of Ayres and into the Confederate rear, then sweep westward down the White Oak Road, rolling up the Confederate defense. However, fatal to proper execution of the plan, the diagram of the Confederate positions proved to be defective.[23]

When Ayres reached and crossed the White Oak Road, the end of the Confederate line was not there. Instead, it was one-half mile to the west. Ayres immediately reacted by turning his division westward. Meanwhile, ignorant of the correction, Crawford and Griffin continued to move north. Chamberlain was posted on the left of Griffin's division, which was in the rear of Crawford's division. Suddenly, the roar of gunfire could be heard to the west, meaning that Ayres was engaged. Chamberlain halted his line and rode to a high clearing on the southeast corner of Sydnor Field. He saw the Second Division fighting alone about 600 yards away. A large gap existed now between Ayres and the other divisions of the Fifth Corps which was not in the plans. The First and Third divisions had marched past the Confederate line and much too far to the east.[24]

Seeing Griffin in that direction, Chamberlain took it upon himself to move against the danger and support Ayres. He pulled his brigade out of the woods to march toward Ayres and directed Gregory to follow with his brigade. Word was also sent to Bartlett. On the way, Chamberlain met Griffin, who ordered him to attack on the right where Confederates, occupying the northern extension of their line from the main works on White Oak Road, were subjecting Ayres' division to a crossfire. Chamberlain, Gregory and Bartlett hit the line obliquely on the flank and rear, causing many of the Confederates to flee or surrender. The crossfire on Ayres was stopped.[25]

Near the angle of the Confederate line, Chamberlain once again ran into Sheridan, this time under favorable circumstances. Having seen Chamberlain lead his men into the battle against the Confederate line, Sheridan exclaimed, "By God, that's what I want to see, general officers at the front!" Sheridan then directed Chamberlain to take command of all of the infantry in the vicinity and break the Rebel line. As he sought to gather scattered groups of men, Chamberlain saw one Union soldier on his hands and knees behind a stump. Rather than berate the young man for cowardice, Chamberlain encouraged him to return to the fight. "But what can I do?" the soldier replied. "I can't stand up against all this alone." "We're forming here," Chamberlain responded. "I want you for guide center." The man stood up—needing only, as Chamberlain recognized, "a token of confidence and appreciation to get possession of himself"—and proudly took his place. In the midst of the confusion and terror of battle, Chamberlain's understanding and quiet compassion restored the young soldier's courage and inspired him to rejoin the battle.[26]

Chamberlain also came upon Brigadier General Edgar Gwyn, leading one of Ayres' brigades. Gwyn had lost touch with Ayres and knew not what to do. Chamberlain told him, "Then come with me. I will take the responsibility. You shall have all the credit. Let me take your brigade for a moment." Chamberlain's soldiers advanced against the northern extension of the Confederate line, as Ayres' division fought at the angle to Chamberlain's left. Sheridan remonstrated against both of them for firing into his cavalry, though Ayres and Chamberlain insisted that they were shooting at the men who were shooting at them. Soon, Chamberlain was, once again, alone with Sheridan. Concerned for his safety, Chamberlain encouraged Sheridan to move himself away from the danger. With a comical look on his face that indicated to Chamberlain that Sheridan did not care much for himself, or for Chamberlain either, Sheridan stated, "Yes, I think I'll go." Then he proceeded to ride directly toward the crossfire they had just discussed. According to Chamberlain, Sheridan did order his cavalry to stop firing into the Union infantry.[27]

The fighting was confused, and the commands were intermingled. At one point, Chamberlain observed a large number of Confederates approaching from behind. He ordered his men to fire to the rear but, as they turned, the Confederates threw down their weapons and surrendered. Others, however, continued to stubbornly resist. When Chamberlain's left center was being held up by a Confederate line near the Ford Road, which ran north from the White Oak Road, he necessarily but impetuously issued this command: "Major Glenn, if you will break that line you shall have a colonel's commission!" Glenn called out, "Boys, will you follow me?" He turned his horse to break the line, without waiting for his regiment. His men did follow and breached the breastworks.[28]

As Chamberlain sought to congratulate Glenn and his regiment, he saw two men carrying Glenn's bleeding body. "General, I have carried out your wishes!" were Glenn's dying words. They pierced Chamberlain deeply:

> It was as if another bullet had cut me through. I almost fell across my saddle-bow. My wish? God in heaven, no more my wish than thine; that this fair body, still part of the unfallen "good," should be smitten to the sod, that this spirit born of thine should be quenched by the accursed!
>
> What dark misgivings searched me as I took the import of these words! What sharp sense of responsibility for those who have committed to them the issues of life and death! Why should I not have let this onset take its general course and men their natural chances? Why choose out him for his death, and so take on myself the awful decision into what home irreparable loss and measureless desolation should cast their unlifted burden? The crowding thought choked utterance. I could only bend my face low to his and answer: "*Colonel*, I will remember my promise; I will remember *you!*"

Chamberlain kept his promise. Immediately after the battle, he recommended Glenn for promotion to colonel in recognition of his conspicuous gallantry and great service at both Quaker Road on March 29 and on the White Oak Road on April 1.[29]

Chamberlain returned to the fight. The Confederates, being struck from the flank and the rear, began to give way, then broke completely. Leading the charge over the breastworks was Sheridan, bearing a battle flag. The confusion caused by the erroneous diagram of the Confederate position was finally rectified, and the Fifth Corps — with Ayres on the left, Griffin in the middle, and Crawford, who had been redirected by Warren to the battle, on the right — swept like a scythe down the Confederate line from east to west along the White Oak Road toward Five Forks. As Confederates ran, throwing down their arms along the way, Sheridan cried out, "Smash 'em! Smash 'em!"[30]

As Ayres' and Griffin's divisions fiercely fought Pickett's division near the White Oak Road, Warren rode to redirect Crawford. Sheridan, who was frustrated with Warren's prior performance and possessed the authority to replace him, now acted. At about 7:30 P.M., Sheridan directed a staff officer to advise Warren that he "wasn't in the fight" and to deliver to him an order relieving him of command. Warren pleaded with Sheridan to reconsider but he refused. Griffin was appointed to command of the Fifth Corps, and Bartlett was elevated to lead the First Division. Warren's humiliating removal from command of the Fifth Corps was a source of great vexation for Chamberlain, who, in Warren's postwar court of inquiry and in Chamberlain's memoirs, did his utmost to explain the actions of Warren and to discredit the reasons given by Sheridan, and sustained by Grant, for Warren's removal.[31]

Though the sun was going down, Sheridan's day was not over. As Chamberlain rode with him, an officer approached exclaiming that Union troops were in the Confederate rear and had captured three guns. Once again seeing the bigger picture, and wanting everyone else to do the same, Sheridan shot back, "I don't care a damn for their guns, or you either, sir! What are you here for? Go back to your business, where you belong! What I want is that Southside Road!" Others were now nearby. Sheridan commanded, "I want you men to understand we have a record to make, before that sun goes down, that will make hell tremble! — I want you there!" gesturing toward the railroad. Sheridan ordered that the advance be pressed so long as "you can see your hand before you!"

Union infantry pressed the Confederates from the east while Sheridan's cavalry blocked a western retreat. The Confederates at the Five Forks intersection were forced to flee to the northwest. There were no more stout defenses, only isolated groups of Confederates resisting as they retreated. Soon, the field was quiet. Confederate prisoners numbered near 5,000. Five Forks was in the hands of Sheridan and the Army of the Potomac, and the Southside Railroad was theirs for the taking.[32]

As Griffin, Chamberlain and others gathered near the Five Forks intersection to discuss the day's momentous events, Sheridan approached out of the darkness. Undoubtedly, the thought occurred to more than one of them it might be his turn to be scolded, reprimanded or summarily dismissed. Instead, Sheridan spoke in words that amazed Chamberlain. "Gentlemen," Sheridan said, "I have come over to see you. I may have spoken harshly to some of you today; but I would not have it hurt you. You know how it is; we had to carry this place, and I fretted all day till it was done. You must forgive me. I know it is hard for the men, too; but we must push. There is more for us to do together. I appreciate and thank you all."

Chamberlain was so taken aback, he was almost willing to blame himself for things he had *not* done wrong. He admittedly liked Sheridan's style of "smash 'em up" fighting and knew there would be no more entrenching. Yet, the injury Sheridan inflicted upon Warren would not be forgotten or forgiven.[33]

Chapter 16

Appomattox

The dam was now broken, though Lee did what he could to stem the flood. He sent three brigades under Bushrod Johnson to Sutherland Station. Johnson, with Pickett and Fitzhugh Lee, would defend the Southside Railroad and the Richmond and Danville Railroad. Lee summoned one of Longstreet's divisions from the defense of Richmond beyond the James River. At 10:00 P.M., Union artillery began shelling the Confederate positions at Petersburg. Early on the morning of Sunday, April 2, Union infantry forces advanced all along the Confederate line, overwhelming the paper-thin defenses. A.P. Hill was killed attempting to rally the men in his broken line, and Lee was forced from his headquarters at the Turnbull House. Before he left, Lee sent a message advising Richmond authorities that he could not hold his position beyond the night and that "all preparation be made for leaving Richmond tonight."[1]

Gordon's Second Corps, posted east and south of Petersburg, had been stretched to the point of breaking by Grant's continued westward movements. Gordon recalled the following: "During the two weeks following the sudden seizure of Fort Stedman and its equally sudden release, my legs were rarely out of my long boots.... Night after night troops were marching, heavy guns were roaring, picket-lines were driven in and had to be reestablished; and the great mortars from both Union and Confederate works were hurling high in the air their ponderous shells, which crossed each other's paths and, with burning fuses, like tails of flying comets, descended in meteoric showers on the opposing entrenchments." Gordon's men were forced back to the inner fortifications but Union forces could push them no farther. Gordon even ordered counterattacks to restore the breach in his line. He had so few men they were standing fifteen feet apart. He stated, "Portions of my line — it was not a line; it was the mere skeleton of a line — had been broken by assaults at daybreak on April 2. There were no troops — not a man in reserve to help us." Before Gordon could initiate another of these moves, he received news from Lee regarding the devastating loss at Five Forks and the Union breach into the Confederate rear.

Gordon was told that no further purpose would be served by attempting to regain his works. His orders were to delay until nightfall, then withdraw to cover the retreat of the Army of Northern Virginia from Richmond and Petersburg. In the opinion of Union soldier and author Morris Schaff, Lee owed more to Gordon than to anyone else for the salvation of Petersburg that day. Meanwhile, Lee and his staff prepared orders for his units near Petersburg to cross to the north of the Appomattox, and his units protecting Richmond to cross to the south of the James for a march towards, and concentration at, Amelia Courthouse, 40 miles to the west. Eventually, Lee hoped to join with Joe Johnston's Army in North Carolina. But Grant was not about to let him get away, and Sheridan tenaciously led the pursuit that would end at Appomattox Courthouse.[2]

By mid-afternoon, Union forces took Sutherland Station on the Southside Railroad. Shortly thereafter, Sheridan moved north from Five Forks to the railroad. Chamberlain's brigade moved north up the Church Road, driving back Confederate skirmishers along the way. The brigade reached the railroad and stopped the last train out of Petersburg. Chamberlain stated, "The officers and soldiers we were obliged to regard as prisoners of war; the rest we let go in peace." Bartlett, now commanding the First Division, directed Chamberlain to move to the Cox Road, where he once again found strong opposition. These Confederates, too, were forced back. Chamberlain's brigade continued to the Namozine Road, where they camped for the night.[3]

Jefferson Davis and the remnants of the Confederate government fled from Richmond — toward Danville, near the North Carolina state line. As Confederate troops retreated from Richmond, they set fire to tobacco warehouses, as well as buildings filled with the munitions that could not be carried with them. Large explosions were heard as each pile was touched off. Soon, wind spread the fire to other buildings. Bridges were also burned to slow the advance of the Union army. With the exit of his corps from Petersburg, Gordon saw that the last hope of Southern independence was shattered. A personal burden also weighed upon him that night. Fanny had recently given birth in Petersburg to their third son and could not travel. She had followed him throughout the war but now he had to leave her behind, having faith that a chivalric Union soldier would protect her from harm. Gordon would not be disappointed.[4]

Despite the events of the past few days, Lee was not discouraged. The infantry units of Longstreet, Ewell, Gordon, Anderson and Mahone, plus the remaining artillerymen and cavalrymen, represented an effective fighting force. Lee rode with Longstreet, Gordon and the remnants of A.P. Hill's corps on the north side of the Appomattox River, while Anderson's men, who had fought on the White Oak Road and at Five Forks, traveled on the south side of the river. Their first stop would be Amelia Courthouse, where Lee had arranged for the delivery of rations from Danville for his hungry army. When Lee arrived there near noon on April 4, he found only ammunition and equipment for his artillery. An error in Danville resulted in no rations having been sent. Lee was forced to halt his army and send foragers into the countryside to find something for his men to eat. They returned on the morning of April 5 with little food, as the country had already been picked clean. Lee had to keep moving.[5]

On April 3, the Fifth Corps, with Chamberlain's brigade, marched all day on the Namozine Road toward the Army of Northern Virginia at Amelia Courthouse. On the morning of the 4th, Union forces reached the Danville Railroad near Jetersville, about five miles southwest of Amelia Courthouse. With the arrival of the Second and Sixth corps, the route to Burkeville, another 12 miles to the southwest, where the Danville and Southside railroads intersected, was now blocked. The Union soldiers remained vigilant for a battle with Lee's army both that day and the next. But Lee knew his army was outnumbered and in no shape to attack. He veered west toward Farmville, eighteen miles away, intending to march south from there toward North Carolina.[6]

Lee's men were in terrible condition. Abandoned muskets and equipment of all kinds littered the road behind the Confederate army. Straggling intensified. Men simply became too weak to go any farther. Some Confederates wandered away from their units in search of something to eat, never to return. When Union soldiers came upon one thin, hungry private from North Carolina, his captors cried out, "Surrender, surrender! We've got you!" The poor ragamuffin replied, "Yes, you've got me, and a hell of a git you got." Meanwhile, the energy and spirit in the Union army was high, as they sensed that the end was near and that each exertion now brought them closer to the end of the war, and home. They also needed little reminding that if Lee got away, Sherman might get the glory for capturing him and ending the war.[7]

Early on the morning of April 6, in the midst of the death knell of the Army of Northern Virginia, Gordon exemplified the dignity and honor of the good man that he was. George, his scout, brought him two soldiers under guard in Confederate uniforms. The men claimed to be in Fitz Lee's cavalry, though George believed they were Yankees. Gordon questioned them and thought that George was mistaken. As they passed a fire, George got a look at their faces. He recognized the men as two of Sheridan's scouts who had, by coincidence, captured George when he was near Grant's headquarters two months before. With a $20 gold piece bribe for the guard, George had managed to escape. By a twist of fate, the men were now in his custody. Upon searching the men, Gordon found an order from Grant to Ord in the boot of one of the soldiers.[8] The younger soldier then admitted that George was right. Gordon said, "Well, you know your fate. Under the laws of war you have forfeited your lives by wearing this uniform, and I shall have you shot at sunrise tomorrow morning." One of them replied, "General, we understand it all.... You have the right to have us shot; but the war can't last much longer, and it would do you no good to have us killed." Gordon had no intention of shooting them but he did not tell them that. On the morning of Lee's surrender at Appomattox Courthouse, Gordon delivered the young soldiers to Sheridan.[9]

Thursday, April 6, would be devastating for Lee and the Army of Northern Virginia. Longstreet led the westward march followed by Anderson and Ewell. Gordon's Second Corps protected the rear, fighting Humphrey's Second Corps along the way. Anderson was forced to stop at times to deal with cavalry attacks on his flank, causing him to become separated from Longstreet. A gap also opened between Ewell and Gordon when Ewell decided to move his corps on a different road but neglected to inform Gordon. As a result, Anderson and Ewell became isolated at Sayler's (sometimes Sailor's) Creek. Sheridan saw the opportunity and acted.[10]

Humphreys kept Gordon occupied in the rear. Lee reported to Jefferson Davis, "Gordon, who all the morning, aided by General W.H.F. Lee's cavalry, had checked the advance of the enemy on the road from Amelia Springs and protected the trains, became exposed to his combined assaults, which he bravely resisted and twice repulsed." Sheridan then sent Wright and the Sixth Corps to hit Anderson and Ewell, who were being held in place by Union cavalry. After an artillery bombardment, Union infantry attacked, routing Anderson's corps. Only one Virginia brigade was able to leave the field as an organized unit. Aside from that exception, from private to general, it was every man for himself. Anderson, Pickett, and Bushrod Johnson escaped but 3,000 others were either killed or captured. Ewell's corps was hit next and fared no better. Ewell himself was captured along with 2,800 weary Confederates. Only about 200 escaped.[11]

Gordon was also roughly handled. Humphreys sent in a division against Gordon's corps, which was slowed by his own wagons. Seventeen hundred Confederates were captured, as well as a number of wagons, colors and guns. When Gordon's losses were added to those of Anderson and Ewell, Confederate prisoners for the day totaled almost 6,000. Chamberlain's brigade participated in the pursuit of Lee's army through Paineville, capturing prisoners and destroying abandoned Confederate property. His brigade camped near Sayler's Creek that evening.[12]

Gordon recalled that, during that awful retreat, it was impossible for Lee's army to bury its dead or even carry its disabled wounded. There was no longer any room in the crowded ambulances that had escaped capture by Union pursuers. Gordon and his men were unable to do anything for the "unfortunate sufferers who were too severely wounded to march, except leave them on the roadside with canteens of water." Thankfully, at this stage of the war, the hatred of many soldiers for their foe had been replaced by Chamberlain's and Gordon's view of a common brotherhood. Gordon related the story of a compassionate Union soldier:

> [He came across a] desperately wounded Confederate shot through legs and body, lying in his blood bed of leaves, groaning with pain and sighing for relief in death. The generous Federal was so moved by the harrowing spectacle that he stopped at the side of the Confederate and asked, "What can I do for you, Johnny? I want to help you if I can."
>
> "Thank you for your sympathy," the sufferer replied, "but no one can help me now. It will not be long till death relieves me."
>
> The Union soldier bade him good-by, and was in the act of leaving, when the wounded Southerner called to him: "Yes, Yank; there is something you might do for me. You might pray for me before you go."
>
> This Union boy had probably never uttered aloud a word of prayer in all his life. But his emotions were deeply stirred, and through his tears he looked around for some one more accustomed to lead in prayer. Discovering some of his comrades passing, he called to them.

The morning of April 7 appeared to bring better fortune to Lee and his army. Lee arrived at Farmville ahead of Longstreet's corps and was able to get some rest. This time, the rations he requested had arrived but there would be no time to cook them. He had left orders that the bridges over the Appomattox River be burned after Gordon crossed. Once accomplished, this would have put the river between the Union and Confederate armies and given him the time and opportunity to maneuver without Grant posing an immediate threat. Unfortunately for Lee and his army, his order to burn the bridges was not successfully carried out. High Bridge was rendered useless but Union forces were able to extinguish the flames on the nearby wagon bridge before significant damage could be done. Soon, Humphreys was marching over the Appomattox toward Farmville.[13]

Lee was forced, once again, to get his unrested and unfed men on their feet. What remained of the Army of Northern Virginia marched on the north side of the Appomattox moving west, followed by the Union Second Corps under Humphreys and the Sixth Corps under Wright. Meanwhile, Sheridan's cavalry, Griffin's Fifth Corps and Ord's Twenty Fourth Corps with Birney's division of the Twenty-Fifth Colored Troops marched a parallel course south of the river. Grant arrived at Burkeville around noon. At about 5:00 P.M., he sent a message through the lines to Lee expressing the view that recent events should have convinced him of the hopelessness of further resistance and requesting the surrender of the Army of Northern Virginia. Lee did not agree that their cause was hopeless but he did accede to a meeting with Grant to determine the terms of a surrender. Apparently, he did not choose his words wisely. When Grant attempted to arrange the meeting, Lee said he did not mean to suggest that he was willing to surrender.[14]

On the night of April 7, Lee issued orders for his army to march to Appomattox Courthouse. Gordon took over the lead from Longstreet. They arrived late in the day on April 8. But Sheridan's cavalry had gotten there first. The rations from Farmville had been sent to Appomattox Station, two to three miles southwest of the town. When the Union cavalry discovered this, they seized the trains and posted themselves on the Lynchburg Pike, the road Lee would need to continue his westward retreat. The Union army was now ahead of Lee. But Sheridan knew that he could not hold back Lee's army with cavalry. He needed the infantry.[15]

Late in the evening of April 8, Confederates moving westward from Appomattox Courthouse ran into the Union cavalry blockade. In addition to the rations, they learned that two dozen Confederate artillery pieces had been captured. With this information, Lee called a meeting of Longstreet, Gordon and Fitz Lee to explain the situation and solicit advice. According to Gordon, "no tongue or pen will ever be able to describe the unutterable anguish of Lee's commanders as they looked into the clouded face of their beloved leader and sought to draw from it some ray of hope." It was decided that the next morning Gordon's Second Corps — down to a mere 2,000 men — supported by Fitz Lee's cavalry and followed by Longstreet's Corps of 6,000, would attempt to break through the Union position on the Lynchburg Pike. Gordon knew that the best that could be achieved was to reach the mountains of Virginia and Tennessee with some part of the army and then join with General Johnston:

> As we rode away from the meeting I directed a staff officer to return to General Lee and ask him if he had any specific directions as to where I should

halt and camp for the night. He said, "Yes; tell General Gordon that I should be glad for him to halt just beyond the Tennessee line." That line was about two hundred miles away, and Grant's battle-lines and breastworks were in our immediate front, ready to check any movement in that direction; but General Lee knew that I would interpret his facetious message exactly as he intended it. His purpose was to let me infer that there was little hope of our escape and that it did not matter where I camped for the night; but if we should succeed in cutting our way out, he expected me to press toward the goal in the mountains.

Gordon noted that about 25,000 Confederates were present at Appomattox but two-thirds of them were "so enfeebled by hunger, so wasted by sickness, and so foot-sore from constant marching that it was difficult for them to keep up with the army."[16]

Meanwhile, the long, daily marches of the Fifth Corps continued on the 8th. That night, after a march of 29 miles, Chamberlain's tired men fell asleep on the Lynchburg Pike, six miles from Appomattox Station. Chamberlain recalled, "After twenty nine miles of this kind of marching, at the blackest hour of night without halting, human nature called a halt. Dropping by the roadside, right and left, wet and dry, down went the men as in a swoon. Officers slid out of saddle, loosened the girth, slipped an arm through a loop of bridle-rein, and sank to sleep. Horses stood with drooping heads just above their masters' faces. All dreaming — one knows not what, of past or coming, possible or fated." In the early hours of April 9, a cavalrymen rushed down the road with an urgent message from Sheridan: "I have cut across the enemy at Appomattox Station, and captured three of his trains. If you can possibly push your infantry up here tonight, we will have great results in the morning." The men were awakened. There was no time to eat, and they had but little rest. The Union infantry was marching again. By sunrise, Chamberlain's brigade arrived at Appomattox Station.[17]

The climactic moment of the Civil War had arrived. Just beyond Appomattox Courthouse in the early morning of April 9, 1865, the Confederates deployed for attack. Initially, it was successful. The Union cavalrymen were flanked and forced away from the Lynchburg Pike. Just as the way to the west appeared open, however, Ord's Union infantry appeared, blocking any further Confederate advance in that direction. According to Ord, Lee was disbelieving when Gordon conveyed this information to him. The gap between Ord's infantry and Sheridan's cavalry to the south soon closed. A cavalryman came riding up to Chamberlain, who, at that time, commanded his and Gregory's brigades, and asked, "General, you command this column?" "Two brigades of it, sir; about half the First

Division, Fifth Corps," was Chamberlain's reply. "Sir, General Sheridan wishes you to break off from the column and come to his support. The rebel infantry is pressing him hard. Our men are falling back. Don't wait for orders through the regular channels, but act on this at once."[18]

Chamberlain led his men and Gregory's through some woods toward Sheridan's battle flag at the edge of an open field. The Fifth Corps joined the Twenty Fourth Corps and Sheridan's cavalry, creating insurmountable odds for Gordon and Fitz Lee. The Confederates could go neither west to Lynchburg nor south to Danville. Sheridan again encouraged the men forward: "Now smash 'em, I tell you; smash 'em!" For Chamberlain, the momentous time had arrived: "It has come at last,—the supreme hour. No thought of human wants or weakness now: all for the front; all for the flag, for the final stroke to make its meaning real—these men of the Potomac and the James, side by side, at the double in time and column, now one and now the other in the road or the fields beside. One striking feature I can never forget—Birney's black men abreast with us, pressing forward to save the white man's country."[19]

In the midst of the final struggle, Chamberlain again demonstrated the humanity and humility that caused him to be held in such high regard by his peers. The Confederates had withdrawn halfway up a slope but had stopped behind a stone wall to make a stand. Chamberlain decided to force them back with artillery and prepared his forces for a charge. Suddenly, Griffin rode up and jokingly scolded Chamberlain for bombarding a blooming peach tree he mistook for a Rebel flag. Attributing the error to his near-sightedness and lack of experience in long-range fighting, Chamberlain apologized.

Shortly thereafter, Griffin again rode up to Chamberlain complaining that Crawford, who commanded the Third Division, was acting in the same way that had gotten Warren into trouble at Five Forks. He was needed desperately but had moved slowly. Griffin proposed to remove Crawford from command and replace him with Chamberlain. Chamberlain protested: "General, pardon me, but you must not do that. It would make trouble for everybody, and I do not desire the position. It would make great disturbance among Crawford's friends, and if you will pardon the suggestion, they may have influence enough at Washington to block your confirmation as Major-General. Besides, I think General Baxter of the Third Division is my senior; that must settle it." Soon, Crawford's men arrived, and the issue was dropped. As things turned out, Chamberlain would command a division in the climactic event at Appomattox Courthouse.[20]

Gordon's 2,000 infantrymen and Fitz Lee's 2,400 cavalrymen were being pressed by 30,000 Union infantrymen, not to mention Sheridan's cavalry preparing to attack the Confederate flank. The Confederates had been pushed back to Appomattox Courthouse. In response to a request from Lee for an update, Gordon responded, "Tell General Lee I have fought my corps to a frazzle and I fear I can do nothing unless I am heavily supported by Longstreet." Lee knew that Longstreet was occupied protecting the rear of the army from Humphreys and could not provide support. With retreat to the west and south now cut off, and with the Second and Sixth corps pressing from the east, Lee knew he had no choice: "Then there is nothing left me to do but go and see General Grant, and I would rather die a thousand deaths."[21]

Gordon continued to fight until he received a message from Lee that there was a flag of truce between himself and General Grant and that Gordon should communicate that fact to the Union commander in his front. At this most critical moment, a somewhat comical scene occurred. Gordon directed Colonel Green Peyton of his staff to take a flag of truce to General Ord. Peyton said that he had no flag of truce. When Gordon told him to use his handkerchief, Peyton replied that he did not have one of those either. "Then tear your shirt, sir, and tie that to a stick," Gordon said. Peyton looked at his own shirt, then at Gordon's, and replied, "General, I have on a flannel shirt, and I see you have. I don't believe there is a white shirt in the army." Obviously exasperated, Gordon shot back, "Get something, sir. Get something and go!"[22] Peyton obtained something that served as a flag of truce and rode off in search of Ord. He found Sheridan instead. Peyton returned to Gordon with Major General George Armstrong Custer, who presented a striking physical appearance but failed to impress with his tactfulness. Custer saluted and said, "I am General Custer, and bear a message to you from General Sheridan. The general desires me to present to you his compliments, and to demand the immediate and unconditional surrender of all the troops under your command."

Believing victory was within his grasp, Sheridan was very unhappy with the cease-fire and suspected a Confederate trick. Aware of the flag of truce between Lee and Grant, Gordon had no intention of acceding to Custer's request. Gordon returned the compliments and declined to surrender his command. Custer responded that, if he did not surrender, Sheridan would annihilate Gordon's command within the hour. Gordon was unmoved by this threat and told Custer that if Sheridan attacked in the face of a flag of truce the blood would be on his hands.[23]

Within a short time, Sheridan arrived on the scene, also with a white flag. As Sheridan approached, one of Gordon's sharpshooters raised his rifle as if to fire on him. Gordon told him he must not fire on a flag of truce, but the soldier did not willingly obey. As he began to raise his gun a second time, Gordon grabbed the gun and reprimanded the man more forcefully. "Well, general," the soldier responded, "let him stay on his own side." Sheridan also demanded Gordon's surrender, apparently unaware of the truce arranged between Lee and Grant. Once Gordon showed Sheridan the note from Lee, Sheridan directed that firing cease and that the lines of each army be withdrawn to certain positions. Sheridan and Gordon dismounted and sat together on the ground.[24]

As Chamberlain continued to advance, he noticed horsemen riding between the lines in front of the cavalry to his right and toward his position. Closer to his front, he saw a Confederate staff officer bearing a white flag. Chamberlain's first thought was to wonder where, in either army, they found a towel so white. The officer approached Chamberlain, dismounted and delivered his message: "Sir, I am from General Gordon. General Lee desires a cessation of hostilities until he can hear from General Grant as to the proposed surrender." Although it was evident to Chamberlain and the soldiers of the Union that Lee and the Army of Northern Virginia were being hard-pressed, they were unaware of the communications between Lee and Grant concerning the possibility of a surrender. The words of the Confederate messenger momentarily left the professor of rhetoric speechless.[25]

Chamberlain had fought many battles, faced death many times, narrowly evaded the deadly path of a minie ball on several occasions, and barely survived when he was struck; yet, now, with peace at hand, his heart was pounding and his mind was racing. With a forced calm, Chamberlain answered the Confederate officer: "Sir, that matter exceeds my authority. I will send to my superior. General Lee is right. He can do no more." The officer remained with Chamberlain as the message was sent to Griffin.

Soon, the other horsemen arrived at his position, also bearing a white flag. The officer, from General Custer's staff, shouted, "This is unconditional surrender! This is the end!" The Confederate rider with him was from Longstreet's staff. The Union officer added, "I am just from Gordon and Longstreet. Gordon says, 'For God's sake, stop this infantry, or hell will be to pay!' I'll go to Sheridan." Some firing continued. As Chamberlain, uncertain of what to do, waited with Longstreet's aide, a cannon shot from the edge of town tore through the chest of Lt. Hiram Clark of the 185th New York, a member of Chamberlain's brigade, and perhaps the last soldier of the Army of the Potomac to die in combat.[26]

The cease-fire began around 10:00 A.M. and was intended to last until

1:00 P.M. During that time, Union and Confederate generals met near the courthouse to talk about their days together at West Point and old friendships. Sheridan's suspicion that Lee had an ulterior motive in seeking a truce was evident, but Gordon and other Confederate officers assured him that Lee was acting in good faith. Time passed and 1:00 P.M. approached without the anticipated word of surrender. The officers, once friends, then enemies, now friends, and soon to be enemies once again, shook hands and said good-bye to rejoin their respective commands. Griffin told Chamberlain, in a low voice, to prepare to deliver or receive an attack within 10 minutes.[27]

Chamberlain mounted his horse, apprehensive of the upcoming struggle, when he sensed a powerful presence. Later he said, "Disquieted, I turned about, and there behind me, riding in between my two lines, appeared a commanding form, superbly mounted, richly accoutred, of imposing bearing, noble countenance, with expression of deep sadness overmastered by deeper strength. It is no other than Robert E. Lee! ... I sat immovable with a certain awe and admiration." Within a short time, Chamberlain saw Grant arrive for the meeting that would end the fighting between the Army of Northern Virginia and the Army of the Potomac. Grant's familiar appearance was plain, simple and unassuming but no less awe-inspiring than was Lee's — so much so that Chamberlain forgot to salute him.[28]

As Lee approached the meeting with Grant near the end of the truce period, one of Gordon's division commanders, recently promoted Major General Bryan Grimes, asked where he should post his troops. Gordon told him he could place them wherever he chose. Puzzled by this answer, Grimes asked what Gordon meant and was told that the Army of Northern Virginia was being surrendered. Grimes was very angry that he had not been told and rode off to tell his men so that those who so wished could try to escape with him to join Joe Johnston in North Carolina. Gordon stopped him and told Grimes that he must not disgrace himself by acting in violation of the flag of truce. Grimes thought about it, then realized that he must do the honorable thing, as painful as it might be. He did not tell his men about the surrender.[29]

At the time Lee sent out his flag of truce mid-morning, Grant had been riding toward Appomattox Courthouse. He received a note from Lee shortly before noon indicating his desire to meet with Grant to ascertain the terms under which Lee could surrender the Army of Northern Virginia. The sick headache from which Grant had been suffering for the past two days suddenly disappeared. Unlike Sheridan, Grant had no doubt of Lee's good faith. Without taking the time to wait for his baggage with a fresh uniform, he proceeded to Appomattox Courthouse and arrived near 1:00

P.M. Grant met Sheridan, who directed him to the McLean house where Lee was waiting.[30]

As the war approached an end, many in the South wandered how harsh would be the terms imposed upon them by the victorious and despotic Federal government. In his second inaugural address, delivered March 4, 1865, Lincoln set the tone which would dictate the South's readmission to the Union. It would be "with malice toward none; with charity for all." Whatever conditions he intended to impose on the Southern politicians and governments who instigated secession, Lincoln emphasized at his meeting on March 24 with Grant and Sherman that he wanted the Southern army to receive generous terms. He believed that if they were simply allowed to return to their homes, they would no longer take up arms against the United States. "Let them all go," he stated, "officers and all, I want submission, and no more bloodshed.... I want no one punished; treat them liberally all around. We want those people to return to their allegiance to the Union and submit to the laws." Again, when Grant met with Lincoln after the fall of Petersburg, Lincoln expressed his wish that thoughts of mercy and magnanimity were uppermost in his heart. The terms Grant offered Lee at Appomattox reflected Lincoln's wishes.[31]

On a soldier's level, Grant, too, favored compassion over revenge. Upon greeting Lee at the McLean house, Grant later noted that Lee concealed his feelings well but that Grant's own feelings, though jubilant upon receiving Lee's note of surrender, were now sad and depressed: "I felt like anything rather than rejoicing at the downfall of a foe who had fought so long and valiantly, and had suffered so much for a cause, though that cause was, I believe, one of the worst for which a people ever fought." Lee and Grant spoke initially of the Mexican War. Grant apologized for his attire but assumed that Lee would not want the meeting to be delayed while Grant waited for his baggage. Lee was appreciative. Eventually, Lee brought the purpose of their meeting into focus.[32]

Grant wrote out the terms of surrender:

Appomattox C.H. Va.,
Apl 9th, 1865

Gen. R.E. Lee,
    Comd'g C.S.A.
Gen: In accordance with the substance of my letter to you of the 8th inst., I propose to receive the surrender of the Army of N. Va. on the following terms, to wit: Rolls of all the officers and men to be made in duplicate. One copy to be given to an officer designated by me, the other to be retained by such officer or officers as you may designate. The officers to give their individual paroles not to take up arms against the Government of the United

States until properly exchanged, and each company or regimental commander sign a like parole for the men of their commands. The arms, artillery, and public property to be parked and stacked, and turned over to the officer appointed by me to receive them. This will not embrace the sidearms of the officers, nor their private horses or baggage. This done, each officer and man will be allowed to return to their homes, not to be disturbed by United States authority so long as they observe their paroles and the laws in force where they may reside.

     Very respectfully,
     U.S. GRANT
     Lt. Gen.

Lee was pleased with the generous terms and said so. Any concerns that Confederate soldiers would be imprisoned or prosecuted for treason by the Federal government were eased. Lee did make one comment. Unlike Union soldiers, Confederate cavalrymen and artillerymen used their own horses in the war and needed those horses for their farms back home. The terms of surrender, as written, permitted only officers to take their horses. Grant readily acceded to Lee's suggestion that any Confederate soldier who owned his own horse be allowed to leave with it.[33]

Having concluded discussion of the terms, the document was copied, and Lee wrote his reply accepting the stipulations. As their business neared an end, Lee stated that, in addition to his own men, he had nearly a thousand Federal prisoners he could not feed. Grant offered to send 25,000 rations to the Confederate lines, which Lee greatly appreciated. Lee and Grant shook hands. Then, around 4:00 P.M., Lee exited the house to a growing crowd of onlookers. As he mounted Traveller, he and Grant tipped their hats to one another before Lee rode off. When Federal artillery began to fire in celebration of the Confederate surrender, Grant ordered them to stop. "The Confederates were now our prisoners," he later stated, "and we did not want to exult over their downfall."[34]

Gordon expressed great admiration for Grant and his treatment of Lee and the Confederate army at the surrender at Appomattox. Before the surrender, Southern soldiers possessed a negative impression of Grant's compassion because of his refusal to exchange prisoners, who often suffered in subhuman conditions. However, the favorable and even lenient terms offered to Lee changed this view significantly. Gordon noted that Grant's "acts and words, did much to alleviate the anguish inseparable from such an ordeal.... [T]here was no trace of exultation at his triumph [and] he was in word and act the embodiment of manly modesty and soldierly magnanimity."[35]

Chapter 17

Going Home

The day after the formal surrender, Chamberlain wrote his sister Sae of the events of the past two weeks and described his feelings as he watched the Confederates on April 12: "I pitied them from the bottom of my heart." They were enemies no longer. "Forgive us, therefore, if from stern, steadfast faces eyes dimmed with tears gazed at each other across that pile of storied relics so dearly there laid down, and brothers' hands were fain to reach across that rushing tide of memories which divided us, yet made us forever one." Gordon understood the sentiment. In his *Reminiscences*, he noted, "At the beginning there was personal antagonism and even bitterness felt by individual soldiers of the two armies toward each other.... But this was all gone long before the conflict had ceased. It was supplanted by a brotherly sympathy." Chamberlain would later say, "What wonder that men who have passed through such things together — no matter on which side arrayed — should be wrought upon by that strange power of a common suffering which so divinely passes into the power of a common love."[1]

The sadness of the Southern soldiers was great at the thought of the sacrifice made for the cause lost. But immeasurable was the pain felt by these men for the one who embodied the cause for which they had fought and died, their beloved commander, Robert E. Lee. Confederates spoke with no regrets, yet with a willingness to accept their future and a gratitude for the benevolent attitude shown them. In this first of many interactions between Americans who had fought as enemies for four years, Southern soldiers were surprised and humbled by the generous treatment shown to them by their former Northern adversary. Gordon recalled, "Marked consideration and courtesy were exhibited at Appomattox by the victorious federals, from the commanding generals to the privates in the ranks."[2]

"General," said one commander to Chamberlain, "this is deeply humiliating; but I console myself with the thought that the whole country will rejoice at this day's business." Yet another told him, "You astonish us by your honorable and generous conduct. I fear we should not have done the same by you had the case been reversed." Still another Confederate stated, "I went into that cause and I meant it. We had our choice of weapons and of ground, and we have lost. Now that is my flag (pointing to the flag of the United States), and I will prove myself as worthy as any of you."[3]

There was one notable exception: Brigadier General Henry A. Wise, former governor of Virginia. Chamberlain noticed him acting restlessly, scolding his men, who snapped back at him. Chamberlain rode to him, hoping to calm him and offer words of encouragement. "This promises well for our coming good-will," Chamberlain said, "brave men may become good friends." "You're mistaken, sir," Wise answered. "You may forgive us but we won't be forgiven. There is rancor in our hearts which you little dream of. We hate you, sir." Unruffled, Chamberlain calmly responded, "Oh, we don't mind much about dreams, nor about hates either. Those two lines of business are closed."[4]

Wise seemed to soften and asked Chamberlain about two bullet holes in his coat. When Chamberlain responded that he was shot at the Quaker Road, Wise erupted again. "I suppose you think you did great things there. I was ordered to attack you and check your advance; and I did it too with a vim, till I found I was fighting three army corps, when I thought it prudent to retire." Chamberlain only made Wise angrier when he told him there was less than one Union division present at Quaker Road.

Wise then saw fit to complain about the way the signing of paroles had been arranged. As Chamberlain turned to ride away, Wise cried out, "You go home, you take these fellows home. That's what will end the war." Chamberlain's patience had run out: "Don't worry about the end of the war. We are going home pretty soon, but not till we see you home." "Home!" Wise yelled. "We haven't any. You have destroyed them. You have invaded Virginia, and ruined her. Her curse is on you." Chamberlain could not resist: "You shouldn't have invited us down here then." Chamberlain noted that the scene had become comical, and that staff officers on both sides were laughing aloud.[5]

Upon returning to camp after the surrender ceremony, Gordon spoke to his men for the last time as their commander. He commended them for their conduct in the past, and consoled them for their sorrow in defeat. He attempted to allay the fears for their futures, and urged them to show the same loyal support to the United States that they had shown to the Confederacy:

I told them of my own grief ... and that I realized most keenly the sorrow that was breaking their hearts, and appreciated fully the countless and stupendous barriers across the paths they were to tread.... As to the thought of their leaving the country that must be abandoned. It was their duty as patriots to remain and work for the recuperation of our stricken section with the same courage, energy and devotion with which they had fought for her in war. I urged them to enter cheerfully and hopefully upon the tasks imposed by the fortunes of war, obeying the laws, and giving, as I knew they would, the same loyal support to the general Government which they had yielded to the Confederacy. I closed with a prophecy that passion would speedily die, and that the brave and magnanimous soldiers of the Union army, when disbanded and scattered among the people, would become promoters of sectional peace and fraternity.

Henry Kyd Douglas saw the crowd standing around Gordon and listening intently to his speech. He stated, "I know no other General in the army who would have attempted to make a speech to the troops at that time, or to whom they would have listened with so much patience and pleasure."[6]

One of those present at Appomattox who listened to Gordon's final impassioned speech to his men was Congressman Elihu Washburne of Illinois, Grant's state representative and long-time guardian angel and the brother of Israel Washburn, Jr., who, as governor of Maine in 1862, had secured Chamberlain's appointment as lieutenant colonel of the 20th Maine. While Gordon reassured his men they would receive benevolent treatment from their Northern conquerors, he apparently was not so sure himself. He asked Washburne how he could be certain that the United States government would be generous to the South. "Because Abraham Lincoln is at its head," was Washburne's answer. They rode together during the next few days toward Petersburg, and Washburne explained much about Lincoln's kind and forgiving character that was, to Gordon, a revelation. In his memoirs, Gordon noted that the prophecy he offered to his soldiers at Appomattox Courthouse would have been fulfilled "but for the calamitous fate that befell the country in the death of President Lincoln." He mused that "if Booth's bullet had not terminated the life filled with 'charity to all and malice toward none,' President Lincoln's benign purposes, seconded by the great-hearted among our Northern countrymen, would have saved the South from those caricatures of government which cursed and crushed her."[7]

On April 13, Gordon telegraphed Fanny from Burkeville to let her know he would arrive in Petersburg the next day. When he arrived there on April 14, he found Fanny recovering from the birth of their son. As Gordon had hoped when he was forced to retreat hastily from Petersburg on April 2, the home in which his wife and infant son had stayed was protected by a Union guard. Once Fanny was able to travel, they departed with Capt. James M. Pace of his staff, who was married to Fanny's sister, and Pace's family. Gordon sold horses to raise money for the journey home. The condition of the railroads and other travel conveyances made the journey difficult. They reached Georgia near the end of April and moved in with his parents in Columbus.[8]

On April 13, the day after the formal surrender, Chamberlain inspected the deserted Confederate camp and collected 400–500 stands of arms, one 12-pounder brass artillery piece, 20 caissons, and many wagons. Also, on that day, Griffin again urged Chamberlain's promotion to brevet major general for his actions on the Quaker Road on March 29. He also mentioned Chamberlain's leadership at Five Forks on April 1 and at Appomattox on April 9. After the Confederates departed, Chamberlain felt strangely alone and lonesome. Without scouts and skirmishers to be vigilant for the approach of the enemy, the Union march away from Appomattox was uninteresting. Eventually, though, thoughts turned to the meaning of what they had endured and he realized that by such things "a step is taken in the homeward march of man."[9]

The Fifth Corps marched out of Appomattox Courthouse toward Burkeville on Saturday morning April 15. Little did they know that at 7:22 that morning in Washington, D.C., President Abraham Lincoln died after having been shot the night before at Ford's Theatre by John Wilkes Booth. The corps reached the vicinity of Farmville, on Sunday afternoon, where a cavalryman rode up with a message, notifying them of the assassination. Concerned for the effect of this news on his men, Chamberlain ordered that a double guard be immediately placed around the whole camp. He then shared the message with his officers. When a lady of a nearby house enquired whether the disturbance meant bad news of Lee or Davis, Chamberlain told her it was Lincoln. She appeared relieved. Chamberlain placed her house under guard, and, sorry to see her face brighten, said, "The South has lost its best friend, madam."[10]

Soon Griffin rode up to get Chamberlain and Ayres for a meeting with Meade. They believed that Lincoln's assassination was an attempt to overthrow the government, and that it might well be necessary to take the army to Washington and make Grant military dictator until constitutional government could be restored. It soon became apparent that Washington civil authorities had matters under control and that such a drastic measure was unnecessary, but the upbeat mood of the army had been crushed.

Chamberlain, now officially in command of the First Division of the Fifth Corps of the Army of the Potomac, led his division in its march eastward. On April 19, the day of Lincoln's funeral in Washington, the army halted its trek at the time the funeral procession passed the capital.[11]

The Fifth Corps was assigned to temporary duty along the railroad between Burkeville and Petersburg. Chamberlain's division was posted from Wilson's Station to Petersburg. While the largest Confederate army in the field had surrendered, the war was not yet over. Though Chamberlain's job was to guard the railroads and surrounding territories, other duties devolved upon him necessitated by the condition of the land and its inhabitants. The countryside was desolated by war, and the people suffered at the hands of marauders, many of whom were emancipated Negroes with no means of support, who took what food and goods the citizens still possessed. Chamberlain used his men to protect the homes and drive off the attackers.[12]

Chamberlain also administered justice because there was no law enforcement and no active court system. They heard complaints against Confederate and Union stragglers, incarcerating them when necessary. Court-martials were established for charges against First Division men. The court was ably and fairly conducted, engendering respect by Virginia civilians who only two weeks before saw these Union soldiers as their hated enemy. The distribution of food often proved difficult. Chamberlain was under strict orders from the government not to provide food from the commissary to Southern citizens until they took an oath of allegiance to the United States. But conditions compelled Chamberlain to seize commissary supplies belonging to the Confederacy and distribute them to those in need. Near the end of April, Chamberlain received orders to prepare to move. A delegation of citizens of Dinwiddie County invited him to a dinner to thank him for his kindness. Chamberlain expressed his deep appreciation for the invitation but declined and told them they should keep the food for themselves.[13]

While Chamberlain and his men were posted at Wilson's Station, the American Civil War finally came to an end. On Thursday, April 13, Joe Johnston, whose Army of the Tennessee was facing Sherman and now also would have to fight Grant, met with Jefferson Davis and P.G.T. Beauregard in Greensboro, North Carolina. After expressing the view that Lee's surrender was not fatal to the Confederate cause, Davis asked Johnston his view. Johnston stated that his men saw the war as lost and were deserting in large numbers and that there was no choice but to seek terms for surrender. Beauregard concurred.[14]

Johnston returned to his headquarters at Hillsboro, North Carolina. Sherman's army occupied Raleigh. They agreed to meet between the lines on Monday, April 17. Shortly before the meeting, Sherman learned of Lincoln's assassination. He shared the news with Johnston before discussing the terms of surrender. The terms Sherman offered were far more generous than those presented to Lee by Grant at Appomattox. They did not require Johnston's army to disarm and they guaranteed that the federal government would recognize existing state governments and the rights of citizens to property. Sherman was clearly going well beyond a military resolution and intruding upon Washington's authority in dealing with the Southern states. Authorities in Washington quickly rejected Sherman's terms, and Grant was required to advise his old friend that Johnston must surrender under the same terms that Grant had given Lee at Appomattox. On April 26, Johnston and Sherman met again and consummated the surrender. The remaining, smaller Confederate armies soon followed the same path. After four long, painful years, the Civil War was over.[15]

On May 2, the Fifth Corps began its march to Petersburg, then turned north through Richmond on its way to Washington. Chamberlain recalled, "A solemn march it was — past so many fields from which visions arose linking life with the immortal." Warren, in Petersburg since his summary dismissal by Sheridan, was asked to appear so the men of the Fifth Corps could pass and pay honor to him. On May 6, they marched through Richmond. That night, they camped by old battlefields near Hanover Court House.

Around midnight, Chamberlain noticed that Charlemagne was pawing nervously at the ground. As he went to investigate, Chamberlain stepped on and crushed the breastbone of a half-buried body. Charlemagne had unearthed two skulls. In the morning, Chamberlain's men were able to identify dead comrades by initials cut into their breastplates. The remains were gathered together to be sent home. On May 10, the Fifth Corps passed Fredericksburg and finally reached Washington on May 12, encamping on Arlington Heights near the Custis-Lee mansion.[16]

A grand review of Union armies was planned for May 23 and 24. Sherman's army arrived on May 20 and camped on the same side of the river as the Army of the Potomac but closer to Alexandria. One civil war was over but, given a chance, another might begin. The armies did not like each other. Sherman's men believed that they had done the lion's share of the fighting, while Grant's men responded that the Westerners had never faced Robert E. Lee. Fortunately, aside from a few skirmishes, no major battles occurred.[17]

17. Going Home

On the night of May 22, Chamberlain, on behalf of the First Division, presented Griffin with a Red Maltese Cross from Tiffany in New York, enhanced by a $1000 diamond in the center, as a token of their respect. Griffin thanked them, singling out Chamberlain, once a youthful subordinate, who through many difficult experiences, had risen to become the division's "tested, trusted, and beloved commander." Men cried and shouted. The night soon came to an end, and within a short time, their military service would draw to a close.[18]

The Fifth Corps crossed the Potomac at 4:00 A.M. on May 23 and was posted near the Capitol. The sidewalks, balconies, windows and rooftops were crowded with onlookers. Battleflags, ribbons, banners and flowers decorated Pennsylvania Avenue from the Capitol to the White House. The review began at 9:00 A.M. When time came for the Fifth Corps to join the procession, a bugle sounded, and Chamberlain mounted Charlemagne. Colonel Ellis Spear and Tom Chamberlain rode behind him. As they passed through the throng, a girl in white pressed close and reached up with a wreath of flowers for Chamberlain. Though accustomed to the fury of battle and having been shot under Chamberlain three times, Charlemagne trembled at her approach. A gallant, undoubtedly appreciative, aide behind Chamberlain took the wreath.[19] Chamberlain described the scene:

> All the way up the Avenue a tumult of sound and motion. Around Griffin is a whirlpool, and far behind swells and rolls the generous acclaim. At the rise of ground near the Treasury a backward glance takes in the mighty spectacle: the broad Avenue for more than a mile solid full, and more, from wall to wall, from door to roof, with straining forms and outwelling hearts. In the midst, onpressing that darker stream, with arms and colors resplendent in the noon-day sun, an army of tested manhood, clothed with power, crowned with glory, marching to its dissolution!

They arrived at the reviewing stand where President Andrew Johnson, his cabinet, and high military and civilian officials awaited. But they missed Lincoln. At President Johnson's direction, Chamberlain was invited to dismount and remain at the reviewing stand for the remainder of the review. As he watched his men march by, Chamberlain was transfixed:

> For me, while this division was passing, no other thing could lure my eyes away, whether looking on or through. These were my men, and those who followed were familiar and dear. They belonged to me, and I to them, by bonds birth cannot create nor death sever. More were passing here than the personages on the stand could see. But to me so seeing, what a review, how great, how far, how near! It was as the morning of the resurrection!

Gordon residence near Atlanta (Kenan Research Center at the Atlanta History Center).

He watched intently as his men passed, recalling where, together, they had fought. He thought not only of those present but also of those who were not there, at least not in body. The passage of the Second Corps completed the review of the first day. Sherman and his army took the stage on May 24.[20]

Now, there was nothing left for the Army of the Potomac to do but disband. The men were allowed to take their equipment home with them and to purchase their arms at a nominal price. Discipline was lax, as there was no motive for its enforcement. Civilians visited freely at camp, as soldiers visited freely in town. The old 20th Maine mustered out of the army on June 4 and took the train from Washington back to their homes in Maine. Chamberlain would have fully agreed with the words of Theodore Gerrish of the 20th Maine describing the feelings of the men upon their separation:

> Then came the last hand-shakings and good-bys. Eyes grew moist, cheeks that had been unblanched amid the horrors of the battle-field became pale and sad in these moments of separation. The ties that bound us together were of the most sacred nature; and they had been begotten in hardships and baptized in blood. Men who lived together in the little shelter tent, slept beneath the same blanket, had divided the scanty ration, and "drank from the same canteen," were now to be separated forever. The last good-by was said, our

ranks were broken for the last time, and we turned our faces homeward. For us there were to be no more weary marches, no more midnight alarms. The strife, dangers, and deaths of a soldier's life were no more to follow our footsteps, but in the more peaceful pursuits of civil life we were to move. No matter how humble the positions we were destined to fill, we were always to derive infinite satisfaction from the thought that in the hour of the country's peril we had not been found wanting, but had cheerfully rendered what little service we could, to defend its honor and preserve its life. Thus we separated; many of us have never met each other since; I presume we shall never in this world; but in that day when the reveille of God shall awaken the slumbering hosts of humanity, may we reform our ranks upon the parade ground of eternity, as the soldiers of the great Prince of Peace.[21]

On July 1, the Fifth Corps received the following order:

> Headquarters, Army of the Potomac,
> June 28, 1865
> By virtue of special orders, No. 339, current series, from the Adjutant General's office, this army, as an organization, ceases to exist.

Chamberlain recalled, "What wonder that a strange thrill went through our hearts." He knew that despite the disbandment, the spirit of the army, soldiers both alive and dead, would never die: "The War Department and the President may cease to give the army orders, may disperse its visible elements, but cannot extinguish them. They will come together again under higher bidding, and will know their place and name. This army will live, and live on, so long as soul shall answer soul, so long as that flag watches with its stars over fields of mighty memory, so long as in its red lines a regenerated people reads the charter of its birthright, and in its field of white God's covenant with man."[22]

Chapter 18

After the War

Unlike the ordinary Confederate soldier, who, while going home to little or nothing, need not fear persecution, Gordon and other high-ranking Confederates could not be so certain. The possibility that they would be indicted for treason was a legitimate fear, at least for several months after the war ended. But Gordon's most immediate problem was to make a living for his family. Although he maintained a financial stake in Georgia coal mines, the mines had been damaged during the war and were closed. He did not have the money he needed to bring them back into operation. At the end of the summer of 1865, he moved his family to Atlanta, and in September 1865, he applied for a presidential pardon from President Johnson. After taking an oath of allegiance to the United States, his rights of full citizenship were restored.[1]

In the latter part of the year, Gordon entered into a partnership that secured financing for the construction of two large sawmills at Brunswick near the Georgia coast. The venture initially proved very successful. Difficulties arose, however, between black troops of the United States government and white citizens of the area. Gordon prevailed upon Grant, who had the black troops removed, and the troubles abated. Gordon and other white citizens did help blacks build a church and schoolhouse in Brunswick in 1866, but Gordon's cooperation was premised upon their willingness to remain subordinate to whites. Gordon clearly believed that God had chosen the white race to be superior. To some degree and for some time, Gordon was associated with the Ku Klux Klan in Georgia. When questioned about this association before a congressional committee, Gordon acknowledged only that he was a member of a secret organization formed for the self-protection of whites.[2]

The lumber business did not do well into 1867. However, Gordon soon found that the reputation he had earned as a military commander in the Confederacy led to other business opportunities. In the latter part of 1867 and early 1868, the Southern Life Insurance Company and Richardson and Company, a publishing firm, sought him offering positions, knowing that association with Gordon's name would be good for business. He did not merely accept a title but worked actively in management to advance the company. Through the publishing firm, Gordon hoped to promote Southern heritage and refute Northern writings portraying Southerners as traitors.[3]

In the late 1860s, Atlanta became the permanent home of the Gordons. They purchased land in Kirkwood, outside the capital, for their residence. Gordon also became interested in politics, another area in which his military career served him well. In early 1868, Georgia still operated under military occupation. To regain normalcy in the Union, Georgia must ratify a constitution and elect state and congressional officers. Leading the Democrats would be John Brown Gordon. He ran for governor against Republican Rufus B. Bullock. Gordon opposed ratification of the new state constitution, even though to do so meant continuation of military occupation. Despite his popularity, Gordon lost, and the constitution was ratified. As a result, federal military troops were withdrawn from Georgia.[4]

In 1872, Gordon's name was mentioned for federal office. In endorsing Gordon over other prospective senatorial nominees, the *Atlanta Constitution* noted his "eminently pure" war record and emphasized that he "combines all essential qualities which may readily serve us and ameliorate our political relations with the Congress of the United States." In January 1873, he was chosen by the Georgia General Assembly to serve in the United States Senate.

Gordon's political stance during Reconstruction was twofold. He possessed a strong desire that the North and South be reunited. When he spoke in the North, this theme was expressed. But his commitment to preserving states rights and traditional Southern liberties went even deeper. Southern audiences often heard those points emphasized. Gordon recognized that both of these goals would have been more readily accomplished had Lincoln not been assassinated. He knew little during the war about Lincoln's views but, after the surrender, learned that Lincoln had meant what he said in his inauguration speech of March 4, 1865: "With malice toward none; with charity for all."[5]

Gordon began his senatorial career in March 1873. In May of that year in South Carolina, Gordon spoke to the Southern wish to remove Republican control and military rule. Yet, he also expressed his desire that the nation would soon put aside the emotions of the war and learn to live in peace. The oratory skills that had motivated his men in battle also served him well in the Capitol and impressed Northerners as well as Southerners. New York newspapers referred to him as the "ablest man from the South in either House of Congress" and "as the representative Southerner, not only of Georgia, but of this entire section of the United States."[6]

Gordon faced attacks by many in Congress who were not willing to forgive Southerners for the Civil War. Efforts by men of the South to regain independence of federal domination met with stern opposition from many Republicans and charges of treachery, murder and intimidation by white Southerners. In a speech before the Senate on January 6, 1875, Gordon responded to these allegations in words much more moderate than reflected the indignation in his heart. He reiterated his desire that sectional differences be buried, and defended his fellow Southerners, explaining that they were living under very difficult circumstances including lack of self-rule and loss of individual rights. Gordon and Northern senator George F. Edmunds exchanged verbal blows during the speech but Gordon's tone of reconciliation over hatred prevailed. As if to amplify his intent, Gordon apologized to Edmunds the next day for any offense he had caused. Edmunds thanked Gordon for his graciousness and apologized to him in turn.[7]

Gordon took great solace knowing that, no matter what Northern politicians thought of him and the South, he always retained the respect of Northern soldiers with whom he had fought and bled on the field of battle. Gordon had been specially invited by General Winfield Hancock to participate in the honors to be paid to the former general president Ulysses S. Grant after his death in July 1885. Hancock requested that Gordon ride with him at the head of the procession. However, the humble Gordon took his place at the rear. Hancock sent one after another of his staff to Gordon directing him to obey Hancock's "order" to join him at the head of the column. Because Gordon's rank as a Confederate general was higher than the other members of Hancock's staff, Gordon sat next to Hancock. Chamberlain, too, attended Grant's funeral and, while assuming the place of an ordinary citizen in his carriage, was also summoned by Hancock to a place of honor in the procession.

After the war, General Meade was department commander of Georgia. During a banquet in Atlanta, Meade proposed a toast to Gordon's health. An objection was lodged that it was too soon after the Civil War to drink to the health of a soldier who had served in the Confederate army. Meade was more indignant at this suggestion than Gordon himself. Meade immediately rose from his seat, raised his glass and emphatically stated, "I propose to drink, and drink now, to my former foe, but now my friend, General Gordon, of Georgia."[8]

In late 1875 or early 1876, the financial condition of the Southern Life Insurance Company deteriorated to the point of bankruptcy. As he often found himself, Gordon was in need of money. During this time, he also became more actively involved in Democratic politics, in particular the drive to win the White House for the Democrats in the election of 1876. Gordon actively campaigned in South Carolina, one of only three Southern states — the other two being Louisiana and Florida — still controlled by Republicans. The election results from these states were contested and, in an effort to sway the results in favor of the Democrats, Gordon provided somewhat suspicious assurances that the elections were fairly conducted. Eventually, a compromise between Republicans and Democrats would result in Republican Rutherford B. Hayes being certified the winner, but only after Gordon and other Democrats, over threat of a filibuster, solicited a promise from Hayes that he would restore home rule to the South.[9]

As might be expected, even a person as popular as Gordon could expect to find himself subject to criticism once he entered politics. Such was the case with the Hayes' compromise. It was seen by many Democrats, and many Georgians, as Gordon's selling out the Democratic nominee for president. For some, the promise that federal troops would be removed from South Carolina, Florida or Louisiana was not a good enough reason for the compromise. Not so in South Carolina, where Gordon was welcomed as a hero after military occupation ended April 2, 1877, less than a month after President Hayes took office. Interestingly, Chamberlain concurred with the policy implemented by Hayes to lessen federal supervision over local affairs, preferring instead to defer to state and local authorities, people he believed were the men of honor he had fought during the Civil War.[10]

In August 1877, the Gordons suffered the loss of an infant daughter, Carolina. After recovering from this traumatic loss, Gordon continued his work in the Senate and with the Hayes' administration. He was reelected, almost unanimously, by the Georgia General Assembly to a second term as senator on November 19, 1878. Federal government domination of the South was no longer the burning issue it had been when he first took office. Now Gordon was dealing with divisions within the Democratic party in his own state. In this endeavor, he came into conflict with Rebecca Latimer Felton, whose husband was an Independent, having broken from the Democratic party. Their jousting would last far longer than the Civil War.[11]

Unexpectedly, Gordon announced his retirement from the United States Senate on May 19, 1880, at the height of his congressional stature. His motives for taking this action were questioned and his honesty was impugned by many in his own state of Georgia. The *Atlanta Constitution* rose to his defense, roundly criticizing those who attempted to assassinate the character of the man who had so well defended the best interests of his native state. Outside of Georgia, Gordon was praised by the *New York Tribune* for his "fairness and moderation" as "one of the most influential members of the Senate" and by the *Washington Post* for his efforts to reunite the divided sections of the country. Gordon had succeeded as a military commander and a politician but not as a businessman. This, to a great extent, motivated his desire to step down from the Senate. Though he would remain active in politics, Gordon accepted a position as general counsel for the Louisville & Nashville Railroad.[12]

In addition to his position with the L & N Railroad, Gordon engaged in business ventures with New York attorney S.L.M. Barlow and worked on another railroad company, the Georgia Western, with his brothers Walter and Eugene. He then formed the Georgia Pacific Company for the purpose of building a railroad from Atlanta to the Mississippi River. His holdings grew, and Gordon became wealthy. In 1884, a presidential election year, Gordon once again turned his attention to national politics. This time, his efforts would be rewarded when Democrat Grover Cleveland was elected. But Gordon could not enjoy the victory. In September, his 19-year-old son, John Brown Gordon, Jr., who had been born in Petersburg in 1865 and protected by a Union guard during the Confederate retreat in the final days of the war, died of typhoid fever. It was a terrible blow to Gordon and Fanny.[13]

John B. Gordon, United States Senator, 1896 (Kenan Research Center at the Atlanta History Center).

Gordon extended his enterprises outside of Georgia to Florida and the Caribbean. While he had enjoyed great success, his acumen as a businessman was still somewhat questionable. According to Gordon's daughter, Caroline Lewis Gordon, "My father was a military genius, a man of imagination and creative ability, and a great states man, but he was not a practical business man." Railroad development slowed, and his wealth deteriorated. As he had needed a break from politics in 1880, now, in 1886, he needed a respite from business. Gordon once again turned his attention to public office, this time in the race for governor of Georgia.[14]

Despite his Civil War heroics and his success as a United States senator, Gordon's nomination as the Democratic candidate for the governorship was not a certainty. But Confederate emotions could be and would be revived. In late April 1886, a monument to Alabama's Confederate war dead was to be dedicated in Montgomery, and Jefferson Davis and Gordon would both attend. Thereafter, on May 1, 1886, a statue dedicated to renowned Georgian Benjamin Hill was to be unveiled in Atlanta. Jefferson Davis had been persuaded to travel to Atlanta to participate with Gordon at the Atlanta ceremony. Their presence together in Montgomery brought many war veterans to the Alabama capital where Gordon spoke and touched the hearts of former Confederate comrades by recounting their bravery against Northern superiority in numbers and materiel. He was able to visit with men of the 6th Alabama he had not seen in many years.[15]

Davis and Gordon then traveled by train to Atlanta for the Hill monument dedication. Crowds along the route wanted Davis to speak to them again but his declining health would not permit it. Gordon spoke instead. He marched with his veterans in Atlanta. He also appeared later on the balcony of a hotel to the cry of "Gordon for Governor." Within a week, he announced his candidacy. Undoubtedly, his appearances with Davis in Montgomery and Atlanta rekindled Southern emotions. His most important asset, his Civil War reputation, started a groundswell of support that would ultimately usher him into the governorship of the State of Georgia. At the state convention on July 28, Gordon received the vast majority of the votes cast and became the Democratic nominee. He was unopposed in the general election in October and was elected governor. He was reelected in 1888 but served a rather uneventful 4 years as Georgia's governor.[16]

Two events during these years which do merit mentioning concern Gordon's unwavering view of the inequality of Negroes. In 1877, Gordon was advised by the board of visitors that white students were attending Atlanta University, which was intended to educate only Negroes. The board recommended that Gordon put a stop to the mixing of the races. Gordon agreed that Negroes and whites should be educated at separate facilities, and that segregation must remain the rule. Gordon also fought a federal effort in 1890 to obtain greater control over local elections in Georgia to protect the Negro vote and Southern efforts to interfere with Negro voters. His response, consistent with his belief in white supremacy, was to let white Southerners handle the problem.[17]

When United States senator Joe Brown of Georgia chose not to seek reelection, Gordon immediately announced his candidacy to return to the Senate. As more time passed from the Civil War, other men and issues arose, and Gordon's influence did not necessarily carry the same weight as before. Yet, when the votes were counted, he once again was elected United States senator, though by a narrow margin. The issues in the Senate in 1891 were different than before, and they provided little interest to Gordon. In his last years of public office, Gordon concentrated on national reconciliation, there no longer being a need to defend the South from Reconstructionists. In July 1894, he said "the American people are a nation and that patriotism and love for the flag now knows no North or South." Gordon left the Senate and public office for the last time in 1896.[18]

Chamberlain arrived back in Brunswick in July 1865. Commencement at Bowdoin College was scheduled for August 2, and its war veterans planned a reunion. As luck would have it, Grant intended to be in Portland at the same time and accepted Chamberlain's invitation to attend the reunion. Upon his arrival in Brunswick, he and Julia Grant were guests in the home of Joshua and Fanny Chamberlain. When the festivities ended, Chamberlain was able to spend precious time with his family. Despite the end of the war, Chamberlain had not left tragedy behind. Within a few days after his family was happily rejoined, their youngest child, seven-month-old Gertrude Loraine, died, leaving Chamberlain, Fanny, Daisy and Wyllys in mourning.[19]

Chamberlain had requested to be relieved from duty to receive surgical treatment for the painful wound he suffered at Petersburg, which would plague him the rest of his life. However, rather than temporary deactivation, Chamberlain was mustered out of the army on August 24, 1865. This meant that the government would not pay for the surgery for the wound he received in service to his country. To address the inequity, Chamberlain was required to request reinstatement. With the help of Grant and others, Chamberlain's muster out order was revoked so that he could obtain the medical treatment he needed.

On January 16, 1866, Chamberlain finally took his place among civilians for good. For the remainder of the 1865-66 school year, he once again became a Bowdoin professor. In 1869, an examining surgeon certified that Chamberlain was permanently disabled from the gunshot wound through both hips and his bladder. He was granted an invalid's pension of $30 per month to date from his discharge from the army, January 15, 1866.[20]

Chamberlain's war experience made him feel alive. It would not be easy for him to return to the mundane life of a college professor. One opportunity which presented itself was to rejoin the regular army as a field officer, but Chamberlain's health would not permit it. However, sooner than Democrats took advantage of Gordon's war reputation in Georgia, Republicans in Maine sought Chamberlain for political office. He was asked to run as the Republican candidate for governor in the fall election of 1866. Chamberlain was enticed by war-related issues. While all but one of the reestablished Southern state governments had ratified the Thirteenth Amendment outlawing slavery, they, including Gordon's Georgia, fought Negro equality with laws that ensured white supremacy. As a result of continued violence directed against Negroes, Congress passed the Fourteenth Amendment, which guaranteed due process and equal protection to all citizens. Ratification of the amendment was an important issue in the fall election.[21]

Chamberlain was far more forgiving of the Southern soldiers he bled with and fought against in the Civil War than he was of the Southern politicians and aristocrats he saw as prompting secession and causing the violence. He wanted guarantees that no such effort would ever recur. In his view, the Southern states must be held strictly accountable until national security could be assured. To simply readmit them to the Union as if nothing had happened was not acceptable. Chamberlain felt that, having chosen to subject the nation to the devastation of war, the South must now face the consequences, including "suspension of certain privileges, the abandonment of certain rights, [and] the forfeiture of certain claims." He decided to run for governor of Maine. The Democratic candidate had opposed Lincoln and the Civil War. Chamberlain won the election by the largest majority received by a candidate for the governorship up to that time. He was reelected in 1867, 1868 and 1869 and stepped down in 1870.[22]

While governor, Chamberlain was elected to the board of trustees of Bowdoin College. Soon after his term as governor ended, the office of president of the college became vacant, and Chamberlain was unanimously elected to the position. He brought his own plans for broad changes to the curriculum, at least one of which did not meet the approval of the students. Undoubtedly influenced by his own military experience, Chamberlain imposed compulsory military training. After a while, students began to complain and then refused to drill. The students, which constituted almost all of the freshmen, sophomore, and junior classes, were suspended, sent home, and threatened with expulsion. The students ultimately returned, but the board of trustees eliminated the mandatory nature of the program.[23]

Some of the reforms instituted by Chamberlain to the Bowdoin curriculum were successful and some were not. By the early 1880s, Chamberlain was suffering more pain from his Civil War wound and needed a change himself. He again underwent surgery. Though he recovered quickly, he resigned the presidency of Bowdoin College in 1883. He remained as a lecturer for two more years but deteriorating health again interfered. In 1885, Chamberlain finally left the college from which he had gone to war and where he had taught almost every subject in the school's curriculum.[24]

Chamberlain became actively involved in a disputed Maine election for governor that demonstrated the depth of his character and the strength of his military reputation. In the election of September 8, 1879, Republican Daniel F. Davis and Greenback Party candidate Joseph L. Smith received most of the votes, with incumbent Democratic governor Dr. Alonzo Garcelon a distant third, but no one possessed a majority. Thus, the election would be decided by the Maine legislature, which was dominated in both houses by Republicans. However, allegations of election corruption surfaced. An investigation by Governor Garcelon resulted in a finding that some Republican seats had been won by bribery and fraud, resulting in a shift of power in the legislature to a Democrat-Greenbacker (Fusionist) majority.[25]

Governor Garcelon summoned Chamberlain to Augusta in January 1880 to deal with the increasingly volatile situation. While some acted moderately, others demanded, and were willing to take, more immediate, decisive action. Chamberlain encouraged the competing sides to permit the issue to be resolved by the Maine supreme court. James G. Blaine, who had served as chairman of the Maine Republican Committee for over 20 years, would not be patient. He set up headquarters in Augusta and encouraged Republicans throughout the state to conduct meetings to intimidate the Fusionists into concessions. Chamberlain feared that such demonstrations would lead to bloodshed and pleaded with Blaine not to promote "incendiary talk." Meanwhile, the situation intensified. Armed men marched to Augusta for both sides. Governor Garcelon declined to call out the state militia, as recommended by some, but did post a guard of 100 armed men around the capitol. The State of Maine stood on the brink of its own civil war.[26]

Chamberlain did his best to keep the flickering situation from erupting into a blaze. Although directed to take command of the state militia, he did not permit any soldiers to come to Augusta. Only he appeared in military uniform, a sign that he was the only authority. Nor did he appear in public armed, despite the presence of many others who were. The mayor of Augusta assured him of full police support. Also, Chamberlain secured the governor's chambers and council rooms, and convinced Governor Garcelon to remove the armed men from around the capitol.[27]

Gordon was strongly aligned to the Democratic party because the North was dominated by Republicans who controlled Reconstruction. In his view, only as a Democrat could he remove the yoke of federal domination and restore the rights and freedoms to which he believed the South justly entitled. Chamberlain's views, on the other hand, particularly concerning treatment of the South after the war, were consistent with those of the Republican Party, but he could easily put party allegiance aside when the situation demanded neutrality, as this one did. Such was evident when Blaine, a fellow Republican, arranged for the state legislature to elect Chamberlain as United States senator if he resolved the election conflict favorably to the Republicans. It is safe to say that the offer was not only not tempting to Chamberlain but affirmatively distasteful. He would not be bribed and would not so blatantly violate the trust imposed upon him by Governor Garcelon on behalf of the citizens of Maine.[28]

The fact that Chamberlain valued integrity above politics does not mean that the respective sides chose to view him as apolitical. His refusal to be bribed made him distrusted by Republicans, while the Fusionists saw him as the former four-time Republican governor of Maine. Feeble efforts were made by partisan civilians to arrest him and plans even surfaced that he would be kidnapped or assassinated. However, his war reputation had not been forgotten. Nor did it pass the notice of many persons that in this crisis Chamberlain was acting in the best interests of his state and not for himself or any political party. One former comrade who had lost a leg at Little Round Top offered to risk the other in defense of his former colonel.[29]

Matters came to a head when an angry crowd of 25–30 men approached the capitol threatening to kill Chamberlain. He put on his coat and walked out to meet them:

> Men, you wish to kill me, I hear. Killing is no new thing to me. I have offered myself to be killed many times, when I no more deserved it than I do now. Some of you, I think, have been with me in those days. You understand what you want, do you? I am here to preserve the peace and honor of this

State, until the rightful government is seated — whichever it may be, it is not for me to say. But it is for me to see the laws of this State are put into effect, without fraud, without force, but with calm thought and purpose. I am here for that, and I shall do it. If anybody wants to kill me for it, here I am. Let him kill!

He threw open his coat and waited, staring into the eyes of his tormentors. At first, they were silent. Then, stirred by not-too-distant memories of comradeship in the Civil War, a veteran stepped forward: "By God, General, the first man that dares to lay a hand on you, I'll kill him on the spot!" Still unhappy but mollified, the crowd dispersed.[30]

Efforts to force Chamberlain to choose a winner and to remove him from his position were fruitless. He insisted throughout that the Maine supreme court should decide whether the election of the legislature was valid, and that the legislature could then determine who should be the governor. He would then resign his authority. Finally, on January 16, 1880, the Maine supreme court upheld the election of a Republican legislature. The legislature elected Davis. Chamberlain recognized him as governor of Maine and, true to his word, resigned his martial position. Chamberlain was praised for his actions during the crisis. But in doing the right thing, in being honorable, in acting in the public interest rather than his own, even at the risk of his life, Chamberlain had made political enemies who would interfere with future political aspirations.[31]

Following his resignation from Bowdoin in 1885, Chamberlain pursued business interests in Florida and in the northeast. Those ventures, as had Gordon's, included railroads. A land development company in Florida initially enjoyed success but later floundered, resulting in Chamberlain's decision in the early 1890s to withdraw from that state. Financial troubles in his northern businesses prompted him to minimize his participation in active management of the businesses and into other interests. He served as president of the Institute for Artists and Artisans in New York City, as well as president of *New England* magazine. Somehow, he also found time to give lectures. Just as Gordon was, Chamberlain was often asked to speak at war reunions and monument dedications, such as the October 3, 1889, dedication of the monuments erected by the State of Maine at Gettysburg.[32]

In that address, Chamberlain blamed secession on the exponents of aristocratic superiority who misled ordinary Southerners and perverted state governments. He defined the Civil War not as a battle to defend states' rights but as a struggle to preserve the existence of the United States. He stated, "The 'lost cause' is not lost liberty and right of self-government.

What is lost is slavery of men and supremacy of States." Then using eloquent, poetic language, as few people could, with words that reached directly into peoples' hearts and souls, Chamberlain spoke these words:

> These monuments are not to commemorate the dead alone. Death was but the divine acceptance of life freely offered by everyone. Service was the central fact. That fact, and that truth, these monuments commemorate. They mark the centres around which stood the manhood of Maine, steadfast in noble service,—to the uttermost, to the uppermost! Those who fell here—those who have fallen before or since—those who linger, yet a little longer, soon to follow; all are mustered in one great company on the shining heights of life, with that star of Maine's armorial ensign upon their foreheads forever—like the ranks of the galaxy.
>
> In great deeds something abides. On great fields something stays. Forms change and pass; bodies disappear; but spirits linger, to consecrate ground for the vision-place of souls. And reverent men and women from afar, and generations that know us not and that we know not of, heart-drawn to see where and by whom great things were suffered and done for them, shall come to this deathless field, to ponder and dream; and lo! the shadow of a mighty presence shall wrap them in its bosom, and the power of the vision pass into their souls.
>
> This is the great reward of service. To live, far out and on, in the life of others; this is the mystery of the Christ,—to give life's best for such high sake that it shall be found again unto life eternal.[33]

Fanny remained precious to Gordon, always. While he was away for long periods of time tending to affairs, she not only maintained their home but also eased Gordon's burden in business and family matters. As she had done on the battlefield at Antietam, Fanny provided love and nurturing to Gordon that sustained him throughout his life. On her 54th birthday, and their anniversary, Gordon wrote the following poem to Fanny to express his continuing love:

> Of all the days I now remember,
> The sweetest far was in September,
> When woods and fields and star-lit skies,
> And mellow suns and Autumn sighs.
>
> Made earth so fair and life so sweet,
> As Heaven bowed this world to greet,
> And threw its sheen o'er Nature's face,
> And clasped all things in love's embrace.
>
> 'Twas natal day to fair young bride,
> 'Twas natal day to new born pride,
> In him whose life and hope and care,
> This fair young bride henceforth must share.

> So young she was, so winsome, coy,
> So lithe her form, so pure her joy,
> So rare her grace, so e'er discreet,
> So trusting, true, so fair and sweet.
>
> That happy man ne'er won for wife,
> To lift his aims and brighten life,
> More helpful hand or mind I ween,
> Than this sweet girl of seventeen.
>
> Though birthdays come and years pass by,
> Though clouds may dim September's sky,
> Though threads of gray may streak thy hair,
> And roses fade from cheeks so fair.
>
> Still beauty's seal is on thy brow,
> No brighter, nobler, then than now,
> And love's still warm, as 'twas when you,
> Were seventeen, I twenty-two.

By 1893, Gordon developed a public lecture about the Civil War, entitled the "Last Days of the Confederacy." He did not detail the battles but cited many incidents "which illustrate the spirit and character of the American soldier and people." He told of the story of Mrs. Rewalt of Wrightsville, Pennsylvania, who fed Gordon and his soldiers after they fought the flames around her home; but then, when it was insinuated that her kindness might be a sign that she was a Southern sympathizer, left no doubt that she was a Union woman who was doing no more than repaying their kindness. Gordon spoke of the Union soldier who swam the Rapidan to visit with his Confederate soldiers only to be caught by Gordon and threatened with imprisonment, and how Gordon's own soldiers, to preserve their honor, refused to permit his capture. Gordon included the story of General Francis Barlow, whom he tended to and left for dead on the field at Gettysburg, only to meet years later, to the pleasant surprise of both.[34]

Gordon first gave the speech in 1893 and soon became much in demand. After Gordon was relieved of his political commitments, he began speaking regularly. The tours kept him away from home but brought needed income to his household. In addition to the incidents, described above, the speech focused extensively on the last days of the war. He talked of the Petersburg retreat and the surrender, the courage and bravery of soldiers on both sides, and the patriotism and sacrifice of women at home. He related humorous incidents, as well as the suffering, captivating the attention and hearts of his listeners. He was a great orator as a young man when he needed to motivate his men for battle, and he always looked every inch a soldier. Now, he could stand before crowds enthralled by his words and

18. After the War

John B. Gordon headstone, Oakland Cemetery, Atlanta, Georgia (author's photograph).

his appearance, speak about people and places close to his heart, and make the Civil War come alive.[35]

Reviews of the speech brought praise far and wide to Gordon, even in the North. On November 5, 1895, the *Boston Daily Globe* described the speech as "a great address. Not great for its finished periods, for its polished rhetoric, for its startling philosophy, for its profound scholarship, but for its abundant human nature, for its grand devotion to the flag, and for its tributes to the men who fought and died for what they believed to be the truth." The paper added that Gordon was one who "with fiery words reaches the human heart and thrills the soul with every utterance." The *Cincinnati Enquirer* reported "a grander, nobler or more eloquent address had never been heard in an Ohio campaign." When Gordon's talk went long, he would apologize and try to finish, only to be met with cries from his audience to keep going.[36] The lecture was enormously popular throughout the country. He made no effort to justify secession. He did not condemn the Union destruction of Southern property in the Shenandoah Valley or in Georgia during Sherman's march to the sea. Instead, he extolled the virtues of soldiers and civilians, North and South. He used the speech to further his efforts at national reconciliation, and he did it masterfully.

Once when Gordon had concluded delivering his address in Vermont, an old man came up to him with tears running down his face. "General Gordon," the man said, "I have hated you for more than thirty years; I have hated everything South. I had cause for hating. You killed the noblest boy in my home, and he lies buried now in an unknown grave. We have mourned his loss all these years, [but] when I had listened to you and heard you tell the history of your hardships, how the soldier marched barefooted, how he lived without a bite some days, how he suffered, I can see that he was fighting for the cause which he esteemed more dear than life." Extending his hand to shake Gordon's, the old man stated, "I will never hate you any more…. My hatred for the South is gone forever."[37]

One of Gordon's proudest honors was his election and annual reelection to the post of commander-in-chief of the United Confederate Veterans (UCV), established in 1889. He was clearly seen as the leading Confederate in the country, being asked to dedicate the monuments of many Confederate war heroes in the 1870s and 1880s. He also expended his efforts for the widows and orphans of Confederate veterans. Enough time had passed since the Civil War that joint reunions between Confederate and Union veterans were being organized. Gordon used the UCV to support these efforts and the goal of further reconciliation.[38]

At one UCV reunion in Nashville, Gordon attempted to relinquish his post as commander-in-chief. As attested to by Stephen D. Lee, who became UCV commander-in-chief after Gordon's death, "The great assemblage (some six thousand persons) rose spontaneously, and with wild acclamation, that would admit of no parleying or delay, commissioned [Gordon] for life as leader and Commander. I doubt if any other man ever had a greater and more effective demonstration of love and confidence." In 1898, when the Spanish-American War broke out, Gordon told the UCV that the fighting of soldiers from southern and northern states side-by-side would lead to "the complete and permanent obliteration of all sectional distrusts, and to the establishment of the too long delayed brotherhood and unity of the American people, which shall neither be broken nor called into question no more forever."[39]

In December 1903, the 71-year-old Gordon traveled to his winter home in Biscayne Bay, Florida, to enjoy warmer weather. On Tuesday January 5, 1904, Gordon and his grandson wandered through the fields and orchards around his home. But the next day, Gordon suddenly fell ill, and his condition deteriorated quickly. Over the next few days, his kidneys began to fail and his heart weakened. He was either unconscious or semi-conscious throughout Saturday, January 9. At 10:05 that night, with Fanny and his children at his bedside, John Brown Gordon died, "as peacefully as a little child falls asleep."[40]

At the request of the people of Miami, Gordon's body was taken to a church to lie in state until the funeral train arrived from Atlanta. The train left for Atlanta on January 12, making stops to accept flowers and, when time allowed, to permit tearful Confederate veterans a last look at their beloved general. The train arrived in Atlanta the next morning. As the pallbearers carried Gordon's casket toward the hearse, an old veteran asked if he could lay his Confederate gray jacket across the coffin. He was allowed to do so, then said, "Now thousands couldn't buy it from me." The procession moved to the state capitol, where Gordon's body would lie in state day and night.[41]

On January 14, a memorial service was held at the state capitol prior to the religious service at Central Presbyterian Church. At Fanny's request, Confederate veterans were given priority seating in the church behind her family. Schools, businesses, and government offices in Atlanta were closed. After the church service, Gordon's body was taken to Oakland Cemetery for burial. The funeral procession "moved to muffled drumbeats through the city streets, all filled with a silent throng and hushed in reverent sorrow: veterans of the Blue and the Gray." In lieu of a place in the Gordon family plot, Gordon was interred at a site donated by the Ladies Memorial Association of Atlanta among other fallen Confederate veterans near the Confederate Memorial Monument.[42]

It would be difficult to find any Confederate soldier who emerged from the war with a more sensational record than John Brown Gordon. Achievement after achievement was awe-inspiring. Author Edward Pollard noted, "His fiery courage, his ardent sentiments, tempered by the highest tone of honour, and regulated by a strong and practical intellect, complete a character to be admired and trusted beyond that of most men." Combined with his political career after the war and efforts at reconciliation, it is safe to say that Gordon had "one of the most spectacular wartime and postbellum careers of any civilian who fought for the Confederacy." Stephen D. Lee commented, "I know of no man more beloved at the South, and he was probably the most popular Southern man among the people of the North." Of Gordon, then-President Theodore Roosevelt said, "A more gallant, generous, and fearless gentlemen and soldier has not been seen by our country."[43]

Joshua L. Chamberlain, 1907 (George J. Mitchell Department of Special Collections & Archives, Bowdoin College Library, Brunswick, Maine).

By the early 1890s, Chamberlain's health was deteriorating. At the prompting of friends and comrades, the United States government, on August 17, 1893, awarded him the Medal of Honor for distinguished gallantry on Little Round Top at the battle of Gettysburg on July 2, 1863. The next few years saw both Chamberlain and Fanny ill. By 1898, Chamberlain spent most of his time in his residence next to the Bowdoin campus in Brunswick. But he was not done yet. With the advent of the Spanish-

Joshua L. Chamberlain headstone, Pine Grove Cemetery, Brunswick, Maine (author's photograph).

American War in 1898, Chamberlain, almost 70 years old, offered his services to the government but was politely turned down. In 1900, he returned to public service as surveyor of the Port of Portland.[44]

On October 18, 1905, Fanny Chamberlain, by then totally blind, died and was buried in Pine Grove Cemetery in Brunswick. Much of Chamberlain's remaining years were filled with speaking engagements. He spoke on the anniversary of Lincoln's 100th birthday in 1909 and planned to attend the 50th anniversary of the Battle of Gettysburg in 1913 with veterans of the Union and Confederate armies. He visited the battlefield in May to prepare for the reunion, but his health did not permit him to return in July. By the beginning of 1914, he was rendered bedridden in Portland by his Petersburg wound. Slowly, he regained strength, then suddenly took a turn for the worse. With his children at his side, Joshua Lawrence Chamberlain died at the age of 85 shortly after 9:30 A.M. on February 24, 1914.[45]

Despite Chamberlain's expressed wish for a simple funeral, he was given a military ceremony with services in both Portland and Brunswick. On February 27, his body was taken by funeral cortege from his home to the Portland city hall past bare-headed crowds lining the streets. An honor guard escorted the casket. After services in Portland, his casket was placed on a train for Brunswick. Businesses closed for the afternoon, and classes at Bowdoin were cancelled. Faculty and undergraduates of Bowdoin College accompanied the casket to the First Parish Church, where Chamberlain had met and married his beloved Fanny. He was interred beside her at Pine Grove Cemetery.[46]

Theodore Gerrish of the 20th Maine remarked that Chamberlain remained the same kind-hearted gentleman throughout his three years of service that he had been when they entered the army together. He was unchanged by rapid promotions and honors. Gerrish stated, "There were but few officers who displayed greater bravery, faced more dangers, and shed their blood on more battle-fields than did General J.L. Chamberlain." Of Chamberlain, his friend and longtime comrade, Ellis Spear wrote, "He rose by force of his own character from the ranks and filled a variety of difficult positions with marked ability and success. I was intimately associated with him and knew no officer of his rank whose services were more valuable to the Government, or creditable to the State."[47]

Afterword

As so many of their time did, Chamberlain and Gordon left their homes and loved ones to fight for a cause. However, they were far from ordinary. Of these two who led their respective armies at the surrender ceremony at Appomattox, most of us have known so very little, if anything at all. Yet, their imprint on history is indelible. Courage made them good soldiers; strength and inspiration made them good leaders. Honor, humility, empathy, compassion, dignity, service, forgiveness, nobility, unselfishness, and morality made them good men. Chamberlain and Gordon did not live without fault. They were, however, remarkable men for an extraordinary time.

In his *Reminiscences*, Gordon, in commenting about the character of a common soldier, stated, "The aggregate character of a people of any country depends upon the personal character of its individual citizens; and the stability of a popular government depends far more upon the character, the individual personal character of its people, than it does upon any constitution that could be adopted or statutes that could be enacted…. [The Civil War] not only gave the occasion for its exhibition, but furnished the food upon which character fed and grew strong." In his own memoirs, Chamberlain disagreed, in part, with Sherman's statement that "war is hell!": "Fighting and destruction are terrible; but are sometimes agencies of heavenly rather than hellish powers. In the privations and sufferings endured as well as in the strenuous action of battle, some of the highest qualities of manhood are called forth — courage, self-command, sacrifice of self for the sake of something held higher — wherein we take it chivalry finds its value; and on another side fortitude, patience, warmth of comradeship, and in the darkest hours tenderness of caring for the wounded and the stricken — exhaustless and unceasing as that of gentlest womanhood which allies us to the highest personality." Chamberlain further said, "[W]e may say war is for the participants a test of character; it makes bad men worse and good men better." In the Civil War, Joshua Lawrence Chamberlain and John Brown Gordon set the standard for this test of character.[1]

Chamberlain and Gordon were highly respected leaders before they met on April 12, 1865. Chamberlain led the victorious Army of the Potomac in saluting their defeated but gallant foe, and Gordon, in the depths of sorrowful defeat, rose to attention in his saddle and directed the Army of Northern Virginia to respond with a similar show of respect. For men in the ranks, and there were undoubtedly many, who wondered whether the surrender could be accomplished peaceably, their actions set a bold example of regard and admiration. Soldiers, both blue and gray, could now look into the eyes of their former enemy and see a foe no longer, but men, as Chamberlain would later write, whose "common suffering ... divinely passes into the power of a common love." The actions of Chamberlain and Gordon at the surrender ceremony exemplified why the American Civil War was unlike any other. On that momentous occasion, two special soldiers demonstrated not only the greatness of their character but also sent a message of reunion and reconciliation to people in the North and the South and set an example of honor and dignity for all to live by.

Notes

Chapter 1

1. Chamberlain, *Passing of the Armies*, 188; Chamberlain, *Bayonet! Forward*, 233; Pullen, *Twentieth Maine*, 268, 270; Gerrish, *Army Life*, 259–60; Winik, *April 1865*, 193; Schaff, *Sunset of the Confederacy*, 57; Wert, *Sword of Lincoln*, 353.
2. Tankersley, *A Study in Gallantry*, 216–17; Freeman, *Lee's Lieutenants*, vol. 3, 741–42; Dowdey and Clifford, eds., *Wartime Papers of R.E. Lee*, 934; OR, Series I, Vol. 46, Pt. III, Ch. 58, 685–86.
3. Chamberlain, *Passing of the Armies*, 186–87; Chamberlain, *Bayonet! Forward*, 226, 234; Wallace, *Soul of the Lion*, 185–86; Pullen, *Twentieth Maine*, 269; Trulock, *Hands of Providence*, 302; OR, Series I, Vol. 46, Pt III, Ch. 58, 691.
4. Grant, *Personal Memoirs of U.S. Grant*, 297–98.
5. Chamberlain, *Passing of the Armies*, 189, 191–93.
6. Schaff, *Sunset of the Confederacy*, 296; Chamberlain, *Bayonet! Forward*, "In Memoriam," 12.
7. Gordon, *Reminiscences*, 445–46; Supp. to OR, Pt. III, Correspondence, Vol. 3, 821.
8. Chamberlain, *Passing of the Armies*, 12, 194–95; Chamberlain, *Bayonet! Forward*, 226–27, 235; Gerrish, *Army Life*, 260–61; Trulock, *Hands of Providence*, 303; Eckert, *Soldier, Southerner, American*, 121; Pullen, *Twentieth Maine*, 271–73; Wallace, *Soul of the Lion*, 187; Bearss, *Fields of Honor*, 411–12.
9. Chamberlain, *Passing of the Armies*, 195–96; Bearss, *Fields of Honor*, 412; Eckert, *Soldier, Southerner, American*, 122; Chamberlain, *Bayonet! Forward*, 235–36.
10. Chamberlain, *Passing of the Armies*, 195–96; Chamberlain, *Bayonet! Forward*, 228, 236; Gordon, *Reminiscences*, 444; Gerrish, *Army Life*, 261; Freeman, *Lee's Lieutenants*, vol. 3, 745–47; Bearss, *Fields of Honor*, 412; Eckert, *Soldier, Southerner, American*, 122; Trulock, *Hands of Providence*, 304–05; Pullen, *Twentieth Maine*, 273; Wallace, *Soul of the Lion*, 188–90; Winik, *April 1865*, 197.
11. Chamberlain, *Passing of the Armies*, 195.
12. Chamberlain, *Passing of the Armies*, 196; Chamberlain, *Bayonet! Forward*, 56, 228, 236–37; Gordon, *Reminiscences*, 445–46; Gerrish, *Army Life*, 261; Bearss, *Fields of Honor*, 412–13; Trulock, *Hands of Providence*, 305–07; Pullen, *Twentieth Maine*, 273.
13. Wallace, *Soul of the Lion*, 189.
14. Chamberlain, *Passing of the Armies*, 196–200, 205; Desjardin, *Stand Firm*, 117–18.
15. Schaff, *Sunset of the Confederacy*, 300–01.
16. Chamberlain, *Passing of the Armies*, 205–06.

Chapter 2

1. Trulock, *Hands of Providence*, 25–27, 34–35; Wallace, *Soul of the Lion*, 17–19.
2. Trulock, *Hands of Providence*, 32–34; Wallace, *Soul of the Lion*, 19–20.

3. Trulock, *Hands of Providence*, 32, 34–35; Wallace, *Soul of the Lion*, 21–22.
4. Trulock, *Hands of Providence*, 32, 36–37, 41; Wallace, *Soul of the Lion*, 22.
5. Trulock, *Hands of Providence*, 40–41.
6. Trulock, *Hands of Providence*, 42–43; Wallace, *Soul of the Lion*, 23–24.
7. Trulock, *Hands of Providence*, 43–44; Wallace, *Soul of the Lion*, 25, 27; 7 June 1852 letter to Fanny from Joshua L. Chamberlain (hereafter JLC), Maine Historical Society.
8. Trulock, *Hands of Providence*, 48, 50, 52; Wallace, *Soul of the Lion*, 28; Longacre, *Joshua Chamberlain: The Soldier and the Man*, 33.
9. Wallace, *Soul of the Lion*, 28–29.
10. Trulock, *Hands of Providence*, 53–57; Wallace, *Soul of the Lion*, 29–32; Longacre, *Joshua Chamberlain*, 44–45.
11. Eckert, *Soldier, Southerner, American*, 7; Gordon, *Reminiscences*, 198–99; Tankersley, *A Study in Gallantry*, 19, 30–31; Buell, *Warrior Generals*, 5.
12. Eckert, *Soldier, Southerner, American*, 8–10; Tankersley, *A Study in Gallantry*, 32–34, 52–53, 64; Gordon, *Reminiscences*, 3.
13. Tankersley, *A Study in Gallantry*, 74–75, 79–82; Eckert, *Soldier, Southerner, American*, 11–13.
14. Buell, *Warrior Generals*, 40; Eckert, *Soldier, Southerner, American*, 13–14.

Chapter 3

1. Gordon, *Reminiscences*, 21.
2. Ibid., 25.
3. Eckert, *Soldier, Southerner, American*, 12–14; Buell, *Warrior Generals*, 40; Gordon, *Reminiscences*, 21.
4. Tankersley, *A Study in Gallantry*, 82; Eckert, *Soldier, Southerner, American*, 15; Gordon, *Reminiscences*, 4, 7.
5. Tankersley, *A Study in Gallantry*, 82–84; Eckert, *Soldier, Southerner, American*, 15–17, 24; Gordon, *Reminiscences*, 4–5, 7–9, 13; Buell, *Warrior Generals*, 41; National Archives, Gordon Military Records.
6. Gordon, *Reminiscences*, 10–12.
7. Tankersley, *A Study in Gallantry*, 83–84, 87; Eckert, *Soldier, Southerner, American*, 17–19; Gordon, *Reminiscences*, 27–28.
8. Cullen, in *Image of War*, vol. 1, pp. 167–78.
9. Ibid.
10. Tankersley, *A Study in Gallantry*, 89–90; Eckert, *Soldier, Southerner, American*, 19–21; Gordon, *Reminiscences*, 27, 38; John B. Gordon Family Papers, Hargrett Library.
11. Trulock, *Hands of Providence*, 59–60; Wallace, *Soul of the Lion*, 34; Chamberlain, *Bayonet! Forward*, 192, 194; Longacre, *Joshua Chamberlain*, 26–27.
12. Trulock, *Hands of Providence*, 60–61; Wallace, *Soul of the Lion*, 34; Chamberlain, *Bayonet! Forward*, 192; Dedication of Maine Monuments at Gettysburg, October 3, 1889.
13. Trulock, *Hands of Providence*, 7, 9–10; Wallace, *Soul of the Lion*, 35; Desjardin, *Stand Firm*, 3.
14. Trulock, *Hands of Providence*, 12; Wallace, *Soul of the Lion*, 36; Desjardin, *Stand Firm*, 3; 8 August 1862 letter to JLC from Gov. Washburn, Library of Congress (hereafter LC).
15. Trulock, *Hands of Providence*, 13, 17; Wallace, *Soul of the Lion*, 38; Pullen, *Twentieth Maine*, 2–3; Desjardin, *Stand Firm*, 3.
16. Pullen, *Twentieth Maine*, 36–38; Spear, *Civil War Recollections*, 7; Longacre, *Joshua Chamberlain: The Soldier and the Man*, 62–63.
17. Gerrish, *Army Life*, 13, 17, 19–20; Pullen, *Twentieth Maine*, 20, 22; Wallace, *Soul of the Lion*, 39–41, 46; Trulock, *Hands of Providence*, 20; Spear, *Civil War Recollections*, 10.

Chapter 4

1. Foote, *Fort Sumter to Perryville*, 99–100; Gordon, *Reminiscences*, 48–51; Newman and Eisenschiml, *An American Iliad*, 71–72.
2. Hassler, in *Image of War*, vol. 2, pp. 12, 14–15, 18; Foote, *Fort Sumter to Perryville*, 268–69, 399–400; Eckert, *Soldier, Southerner, American*, 21–22; Gordon, *Reminiscences*, 52; Newman and Eisenschiml, *An American Iliad*, 82–83.
3. Foote, *Fort Sumter to Perryville*, 410–11; Gordon, *Reminiscences*, 53.
4. Thomas, in *Image of War*, vol. 2, pp. 116–117; Tankersley, *A Study in Gallantry*, 92; Eckert, *Soldier, Southerner, American*, 21–22; National Archives, Gordon Military Records; OR, Vol. 11, Pt. 1, 943.
5. Tankersley, *A Study in Gallantry*, 94; Eckert, *Soldier, Southerner, American*, 23–24; Gordon, *Reminiscences*, 56; Freeman, *Lee's Lieutenants*, vol. 1, pp. 251–52; Buell,

Warrior Generals, 66; Pollard, *Companions in Arms*, 537; OR, Series I, Vol. 11, Pt. I, Ch. 23, pp. 943–44.

6. Tankersley, *A Study in Gallantry*, 94–95; Eckert, *Soldier, Southerner, American*, 24–25, 27; Gordon, *Reminiscences*, 56–58; Freeman, *Lee's Lieutenants*, vol. 1, pp. 251–52; Buell, *Warrior Generals*, 67; Pollard, *Companions in Arms*, 537; OR, Series I, Vol. 11, Pt. I, Ch. 23, pp. 971, 973–76, 979–80.

7. Eckert, *Soldier, Southerner, American*, 26; Gordon, *Reminiscences*, 56, 70–71.

8. Gordon, *Reminiscences*, 59.

9. Thomas, in *Image of War*, vol. 2, pp. 117–19.

10. Tankersley, *A Study in Gallantry*, 97; Freeman, *Lee's Lieutenants*, vol. 1, p. 533; Thomas, in *Image of War*, vol. 2, pp. 120–22; Eckert, *Soldier, Southerner, American*, 28; Buell, *Warrior Generals*, 80; OR, Series I, Vol. 11, Pt. II, Ch. 23, p. 631.

11. Thomas, in *Image of War*, vol. 2, pp. 120–22; Eckert, *Soldier, Southerner, American*, 28.

12. Freeman, *Lee's Lieutenants*, vol. 1, pp. 589, 602; Thomas, in *Image of War*, vol. 2, pp. 122–23; Eckert, *Soldier, Southerner, American*, 29; Foote, *Fort Sumter to Perryville*, 511–12; OR, Series I, Vol. 11, Pt. II, Ch. 23, p. 632.

13. Tankersley, *A Study in Gallantry*, 98–99; Freeman, *Lee's Lieutenants*, vol. 1, pp. 589, 602; Thomas, in *Image of War*, vol. 2, pp. 122–23; Eckert, *Soldier, Southerner, American*, 29; Gordon, *Reminiscences*, 73–75; Buell, *Warrior Generals*, 89–90; Pollard, *Companions in Arms*, 537; OR, Series I, Vol. 11, Pt. II, Ch. 23, p. 634.

14. Lindsey, in *Image of War*, vol. 2, pp. 348–49, 360–61; Eckert, *Soldier, Southerner, American*, 30.

Chapter 5

1. Horn, ed., *Robert E. Lee Reader*, 235–36; Foote, *Fort Sumter to Perryville*, 662–63, 665; Sears, *Landscape Turned Red*, 64–66, 69.

2. Tankersley, *A Study in Gallantry*, 103; Foote, *Fort Sumter to Perryville*, 663; Robertson, in *Image of War*, vol. 3, p. 13; Sears, *Landscape Turned Red*, 71, 85; Gordon, *Reminiscences*, 138.

3. Foote, *Fort Sumter to Perryville*, 666–69; Robertson, in *Image of War*, vol. 3, pp. 16–17.

4. Robertson, in *Image of War*, vol. 3, pp. 14, 17; Foote, *Fort Sumter to Perryville*, 670–71.

5. Robertson, "The Bloodiest Day," in *Image of War*, vol. 3, *Embattled Confederacy*, 18; Foote, *Fort Sumter to Perryville*, 674–75.

6. Tankersley, *A Study in Gallantry*, 104–05; Freeman, *Lee's Lieutenants*, vol. 2, pp. 180, 182; Robertson, in *Image of War*, vol. 3, p. 19; Sears, *Landscape Turned Red*, 137–43; Taylor, *Four Years with General Lee*, 67–68; Buell, *Warrior Generals*, 112–13; Foote, *Fort Sumter to Perryville*, 675–76; Eckert, *Soldier, Southerner, American*, 31–32; OR, Series I, Vol. 19, Pt. I, Ch. 31, pp. 1034–36.

7. Bearss, *Fields of Honor*, 95–97.

8. Sears, *Landscape Turned Red*, 175; Foote, *Fort Sumter to Perryville*, 685–86, Gordon, *Reminiscences*, 83.

9. Bearss, *Fields of Honor*, 97–99; Sears, *Landscape Turned Red*, 190, 197–98; Foote, *Fort Sumter to Perryville*, 688–89, 692, Gordon, *Reminiscences*, 81, 83.

10. Foote, *Fort Sumter to Perryville*, 690–92; Bearss, *Fields of Honor*, 100–01, 104; Sears, *Landscape Turned Red*, 206, 220, 223; Robertson, in *Image of War*, vol. 3, pp. 28–29.

11. Bearss, *Fields of Honor*, 105–06; Foote, *Fort Sumter to Perryville*, 692, Gordon, *Reminiscences*, 84.

12. Bearss, *Fields of Honor*, 106–07; Foote, *Fort Sumter to Perryville*, 693; Eckert, *Soldier, Southerner, American*, 33; Sears, *Landscape Turned Red*, 236.

13. Tankersley, *A Study in Gallantry*, 106; Gordon, *Reminiscences,* 82, 84–85; Freeman, *Lee's Lieutenants*, vol. 2, p. 211.

14. Gordon, *Reminiscences*, 85–87.

15. Gordon, *Reminiscences,* 87; Eckert, *Soldier, Southerner, American*, 35; Buell, *Warrior Generals*, 118.

16. Gordon, *Reminiscences*, 88–89; Tankersley, *A Study in Gallantry*, 108; Pollard, *Companions in Arms*, 538–39; Buell, *Warrior Generals*, 119; Sears, *Landscape Turned Red*, 246.

17. Gordon, *Reminiscences* 89–90; Tankersley, *A Study in Gallantry*, 108; Pollard, *Companions in Arms*, 539; Buell, *Warrior Generals*, 119.

18. Bearss, *Fields of Honor*, 109–10; Sears, *Landscape Turned Red*, 246–47; OR, Vol. 19, Ch. 31, pp. 1037–38.

19. Tankersley, *A Study in Gallantry*, 108–09; Eckert, *Soldier, Southerner, Amer-*

ican, 36; Sears, *Landscape Turned Red*, 247, 251–57; Foote, *Fort Sumter to Perryville*, 694–95; Robertson, in *Image of War*, vol. 3, p. 32; Bearss, *Fields of Honor*, 109–110; Gordon, *Reminiscences*, 88.

20. Freeman, *Lee's Lieutenants*, vol. 2, p. 262; Gordon, *Reminiscences*, 90–91; Buell, *Warrior Generals*, 125.

21. Gordon, *Reminiscences*, 91; Freeman, *Lee's Lieutenants*, vol. 2, p. 262; Pollard, *Companions in Arms*, 539–40; Buell, *Warrior Generals*, 125; Munson, in *The Photographic History of the Civil War*, vol. 4.

22. Freeman, *Lee's Lieutenants*, vol. 2, pp. 262, 265–66; Eckert, *Soldier, Southerner, American*, 38; OR, Series I, Vol. 19, Ch. 31, pp. 683–84, 697–98, 1021, 1027–28, 1038.

23. Bearss, *Fields of Honor*, 111–13; Foote, *Fort Sumter to Perryville*, 695–97; Sears, *Landscape Turned Red*, 260.

24. Foote, *Fort Sumter to Perryville*, 697–98; Bearss, *Fields of Honor*, 114–15; Sears, *Landscape Turned Red*, 265–67, 276.

25. Sears, *Landscape Turned Red*, 284–87, 292–93; Bearss, *Fields of Honor*, 115; Robertson, in *Image of War*, vol. 3, p. 34.

26. Sears, *Landscape Turned Red*, 294–97, 299, 302–04, 307; Bearss, *Fields of Honor*, 116; Robertson, in *Image of War*, vol. 3, p. 36.

27. Pullen, *Twentieth Maine*, 22; Gerrish, *Army Life*, 25, 27.

28. Gerrish, *Army Life*, 25, 27–28; Trulock, *Hands of Providence*, 67–69.

29. Pullen, *Twentieth Maine*, 25; Gerrish, *Army Life*, 30–31, 33–40; Trulock, *Hands of Providence*, 72; Longacre, *Joshua Chamberlain: The Soldier and the Man*, 73.

30. Pullen, *Twentieth Maine*, 27–30; Wallace, *Soul of the Lion*, 41–42; Trulock, *Hands of Providence*, 75; *Civil War Recollections*, 12–13.

31. Chamberlain, *Bayonet! Forward*, 1.

32. Foote, *Fort Sumter to Perryville*, 707–11.

33. Wallace, *Soul of the Lion*, 42–43; Foote, *Fort Sumter to Perryville*, 707–11.

Chapter 6

1. Wallace, *Soul of the Lion*, 44–46; Trulock, *Hands of Providence*, 79; JLC to Fanny, 10 October 1862 and 10 October 1862 (LC).

2. Wallace, *Soul of the Lion*, 43–44; Pullen, *Twentieth Maine*, 33–38; Gerrish, *Army Life*, 50–54, 62–63; Desjardin, *Stand Firm*, 8.

3. Foote, *Fort Sumter to Perryville*, 748–49, 751–55; Sears, *Landscape Turned Red*, 338; Wallace, *Soul of the Lion*, 47, 49–50.

4. Foote, *Fort Sumter to Perryville*, 765–66; Gerrish, *Army Life*, 72; Pullen, *Twentieth Maine*, 44; Parrish, in *Image of War*, vol. 3, pp. 64, 66; Wallace, *Soul of the Lion*, 51; Trulock, *Hands of Providence*, 87.

5. Foote, *Fort Sumter to Perryville*, 766–67; Pullen, *Twentieth Maine*, 44–46; Chamberlain, *Bayonet! Forward*, 2; Trulock, *Hands of Providence*, 88.

6. Foote, *Fredericksburg to Meridian*, 26–29.

7. Ibid., 30–31, 36–37.

8. Foote, *Fredericksburg to Meridian*, 35; Pullen, *Twentieth Maine*, 49–50; Chamberlain, *Bayonet! Forward*, 2–3; Horn, ed., *Robert E. Lee Reader*, 270.

9. Foote, *Fredericksburg to Meridian*, 34–35, 38–40; Gerrish, *Army Life*, 76; Chamberlain, *Bayonet! Forward*, 5.

10. Chamberlain, *Bayonet! Forward*, 4–6.

11. Foote, *Fredericksburg to Meridian*, 40; Chamberlain, *Bayonet! Forward*, 6–7; Pullen, *Twentieth Maine*, 53; Gerrish, *Army Life*, 77–78; Spear, *Civil War Recollections*, 20.

12. Chamberlain, *Bayonet! Forward*, 7–8; Pullen, *Twentieth Maine*, 53; Gerrish, *Army Life*, 78.

13. Chamberlain, *Bayonet! Forward*, 8–9; Pullen, *Twentieth Maine*, 53.

14. Foote, *Fredericksburg to Meridian*, 41–42; Chamberlain, *Bayonet! Forward*, 9; Gerrish, *Army Life*, 79; Pullen, *Twentieth Maine*, 55; OR, Vol. 21, pp. 411–12.

15. Chamberlain, *Bayonet! Forward*, 10; Gerrish, *Army Life*, 79–80; Pullen, *Twentieth Maine*, 55–56.

16. Chamberlain, *Bayonet! Forward*, 10–11; Gerrish, *Army Life*, 80; Pullen, *Twentieth Maine*, 57.

17. Chamberlain, *Bayonet! Forward*, 11–12; Gerrish, *Army Life*, 80; Pullen, *Twentieth Maine*, 57. 18. Chamberlain, *Bayonet! Forward*, 12; Pullen, *Twentieth Maine*, 57–9.

19. Chamberlain, *Bayonet! Forward*, 14; Pullen, *Twentieth Maine*, 57; Foote, *Fredericksburg to Meridian*, 44.

20. Foote, *Fredericksburg to Meridian*, 128–31; Pullen, *Twentieth Maine*, 68–70.

Chapter 7

1. Freeman, *Lee's Lieutenants*, vol. 2, p. 508; Eckert, *Soldier, Southerner, American*, 38; Alexander, *Fighting for the Confederacy*, 193.
2. Freeman, *Lee's Lieutenants*, vol. 2, p. 508; Eckert, *Soldier, Southerner, American*, 39–40; OR, Series I, Pt. I, Vol. 25, Ch. 37, 792; Pt. II, p. 717; Gordon, *Reminiscences*, 95.
3. Foote, *Fredericksburg to Meridian*, 262–67; Bearss, *Fields of Honor*, 121.
4. Foote, *Fredericksburg to Meridian*, 270–71, 274–75; Bearss, *Fields of Honor*, 121–23, 126.
5. Foote, *Fredericksburg to Meridian*, 277–79; Bearss, *Fields of Honor*, 127.
6. Foote, *Fredericksburg to Meridian*, 280–83, 285, 291; Bearss, *Fields of Honor*, 129–30.
7. Foote, *Fredericksburg to Meridian*, 292, 295–96; Bearss, *Fields of Honor*, 135–36.
8. Foote, *Fredericksburg to Meridian*, 292, 300–02; Bearss, *Fields of Honor*, 131, 136–39.
9. Foote, *Fredericksburg to Meridian*, 305–07; Bearss, *Fields of Honor*, 144, 149.
10. Foote, *Fredericksburg to Meridian*, 308–09; Bearss, *Fields of Honor*, 146–49.
11. Tankersley, *A Study in Gallantry*, 114–15; Foote, *Fredericksburg to Meridian*, 310; Bearss, *Fields of Honor*, 150–51; Gordon, *Reminiscences*, 100–01; Freeman, *Lee's Lieutenants*, vol. 2, pp. 628–29; OR, Series I, Pt. I, Vol. 25, Ch. 37, pp. 841, 1001; Early, *Autobiographical Sketch*, 209, 221–25.
12. Gordon, *Reminiscences*, 101–02.
13. Freeman, *Lee's Lieutenants*, vol. 2, pp. 633, 635; Foote, *Fredericksburg to Meridian*, 311–14; Bearss, *Fields of Honor*, 151–53; OR, Series I, Pt. I, Vol. 25, Ch. 37, p. 1002; Early, *Autobiographical Sketch*, 229–30.
14. *Atlanta Georgia Journal* 29, "Sanders, Col. C.C.," p. 170.
15. Tankersley, *A Study in Gallantry*, 226; Foote, *Fredericksburg to Meridian*, 314, 317–19; Gordon, *Reminiscences*, 64–65.
16. Trulock, *Hands of Providence*, 110–11; Wallace, *Soul of the Lion*, 66; Supp. to OR, Series I, Pt. II, Vol. 25, Series 37, p. 706; Gerrish, *Army Life*, 86; Pullen, *Twentieth Maine*, 73–75; Spear, *Civil War Recollections*, 26; Longacre, *Joshua Chamberlain: The Soldier and the Man*, 109.
17. Trulock, *Hands of Providence*, 111–12, 114; Wallace, *Soul of the Lion*, 67; Pullen, *Twentieth Maine*, 76–77; Letter dated July 11, 1863, acknowledging JLC's promotion to colonel, Pejebscot Historical Society.
18. Trulock, *Hands of Providence*, 114; Wallace, *Soul of the Lion*, 67–68; Pullen, *Twentieth Maine*, 77, 79; Chamberlain, *Bayonet! Forward*, 23; Desjardin, *Stand Firm*, 16; Longacre, *Joshua Chamberlain: The Soldier and the Man*, 116.
19. Trulock, *Hands of Providence*, 115; Wallace, *Soul of the Lion*, 68–69; Pullen, *Twentieth Maine*, 77–78, 80–81; Chamberlain, *Bayonet! Forward*, 24; Desjardin, *Stand Firm*, 17; Longacre, *Joshua Chamberlain: The Soldier and the Man*, 116–17.
20. Trulock, *Hands of Providence*, 115; Wallace, *Soul of the Lion*, 68–69; Pullen, *Twentieth Maine*, 77–78, 80–81; Chamberlain, *Bayonet! Forward*, 24; Longacre, *Joshua Chamberlain: The Soldier and the Man*, 116–17.

Chapter 8

1. OR, Series I, Pt. II, Vol. 25, Ch. 37, p. 810; Eckert, *Soldier, Southerner, American*, 41; Dowdey and Manarin, eds., *Wartime Papers of R.E. Lee*, 488; Buell, *Warrior Generals*, 220; John B. Gordon Family Papers, Hargrett Library.
2. Eckert, *Soldier, Southerner, American*, 42.
3. Foote, *Fredericksburg to Meridian*, 431; Bearss, *Fields of Honor*, 154; Gordon, *Reminiscences*, 137, 139.
4. Foote, *Fredericksburg to Meridian*, 439–40; Eckert, *Soldier, Southerner, American*, 42–45; Gordon, *Reminiscences*, 60–69; OR, Series I, Vol. 27, Pt. II, Ch. 39, pp. 451, 462–64, 491; Early, *Autobiographical Sketch*, 250; Buell, *Warrior Generals*, 224–25.
5. Gordon, *Reminiscences*, 140; Early, *Autobiographical Sketch*, 256–57.
6. Eckert, *Soldier, Southerner, American*, 46–47; Gordon, *Reminiscences*, 142–43, 145; OR, Series I, Vol. 27, Pt. II, Ch. 39, pp. 466, 491–92; Buell, *Warrior Generals*, 226.
7. Tankersley, *A Study in Gallantry*, 123; Eckert, *Soldier, Southerner, American*, 49; Gordon, *Reminiscences*, 143–44, 147–48; Freeman, *Lee's Lieutenants*, vol. 3, p. 33; OR, Series I, Vol. 27, Pt. II, Ch. 39, pp.

443, 466–67, 491–92; Early, *Autobiographical Sketch*, 258–60; Buell, *Warrior Generals*, 226.

8. Gordon, *Reminiscences*, 148–49; Eckert, *Soldier, Southerner, American*, 49–50.

9. Foote, *Fredericksburg to Meridian*, 441, 456–57, 462–63; OR, Series I, Vol. 27, Pt. II, Ch. 39, pp. 467–68; Bearss, *Fields of Honor*, 156; Dowdey and Manarin, eds., *Wartime Papers of R.E. Lee*, 534–35; Sorrel, *Recollections of a Confederate Staff Officer*, 161–62.

10. Foote, *Fredericksburg to Meridian*, 446–51, 455; Bearss, *Fields of Honor*, 155.

11. Foote, *Fredericksburg to Meridian*, 448, 453, 465; Bearss, *Fields of Honor*, 157–58.

12. Foote, *Fredericksburg to Meridian*, 465, 467–68; Bearss, *Fields of Honor*, 159–60.

13. Foote, *Fredericksburg to Meridian*, 469–71; Bearss, *Fields of Honor*, 161, 164–65.

14. Foote, *Fredericksburg to Meridian*, 471–76; Bearss, *Fields of Honor*, 166–67.

15. Freeman, *Lee's Lieutenants*, vol. 3, pp. 87–88; Foote, *Fredericksburg to Meridian*, 476–77; Eckert, *Soldier, Southerner, American*, 52–53; Bearss, *Fields of Honor*, 168–69; Gordon, *Reminiscences*, 150–53; OR, Series I, Vol. 27, Pt. II, Ch. 39, pp. 445, 468–69, 492–93; Early, *Autobiographical Sketch*, 267–68.

16. Tankersley, *A Study in Gallantry*, 126; Gordon, *Reminiscences*, 151–52; Southern Historical Society Papers, vol. 21, pp. 337–339.

17. Tankersley, *A Study in Gallantry*, 127; Gordon, *Reminiscences*, 152–53; Eckert, *Soldier, Southerner, American*, 53–54.

18. Foote, *Fredericksburg to Meridian*, 478–81, 486–87; OR, Series I, Vol. 27, Pt. II, Ch. 39, pp. 468–69, 493.

19. Tankersley, *A Study in Gallantry*, 127–29; Gordon, *Reminiscences*, 153–57; Freeman, *Lee's Lieutenants*, vol. pp. 3, 92–93; Eckert, *Soldier, Southerner, American*, 54–57; Early, *Autobiographical Sketch*, 271.

20. Foote, *Fredericksburg to Meridian*, 482–86; Bearss, *Fields of Honor*, 171–72.

21. Foote, *Fredericksburg to Meridian*, 479–80, 488–92; Bearss, *Fields of Honor*, 173–74.

22. Foote, *Fredericksburg to Meridian*, 493–95; Bearss, *Fields of Honor*, 175–76.

23. Foote, *Fredericksburg to Meridian*, 495–96; Bearss, *Fields of Honor*, 175–76.

24. Foote, *Fredericksburg to Meridian*, 498–501; Bearss, *Fields of Honor*, 178–80.

25. Oates, *The War Between the Union and The Confederacy*, 211–12; Foote, *Fredericksburg to Meridian*, 502; Bearss, *Fields of Honor*, 180.

26. Desjardin, *Stand Firm*, 7, 19; Pullen, *Twentieth Maine*, 86, 90, 96; Chamberlain, *Bayonet! Forward*, 16–21; Pullen, *Twentieth Maine*, 108; *Civil War Recollections*, 33; OR, Series I, Vol. 27, Pt. 2, Ch. 39, pp. 622–23; Longacre, *Joshua Chamberlain: The Soldier and the Man*, 121–23.

27. Foote, *Fredericksburg to Meridian*, 503; Bearss, *Fields of Honor*, 180–81; Pullen, *Twentieth Maine*, 107, 109; Desjardin, *Stand Firm*, 36–37; Chamberlain, *Bayonet! Forward*, 21; Spear, *Civil War Recollections*, 33.

28. Desjardin, *Stand Firm*, 37; Chamberlain, *Bayonet! Forward*, 22; Spear, *Civil War Recollections*, 33; Longacre, *Joshua Chamberlain: The Soldier and the Man*, 127–28.

29. Bearss, *Fields of Honor*, 181; Pullen, *Twentieth Maine*, 110–11; Chamberlain, *Bayonet! Forward*, 23; OR, Series I, Vol. 27, Pt. 2, Ch. 39, p. 623.

30. Bearss, *Fields of Honor*, 181–82; Pullen, *Twentieth Maine*, 116; Desjardin, *Stand Firm*, 38, 41, 44, 50; Chamberlain, *Bayonet! Forward*, 23, 26–27; Oates, *The War Between the Union and The Confederacy*, 214; Trulock, *Hands of Providence*, 142; OR, Series I, Vol. 27, Pt. 2, Ch. 39, p. 623.

31. Bearss, *Fields of Honor*, 183–84; Pullen, *Twentieth Maine*, 117–18; Desjardin, *Stand Firm*, 51–54; Chamberlain, *Bayonet! Forward*, 26–27, 185; Gerrish, *Army Life*, 107; Norton, *Attack and Defense of Little Round Top*, 261; Spear, *Civil War Recollections*, 33–34; OR, Series I, Vol. 27, Pt. 2, Ch. 39, p. 623; Longacre, *Joshua Chamberlain: The Soldier and the Man*, 135.

32. Pullen, *Twentieth Maine*, 118–19, 121–22; Desjardin, *Stand Firm*, 54, 58; Oates, *The War Between the Union and The Confederacy*, 214, 218–19; OR, Series I, Vol. 27, Pt. 2, Ch. 39, pp. 623–24.

33. Chamberlain, *Bayonet! Forward*, 28; Oates, *The War Between the Union and The Confederacy*, 220; Gerrish, *Army Life*, 108.

34. Desjardin, *Stand Firm*, 58, 60–63, 65, 131–32; Chamberlain, *Bayonet! Forward*, 29–31; Gerrish, *Army Life*, 69–70, 109; Norton, *Attack and Defense of Little Round Top*, 261; Longacre, *Joshua Chamberlain: The Soldier and the Man*, 137.

35. Desjardin, *Stand Firm*, 64; Cham-

berlain, *Bayonet! Forward*, 31–32; Welsh, *Medical Histories*, 63.

36. OR, Series I, Vol. 27, Pt. 1, Ch. 39, p. 603; Pullen, *Twentieth Maine*, 123; Desjardin, *Stand Firm*, 58,69; Gerrish, *Army Life*, 109; Norton, *Attack and Defense of Little Round Top*, 261; Chamberlain, *Bayonet! Forward*, 32–33; OR, Series I, Vol. 27, Pt. 2, Ch. 39, p. 624; Longacre, *Joshua Chamberlain: The Soldier and the Man*, 138.

37. OR, Series I, Vol. 27, Pt. 2, Ch. 39, pp. 392–93; Oates, *The War Between the Union and The Confederacy*, 206, 219–21; Desjardin, *Stand Firm*, 69.

38. Chamberlain, *Bayonet! Forward*, 33; Oates, *The War Between the Union and The Confederacy*, 221; Gerrish, *Army Life*, 110; Pullen, *Twentieth Maine*, 124–25; Desjardin, *Stand Firm*, 69–71; Spear, *Civil War Recollections*, 34–36; OR, Series I, Vol. 27, Pt. 1, Ch. 39, pp. 603,624.

39. Oates, *The War Between the Union and The Confederacy*, 220; Foote, *Fredericksburg to Meridian*, 505; Desjardin, *Stand Firm*, 73–74; Pullen, *Twentieth Maine*, 125; Spear, *Civil War Recollections*, 35.

40. Chamberlain, *Bayonet! Forward*, 33–34; Desjardin, *Stand Firm*, 73–75, 81–82, 117; Pullen, *Twentieth Maine*, 126–27; OR, Series I, Vol. 27, Pt. 1, Ch. 39, pp. 603, 624–25.

41. Foote, *Fredericksburg to Meridian*, 506–09; Bearss, *Fields of Honor*, 185–87.

42. Foote, *Fredericksburg to Meridian*, 509–12; Bearss, *Fields of Honor*, 188–90.

43. OR, Series I, Vol. 27, Pt. II, Ch. 39, p. 493; Foote, *Fredericksburg to Meridian*, 514–20; Bearss, *Fields of Honor*, 190–93; Early, *Autobiographical Sketch*, 272–74.

44. Desjardin, *Stand Firm*, 83–86, 88; Pullen, *Twentieth Maine*, 130–31; OR, Series I, Vol. 27, Pt. 1, Ch. 39, pp. 618, 625–26.

45. JLC to Fanny, letter dated July 4, 1863 (LC); OR, Series I, Vol. 27, Pt. 1, Ch. 39, p. 620; Desjardin, *Stand Firm*, 91; Oates, *The War Between the Union and The Confederacy*, 219.

46. Foote, *Fredericksburg to Meridian*, 523–28; Bearss, *Fields of Honor*, 194.

47. Foote, *Fredericksburg to Meridian*, 528–30, 540–41; Bearss, *Fields of Honor*, 194–95.

48. Foote, *Fredericksburg to Meridian*, 546–49; Bearss, *Fields of Honor*, 195–97; Eckert, *Soldier, Southerner, American*, 57; Wallace, *Soul of the Lion*, 107; Wert, *Gettysburg: Day Three*, 172–73, 181.

49. Foote, *Fredericksburg to Meridian*, 536–37, 543, 548; Bearss, *Fields of Honor*, 198.

50. Foote, *Fredericksburg to Meridian*, 525, 543–44; Haskell, *Eyewitness Account of Col. Frank A Haskell*, 73.

51. Foote, *Fredericksburg to Meridian*, 553–57; Bearss, *Fields of Honor*, 198–99; Wert, *Gettysburg: Day Three*, 201.

52. Foote, *Fredericksburg to Meridian*, 555, 559–62; Haskell, *Eyewitness Account of Col. Frank A Haskell*, 91–100; Bearss, *Fields of Honor*, 200–01; Wert, *Gettysburg: Day Three*, 226–27.

53. Foote, *Fredericksburg to Meridian*, 563–69; Wert, *Gettysburg: Day Three*, 250–51.

54. Foote, *Fredericksburg to Meridian*, 576, 578.

55. Gordon, *Reminiscences*, 160–61, 168–69.

56. Foote, *Fredericksburg to Meridian*, 566, 581–85, 588–92; Bearss, *Fields of Honor*, 202; Gordon, *Reminiscences*, 172; OR, Series I, Vol. 27, Pt. II, Ch. 39, pp. 448, 471, 493.

57. Chamberlain, *Bayonet! Forward*, 36; OR, Series I, Vol. 27, Pt. 1, Ch. 39, p. 626.

58. 07/04/1863 letter to Fanny from JLC.

59. Foote, *Fredericksburg to Meridian*, 827, 831–33.

Chapter 9

1. Desjardin, *Stand Firm*, 108–09; Pullen, *Twentieth Maine*, 147, 151.

2. Pullen, *Twentieth Maine*, 158; Gerrish, *Army Life*, 122; Desjardin, *Stand Firm*, 118; Wallace, *Soul of the Lion*, 115–16; Trulock, *Hands of Providence*, 167; National Archives, Joshua L. Chamberlain Military Records; OR, Series I, Vol. 29, Pt. 1, Ch. 41, p. 917; Welsh, *Medical Histories*, 63.

3. Wallace, *Soul of the Lion*, 116; Trulock, *Hands of Providence*, 169.

4. Trulock, *Hands of Providence*, 164; Gerrish, *Army Life*, 123; Pullen, *Twentieth Maine*, 154–55.

5. Gerrish, *Army Life*, 124–26; Trulock, *Hands of Providence*, 164–65; Pullen, *Twentieth Maine*, 155–56.

6. Gerrish, *Army Life*, 126–28; Trulock, *Hands of Providence*, 164–65; Pullen, *Twentieth Maine*, 156–57; Spear, *Civil War Recollections*, 47–48.

7. Trulock, *Hands of Providence*, 165, 167,

170, 201; Wallace, *Soul of the Lion*, 118–19, 144; Horn, ed., *Robert E. Lee Reader*, 342–43; Foote, *Fredericksburg to Meridian*, 791–93, 795, 801; Pullen, *Twentieth Maine*, 210, 244.

8. Trulock, *Hands of Providence*, 171–73; Wallace, *Soul of the Lion*, 118–19; Gerrish, *Army Life*, 129; Pullen, *Twentieth Maine*, 160–66; Spear, *Civil War Recollections*, 62; OR, Series I, Vol. 29, Pt. 1, Ch. 41, pp. 581–82, 621–22.

9. Wallace, *Soul of the Lion*, 119–21; Trulock, *Hands of Providence*, 173–74; Pullen, *Twentieth Maine*, 166; Welsh, *Medical Histories*, 63; National Archives, Joshua L. Chamberlain Military Records; 11/16/1863 letter to Fanny from Lt. Wm. E. Donnell, LC; Longacre, *Joshua Chamberlain: The Soldier and the Man*, 171–72.

10. Gerrish, *Army Life*, 132–33; Foote, *Fredericksburg to Meridian*, 870, 875–77; OR, Series I, Vol. 29, Pt. 1, Ch. 41, pp. 843–45.

11. Trulock, *Hands of Providence*, 174; Gerrish, *Army Life*, 136; Berkley, *Four Years in the Confederate Artillery*, 63–71, Gordon, *Reminiscences*, 229–30, 233; Foote, *Fredericksburg to Meridian*, 870, 888.

12. Gerrish, *Army Life*, 136, 142–144; Pullen, *Twentieth Maine*, 169.

13. Gordon, *Reminiscences*, 110, 229.

14. Ibid., 110–11.

15. Ibid., 111–12.

16. Ibid.

17. Freeman, *Lee's Lieutenants*, vol. 3, pp. 325, 332–33; Dowdey and Manarin, eds., *Wartime Papers of R.E. Lee*, 662; Eckert, *Soldier, Southerner, American*, 60; OR, Series I, Vol. 33, Pt. 1, Ch. 45, pp. 1124, 1131.

Chapter 10

1. Foote, *Fredericksburg to Meridian*, 962–63; Grant, *Personal Memoirs of U.S. Grant*, vol. 2, p. 114.

2. Trulock, *Hands of Providence*, 169, 175; Grant, *Personal Memoirs of U.S. Grant*, vol. 2, pp. 116–117; Foote, *Red River to Appomattox*, 10; Bearss, *Fields of Honor*, 274.

3. Grant, *Personal Memoirs of U.S. Grant*, vol. 2, pp. 119–20, 130–33; Foote, *Red River to Appomattox*, 135–38; Bearss, *Fields of Honor*, 274.

4. Foote, *Red River to Appomattox*, 133, 145–48, 150; Bearss, *Fields of Honor*, 275, 277.

5. Tankersley, *A Study in Gallantry*, 137;

Foote, *Red River to Appomattox*, 154–55, 158–59; Bearss, *Fields of Honor*, 278; Gordon, *Reminiscences*, 238–39; Pullen, *Twentieth Maine*, 184–86; Freeman, *Lee's Lieutenants*, vol. 3, p. 350; Pollard, *Companions in Arms*, 542–43; Spear, *Civil War Recollections*, 94–96.

6. Tankersley, *A Study in Gallantry*, 137–38; Freeman, *Lee's Lieutenants*, vol. 3, p. 350; Foote, *Red River to Appomattox*, 155; Early, *Autobiographical Sketch*, 346–47; Gordon, *Reminiscences*, 239–41; Eckert, *Soldier, Southerner, American*, 63–64; OR, Series I, Vol. 36, Pt. I, Ch. 48, pp. 1070, 1076–77; Pullen, *Twentieth Maine*, 184–87; Gerrish, *Army Life*, 162; Buell, *Warrior Generals*, 310.

7. Foote, *Red River to Appomattox*, 156, 160; Early, *Autobiographical Sketch*, 347; OR, Series I, Vol. 36, Pt. I, Ch. 48, p. 1077; Bearss, *Fields of Honor*, 287–88.

8. Foote, *Red River to Appomattox*, 156, 161–63; Bearss, *Fields of Honor*, 286–87.

9. Foote, *Red River to Appomattox*, 164–71, 175–81; Bearss, *Fields of Honor*, 288–92; Sorrel, *Recollections of a Confederate Staff Officer*, 241–44; Longstreet, *From Manassas to Appomattox*, 564.

10. Freeman, *Lee's Lieutenants*, vol. 3, p. 368; Foote, *Red River to Appomattox*, 173, 181; Bearss, *Fields of Honor*, 293–94; Gordon, *Reminiscences*, 243; Buell, *Warrior Generals*, 310; OR, Series I, Vol. 36, Pt. I, Ch. 48, pp. 1040, 1071, 1077, 1085.

11. Freeman, *Lee's Lieutenants*, vol. 3, pp. 369–70; Foote, *Red River to Appomattox*, 173; Bearss, *Fields of Honor*, 294; Gordon, *Reminiscences*, 245–46, 255; Early, *Autobiographical Sketch*, 348; OR, Supplement, Vol. 6, pp. 670–73.

12. Tankersley, *A Study in Gallantry*, 141–42; Freeman, *Lee's Lieutenants*, vol. 3, pp. 370–71; Foote, *Red River to Appomattox*, 181; Bearss, *Fields of Honor*, 294; Gordon, *Reminiscences*, 258; Early, *Autobiographical Sketch*, 348.

13. Tankersley, *A Study in Gallantry*, 142; Freeman, *Lee's Lieutenants*, vol. 3, pp. 371–72; Foote, *Red River to Appomattox*, 181–82; Bearss, *Fields of Honor*, 294–95; Gordon, *Reminiscences*, 249–50; Early, *Autobiographical Sketch*, 349–50; Horn, ed., *Robert E. Lee Reader*, 371; OR, Series I, Vol. 36, Pt. I, Ch. 48, pp. 1077–78; OR, Series I, Vol. 36, Pt. II, Ch. 48, pp. 966; OR, Series I, Vol. 51, Pt. II, Ch. 63, pp. 889–90.

14. Gordon, *Reminiscences*, 245, 252–

53, 259–61; OR, Series I, Vol. 36, Pt. I, Ch. 48, p. 1078.
15. Pollard, *Companions in Arms*, 544; Gordon, *Reminiscences*, 263–66.
16. Foote, *Red River to Appomattox*, 183; Bearss, *Fields of Honor*, 293; Gordon, *Reminiscences*, 267.
17. Bearss, *Fields of Honor*, 296; Gordon, *Reminiscences*, 268–69; Pullen, *Twentieth Maine*, 193.
18. Foote, *Red River to Appomattox*, 185, 187–91; Bearss, *Fields of Honor*, 295; Gordon, *Reminiscences*, 268–69; Pullen, *Twentieth Maine*, 194.
19. Trulock, *Hands of Providence*, 176–77; Wallace, *Soul of the Lion*, 121–23; *Civil War Recollections*, 109; National Archives, Joshua L. Chamberlain Military Records; Longacre, *Joshua Chamberlain: The Soldier and the Man*, 173.

Chapter 11

1. Foote, *Red River to Appomattox*, 189, 193; Bearss, *Fields of Honor*, 298–99, 302.
2. Foote, *Red River to Appomattox*, 193; Early, *Autobiographical Sketch*, 351; Dowdey and Manarin, eds., *Wartime Papers of R.E. Lee*, 725; Freeman, *Lee's Lieutenants*, vol. 3, p. 391; OR, Series I, Vol. 33, Pt. 1, Ch. 45, p. 1131; OR, Series I, Vol. 36, Pt. 1, Ch. 48, p. 1071; OR, Series I, Vol. 51, Pt. II, Ch. 63, pp. 902–03.
3. Foote, *Red River to Appomattox*, 203; Bearss, *Fields of Honor*, 305–07; Krick, in *Image of War*, vol. 5, p. 178; Grant, *Personal Memoirs of U.S. Grant*, 218–20.
4. Foote, *Red River to Appomattox*, 205–08; Bearss, *Fields of Honor*, 308–09; Krick, in *Image of War*, vol. 5, p. 178; Grant, *Personal Memoirs of U.S. Grant*, 220–23.
5. Foote, *Red River to Appomattox*, 208–09; Bearss, *Fields of Honor*, 310–12; Gordon, *Reminiscences*, 272–73; Grant, *Personal Memoirs of U.S. Grant*, 224.
6. Tankersley, *A Study in Gallantry*, 148; Foote, *Red River to Appomattox*, 210; Bearss, *Fields of Honor*, 312–13; Gordon, *Reminiscences*, 272–73; Grant, *Personal Memoirs of U.S. Grant*, 224; OR, Series I, Vol. 36, Pt. I, Ch. 48, p. 1078.
7. Foote, *Red River to Appomattox*, 210, 213–17; Bearss, *Fields of Honor*, 313–15; Grant, *Personal Memoirs of U.S. Grant*, 230–31.
8. Foote, *Red River to Appomattox*, 216–18; Gordon, *Reminiscences*, 272, 275–77; Freeman, *Lee's Lieutenants*, vol. 3, p. 405; Buell, *Warrior Generals*, 322; OR, Series I, Vol. 36, Pt. I, Ch. 48, pp. 1078–79.
9. Gordon, *Reminiscences*, 277.
10. Foote, *Red River to Appomattox*, 218; Gordon, *Reminiscences*, 278–79; Freeman, *Lee's Lieutenants*, vol. 3, pp. 405–06; Bearss, *Fields of Honor*, 316; Horn, *Robert E. Lee Reader*, 377; Buell, *Warrior Generals*, 323.
11. Foote, *Red River to Appomattox*, 218–19; Bearss, *Fields of Honor*, 316; Gordon, *Reminiscences*, 279–80; Grant, *Personal Memoirs of U.S. Grant*, 231; Freeman, *Lee's Lieutenants*, vol. 3, p. 408; Alexander, *Fighting for the Confederacy*, 377; Buell, *Warrior Generals*, 324; Pollard, *Companions in Arms*, 544–45; OR, Series I, Vol. 36, Pt. I, Ch. 48, pp. 1057, 1072, 1079; OR, Supplement, Vol. 6, p. 523.
12. Foote, *Red River to Appomattox*, 221–22; Bearss, *Fields of Honor*, 317–18; Gordon, *Reminiscences*, 284–85.
13. Foote, *Red River to Appomattox*, 222–23; Bearss, *Fields of Honor*, 317–18; Gordon, *Reminiscences*, 285; OR, Series I, Vol. 36, Pt. I, Ch. 48, pp. 1057, 1073.
14. Foote, *Red River to Appomattox*, 236–39, 241–42; Bearss, *Fields of Honor*, 318–19; Gordon, *Reminiscences*, 289–90; Grant, *Personal Memoirs of U.S. Grant*, 234, 242; Eckert, *Soldier, Southerner, American*, 79; Freeman, *Lee's Lieutenants*, vol. 3, p. 434; Early, *Autobiographical Sketch*, 359; Buell, *Warrior Generals*, 325, 329; OR, Series I, Vol. 36, Pt. I, Ch. 48, p. 1073; OR, Series I, Vol. 36, Pt. III, Ch. 48, pp. 813–14, 873–74.

Chapter 12

1. Foote, *Red River to Appomattox*, 247–64; Bearss, *Fields of Honor*, 319; Grant, *Personal Memoirs of U.S. Grant*, 238.
2. Foote, *Red River to Appomattox*, 265–66; Bearss, *Fields of Honor*, 322; Wallace, *Soul of the Lion*, 123–24; Trulock, *Hands of Providence*, 181–82; Pullen, *Twentieth Maine*, 203–04: Grant, *Personal Memoirs of U.S. Grant*, 243–45; OR, Series I, Vol. 36, Pt. 1, Ch. 48, pp. 574, 591–92.
3. Foote, *Red River to Appomattox*, 265–67, 274–75; Bearss, *Fields of Honor*, 323–24; Wallace, *Soul of the Lion*, 125; Trulock, *Hands of Providence*, 183; Grant, *Personal Memoirs of U.S. Grant*, 246–48.
4. Foote, *Red River to Appomattox*, 265–

71, 274–76; Bearss, *Fields of Honor*, 323–24; Grant, *Personal Memoirs of U.S. Grant*, 249; Krick, in *Image of War*, vol. 5, pp. 182–83.

5. Foote, *Red River to Appomattox*, 270–71, 277–79; Bearss, *Fields of Honor*, 327; Wallace, *Soul of the Lion*, 125; Trulock, *Hands of Providence*, 185; Pullen, *Twentieth Maine*, 204; Grant, *Personal Memoirs of U.S. Grant*, 260–63; Krick, in *Image of War*, vol. 5, pp. 183–85.

6. Foote, *Red River to Appomattox*, 281–90; Bearss, *Fields of Honor*, 326–28, 331; Grant, *Personal Memoirs of U.S. Grant*, 264–70; Eckert, *Soldier, Southerner, American*, 81; Early, *Autobiographical Sketch*, 363; Winik, *April 1865*, 96.

7. Foote, *Red River to Appomattox*, 281–90; Bearss, *Fields of Honor*, 326–28, 331; Grant, *Personal Memoirs of U.S. Grant*, 264–70; Early, *Autobiographical Sketch*, 363; Winik, *April 1865*, 96.

8. Foote, *Red River to Appomattox*, 290–96; Bearss, *Fields of Honor*, 328–31; Grant, *Personal Memoirs of U.S. Grant*, 270–76.

9. Foote, *Red River to Appomattox*, 290–96; Bearss, *Fields of Honor*, 328–31; Grant, *Personal Memoirs of U.S. Grant*, 270–76.

10. Bearss, *Fields of Honor*, 331–33; Grant, *Personal Memoirs of U.S. Grant*, 251, 278; Krick, in *Image of War*, vol. 5, p. 187; Smith, in *Image of War*, vol. 5, pp. 304–05.

11. Foote, *Red River to Appomattox*, 270, 295, 301–02, 309–10, 312; Bearss, *Fields of Honor*, 331–33; Grant, *Personal Memoirs of U.S. Grant*, 251, 278, 282, 288–89, 294–95; Krick, in *Image of War*, vol. 5, p. 187; Smith, in *Image of War*, vol. 5, pp. 304–05.

12. Foote, *Red River to Appomattox*, 315–16, 427–29; Bearss, *Fields of Honor*, 333–34; Grant, *Personal Memoirs of U.S. Grant*, 295–96; Krick, in *Image of War*, vol. 5, p. 187.

13. Foote, *Red River to Appomattox*, 429–31; Bearss, *Fields of Honor*, 334–35; Grant, *Personal Memoirs of U.S. Grant*, 295–96; Krick, in *Image of War*, vol. 5, p. 187.

14. Foote, *Red River to Appomattox*, 431–37; Bearss, *Fields of Honor*, 336–40; Grant, *Personal Memoirs of U.S. Grant*, 296–97.

15. Foote, *Red River to Appomattox*, 439–41; Bearss, *Fields of Honor*, 341–42.

16. Wallace, *Soul of the Lion*, 125–26, 128–29; Trulock, *Hands of Providence*, 188, 193–94; Spear, *Civil War Recollections*, 120; OR, Series I, Vol. 36, Pt. 1, Ch. 48, pp. 169, 652; OR, Series I, Vol. 36, Pt. III, Ch. 48, pp. 613, 653, 709–10.

17. Chamberlain, *Bayonet! Forward*, 46–47; Wallace, *Soul of the Lion*, 128–29; Trulock, *Hands of Providence*, 199–201; Pullen, *Twentieth Maine*, 209–10.

18. Chamberlain, *Bayonet! Forward*, 47; Wallace, *Soul of the Lion*, 129; Trulock, *Hands of Providence*, 201–03; Pullen, *Twentieth Maine*, 210.

19. Chamberlain, *Bayonet! Forward*, 47–48; Wallace, *Soul of the Lion*, 129; Trulock, *Hands of Providence*, 203; Pullen, *Twentieth Maine*, 210.

20. Wallace, *Soul of the Lion*, 129–30; Trulock, *Hands of Providence*, 203–04; Pullen, *Twentieth Maine*, 210–11.

21. Chamberlain, *Bayonet! Forward*, 48; Wallace, *Soul of the Lion*, 131; Trulock, *Hands of Providence*, 204–10.

22. Chamberlain, *Bayonet! Forward*, 48; Wallace, *Soul of the Lion*, 131–32; Trulock, *Hands of Providence*, 208–09; Pullen, *Twentieth Maine*, 211.

23. Chamberlain, *Bayonet! Forward*, 48; Wallace, *Soul of the Lion*, 132–33; Trulock, *Hands of Providence*, 210, 212–13; Pullen, *Twentieth Maine*, 211; Bearss, *Fields of Honor*, 343; Longacre, *Joshua Chamberlain: The Soldier and the Man*, 196.

24. 6/19/1864 letter to Meade from Warren, LC, Special Orders, No. 39, June 20, 1864; LC, Grant to Stanton, June 20, 1864; Grant, *Personal Memoirs of U.S. Grant*, 297–98; OR, Series I, Vol. 40, Ch. 52, Pt. I, pp. 216–17, 236–37, 421; OR, Series I, Vol. 40, Ch. 52, Pt. III, p. 520.

25. Welsh, *Medical Histories*, 63–64, Pejebscot Historical Society; *Medical and Surgical History*, 363; Wallace, *Soul of the Lion*, 133–34; Trulock, *Hands of Providence*, 213; Pullen, *Twentieth Maine*, 211–12.

26. 6/20/1864 letter to Fanny from JLC, LC; Trulock, *Hands of Providence*, 215–16; Welsh, *Medical Histories*, 64; Wallace, *Soul of the Lion*, 135–36.

27. Foote, *Red River to Appomattox*, 444, 531–34; Bearss, *Fields of Honor*, 343–46; Grant, *Personal Memoirs of U.S. Grant*, 307–13.

28. Foote, *Red River to Appomattox*, 535–38; Bearss, *Fields of Honor*, 346–51; Grant, *Personal Memoirs of U.S. Grant*, 313–15.

Chapter 13

1. Foote, *Red River to Appomattox*, 445–46; Dowdey and Manarin, eds., *Wartime*

Papers of R.E. Lee, 806–07, 811; Gordon, *Reminiscences*, 300–03.

2. Foote, *Red River to Appomattox*, 447–50; Eckert, *Soldier, Southerner, American*, 82–83; Freeman, *Lee's Lieutenants*, vol. 3, pp. 557–58, 562–63; OR, Series I, Vol. 37, Pt. I, Ch. 49, p. 768; Early, *Autobiographical Sketch*, 381, 387–88; Douglas, *I Rode with Stonewall*, 281.

3. Tankersley, *A Study in Gallantry*, 157–60; Foote, *Red River to Appomattox*, 450–52; Gordon, *Reminiscences*, 309–13; Eckert, *Soldier, Southerner, American*, 83–85; Freeman, *Lee's Lieutenants*, vol. 3, pp. 557–58, 562–63; OR, Series I, Vol. 37, Pt. I, Ch. 49, pp. 350–52; Early, *Autobiographical Sketch*, 387–88; Douglas, *I Rode with Stonewall*, 281; Buell, *Warrior Generals*, 338–39.

4. Foote, *Red River to Appomattox*, 450, 453–57; Eckert, *Soldier, Southerner, American*, 85–86; Gordon, *Reminiscences*, 314; Grant, *Personal Memoirs of U.S. Grant*, 305–06; Early, *Autobiographical Sketch*, 391–92; Letter to Fanny, dated 7/11/1864, Hargrett Library.

5. Foote, *Red River to Appomattox*, 457–61; Eckert, *Soldier, Southerner, American*, 86; Gordon, *Reminiscences*, 315–16; Grant, *Personal Memoirs of U.S. Grant*, 306; Early, *Autobiographical Sketch*, 392; Douglas, *I Rode with Stonewall*, 283–84; Freeman, *Lee's Lieutenants*, vol. 3, pp. 566–67; Buell, *Warrior Generals*, 339–40.

6. Foote, *Red River to Appomattox*, 544–45; Eckert, *Soldier, Southerner, American*, 87; Gordon, *Reminiscences*, 317; Grant, *Personal Memoirs of U.S. Grant*, 316–21, 327, 581–82; Douglas, *I Rode with Stonewall*, 288, 293–96; Early, *Autobiographical Sketch*, 406–13; Sheridan, *Personal Memoirs of P.H. Sheridan*, 254; OR, Supplement, Vol. 7, pp. 274–75; Smith, in *Image of War*, vol. 5, p. 311.

7. Gordon, *Reminiscences*, 302–06, 327–28.

8. Gordon, *Reminiscences*, 302–06, 327–28; Smith, in *Image of War*, vol. 5, pp. 304–05, 309–11, 315.

9. Tankersley, *A Study in Gallantry*, 162; Foote, *Red River to Appomattox*, 554–55; Gordon, *Reminiscences*, 320–22: Douglas, *I Rode with Stonewall*, 296–97; Early, *Autobiographical Sketch*, 420–27; Sheridan, *Personal Memoirs of P.H. Sheridan*, 280–95; Freeman, *Lee's Lieutenants*, vol. 3, pp. 577–78; OR, Series I, Vol. 43, Ch. 55, Pt. I, 554–56; OR, Supplement, Vol. 7, pp. 600–01.

10. Gordon, *Reminiscences*, 318–19, 322; Freeman, *Lee's Lieutenants*, vol. 3, p. 328; Buell, *Warrior Generals*, 340.

11. Gordon, *Reminiscences*, 42, 323; Freeman, *Lee's Lieutenants*, vol. 3, pp. 580–81; Douglas, *I Rode with Stonewall*, 298.

12. Gordon, *Reminiscences*, 326; Sheridan, *Personal Memoirs of P.H. Sheridan*, 299–301; Foote, *Red River to Appomattox*, 555–58; Early, *Autobiographical Sketch*, 430; Eckert, *Soldier, Southerner, American*, 91.

13. Douglas, *I Rode with Stonewall*, 300–02; Sheridan, *Personal Memoirs of P.H. Sheridan*, 306, 310–12; Foote, *Red River to Appomattox*, 563–65; Grant, *Personal Memoirs of U.S. Grant*, 331, 335–38; Early, *Autobiographical Sketch*, 437; Gordon, *Reminiscences*, 332; Eckert, *Soldier, Southerner, American*, 92.

14. Foote, *Red River to Appomattox*, 566; Early, *Autobiographical Sketch*, 438–39; Gordon, *Reminiscences*, 332–35; Eckert, *Soldier, Southerner, American*, 93; Freeman, *Lee's Lieutenants*, vol. 3, p. 597; OR, Series I, Vol. 43, Ch. 55, Pt. I, pp. 561–62, 580.

15. Tankersley, *A Study in Gallantry*, 165–66; Freeman, *Lee's Lieutenants*, vol. 3, p. 598; Foote, *Red River to Appomattox*, 566–67; Early, *Autobiographical Sketch*, 439–43; Gordon, *Reminiscences*, 334–36; Eckert, *Soldier, Southerner, American*, 94–95.

16. Gordon, *Reminiscences*, 63–64, 338; Foote, *Red River to Appomattox*, 571.

17. Gordon, *Reminiscences*, 337.

18. Foote, *Red River to Appomattox*, 567–68; Douglas, *I Rode with Stonewall*, 302–03; Early, *Autobiographical Sketch*, 443–47; Gordon, *Reminiscences*, 338–40; Sheridan, *Personal Memoirs of P.H. Sheridan*, 335; Catton, *A Stillness at Appomattox*, 308–10; Pollard, *Companions in Arms*, 545–46; Freeman, *Lee's Lieutenants*, vol. 3, pp. 601–02; OR, Series I, Vol. 43, Ch. 55, Pt. I, pp. 561–62, 581; OR, Supplement, Vol. 7, pp. 591, 605, 607; Eckert, *Soldier, Southerner, American*, 97.

19. Tankersley, *A Study in Gallantry*, 168; Foote, *Red River to Appomattox*, 568–69; Gordon, *Reminiscences*, 340–41; Catton, *A Stillness at Appomattox*, 311; Freeman, *Lee's Lieutenants*, vol. 3, pp. 603–04; OR, Supplement, Vol. 7, pp. 589, 612; Eckert, *Soldier, Southerner, American*, 98.

20. Tankersley, *A Study in Gallantry*, 168; Foote, *Red River to Appomattox*, 568–69; Douglas, *I Rode with Stonewall*, 303; Gordon, *Reminiscences*, 340–43.

21. Foote, *Red River to Appomattox*, 569–71; Catton, *A Stillness at Appomattox*, 312–16; Sheridan, *Personal Memoirs of P.H. Sheridan*, 321–33; Early, *Autobiographical Sketch*, 447–48; Douglas, *I Rode with Stonewall*, 303; Gordon, *Reminiscences*, 345–47; Grant, *Personal Memoirs of U.S. Grant*, 338–39; OR, Supplement, Vol. 7, pp. 610–11; Eckert, *Soldier, Southerner, American*, 99–100.

22. Tankersley, *A Study in Gallantry*, 170; Foote, *Red River to Appomattox*, 571; Early, *Autobiographical Sketch*, 448–50; Douglas, *I Rode with Stonewall*, 303; Gordon, *Reminiscences*, 347–49; Grant, *Personal Memoirs of U.S. Grant*, 339–40; Pollard, *Companions in Arms*, 546–47; Freeman, *Lee's Lieutenants*, vol. 3, p. 608; OR, Supplement, Vol. 7, pp. 594–95, 605, 611; Eckert, *Soldier, Southerner, American*, 100–01.

23. Gordon, *Reminiscences*, 347–49.

24. Ibid., 352–72.

25. Gordon, *Reminiscences*, 351, 354–72; Douglas, *I Rode with Stonewall*, 304–05; OR, Series I, Vol. 43, Pt. I, Ch. 55, p. 563; OR, Series I, Vol. 46, Pt. II, Ch. 58, pp. 385–86.

26. Foote, *Red River to Appomattox*, 571–72, 806–09; Sheridan, *Personal Memoirs of P.H. Sheridan*, 346–47; Early, *Autobiographical Sketch*, 453–55; Douglas, *I Rode with Stonewall*, 306.

27. Tankersley, *A Study in Gallantry*, 173; Foote, *Red River to Appomattox*, 637–38; Gordon, *Reminiscences*, 374; Sheridan, *Personal Memoirs of P.H. Sheridan*, 353; Freeman, *Lee's Lieutenants*, vol. 3, pp. 617, 628; Buell, *Warrior Generals*, 415.

Chapter 14

1. Trulock, *Hands of Providence*, 218–20; Wallace, *Soul of the Lion*, 137–39; Welsh, *Medical Histories*, 63; OR, Series I, Vol. 42, Ch. 54, Pt. III, pp. 663, 1117.

2. Trulock, *Hands of Providence*, 220; Pullen, *Twentieth Maine*, 230.

3. Trulock, *Hands of Providence*, 221; Pullen, *Twentieth Maine*, 231–32; Chamberlain, *Passing of the Armies*, 9–10; Gerrish, *Army Life*, 229

4. Foote, *Red River to Appomattox*, 628; Trulock, *Hands of Providence*, 220–22; Wallace, *Soul of the Lion*, 139–40; Gerrish, *Army Life*, 220–22; Pullen, *Twentieth Maine*, 232–34; Spear, *Civil War Recollections*, 157, 159.

5. Foote, *Red River to Appomattox*, 784–85; Gordon, *Reminiscences*, 376; Trulock, *Hands of Providence*, 224–26; Wallace, *Soul of the Lion*, 140; Douglas, *I Rode with Stonewall*, 311–12; OR, Supplement, Vol. 7, p. 717; Eckert, *Soldier, Southerner, American*, 106; Dowdey and Manarin, eds., *Wartime Papers of R.E. Lee*, 889; Gerrish, *Army Life*, 223; OR, Series I, Vol. 46, Ch. 58, Pt. I, 390.

6. Foote, *Red River to Appomattox*, 628–30, 632, 639–40, 785; Gordon, *Reminiscences*, 377–78, 381–82, 416; Wheeler, *Witness to Appomattox*, 9–10; Dowdey and Manarin, eds., *Wartime Papers of R.E. Lee*, 890.

7. Foote, *Red River to Appomattox*, 754; Letter, dated 2/26/1865, Hargrett Library; OR, Series I, Vol. 51, Pt. II, Ch. 63, p. 1063.

8. Foote, *Red River to Appomattox*, 755, 859–60; Dowdey and Manarin, eds., *Wartime Papers of R.E. Lee*, 914; Winik, *April 1865*, 61–62.

9. Foote, *Red River to Appomattox*, 770–75; Grant, *Personal Memoirs of U.S. Grant*, 420–22.

10. Foote, *Red River to Appomattox*, 776–77; Grant, *Personal Memoirs of U.S. Grant*, 422–23; Winik, *April 1865*, 33–34.

11. Foote, *Red River to Appomattox*, 809–10; Dowdey and Manarin, eds., *Wartime Papers of R.E. Lee*, 911–12.

12. Foote, *Red River to Appomattox*, 768–69, 786; Dowdey and Manarin, eds., *Wartime Papers of R.E. Lee*, 892–93, 910.

13. Foote, *Red River to Appomattox*, 839–40; Gordon, *Reminiscences*, 385–86, 391.

14. Gordon, *Reminiscences*, 385–88; Winik, *April 1865*, 32–33.

15. Tankersley, *A Study in Gallantry*, 174–76; Gordon, *Reminiscences*, 389–93.

16. Freeman, *Lee's Lieutenants*, vol. 3, p. 646; Gordon, *Reminiscences*, 394, 397–400; Eckert, *Soldier, Southerner, American*, 107–08.

17. Gordon, *Reminiscences*, 401–04; Freeman, *Lee's Lieutenants*, vol. 3, pp. 646–47; Foote, *Red River to Appomattox*, 840–41; Eckert, *Soldier, Southerner, American*, 109.

18. Gordon, *Reminiscences*, 405–07; Foote, *Red River to Appomattox*, 841–42; Eckert, *Soldier, Southerner, American*, 110.

19. Gordon, *Reminiscences*, 397–97.

20. Gordon, *Reminiscences*, 408; Freeman, *Lee's Lieutenants*, vol. 3, p. 647; Eckert, *Soldier, Southerner, American*, 111.

21. Gordon, *Reminiscences*, 409–10; Freeman, *Lee's Lieutenants*, vol. 3, p. 648; Eckert, *Soldier, Southerner, American*, 111.

22. Tankersley, *A Study in Gallantry*, 184–85; Gordon, *Reminiscences*, 410; Foote, *Red River to Appomattox*, 842; Eckert, *Soldier, Southerner, American*, 111–12; Douglas, *I Rode with Stonewall*, 313–14; Wert, *Sword of Lincoln*, 397; Freeman, *Lee's Lieutenants*, vol. 3, pp. 648–49; Buell, *Warrior Generals*, 416; OR, Series I, Vol. 46, Pt. I, Ch. 58, pp. 173, 317.

23. Gordon, *Reminiscences*, 411; Foote, *Red River to Appomattox*, 842–43; Eckert, *Soldier, Southerner, American*, 112; Dowdey and Manarin, eds., *Wartime Papers of R.E. Lee*, 916; Grant, *Personal Memoirs of U.S. Grant* 433; Douglas, *I Rode with Stonewall*, 314; Wert, *Sword of Lincoln*, 398; Freeman, *Lee's Lieutenants*, vol. 3, pp. 650–51; Buell, *Warrior Generals*, 416; OR, Series I, Vol. 46, Pt. I, Ch. 58, pp. 318, 321.

24. Foote, *Red River to Appomattox*, 843–45; Gordon, *Reminiscences*, 412; *Personal Memoirs of U.S. Grant*, 431; Freeman, *Lee's Lieutenants*, vol. 3, p. 655; Dowdey and Manarin, eds., *Wartime Papers of R.E. Lee*, 916–18.

Chapter 15

1. Foote, *Red River to Appomattox*, 852, 857, 862–63; Sheridan, *Personal Memoirs of P.H. Sheridan*, 362; Grant, *Personal Memoirs of U.S. Grant*, 434–35; Trulock, *Hands of Providence*, 227; Chamberlain, *Passing of the Armies*, 29.

2. Chamberlain, *Passing of the Armies*, 25.

3. Chamberlain, *Passing of the Armies*, 30–31; Trulock, *Hands of Providence*, 232–33.

4. Chamberlain, *Passing of the Armies*, 30–33; Wallace, *Soul of the Lion*, 142; Pullen, *Twentieth Maine*, 243; Trulock, *Hands of Providence*, 230; OR, Series I, Vol. 46, Pt. I, Ch. 58, p. 847.

5. Chamberlain, *Passing of the Armies*, 33; Pullen, *Twentieth Maine*, 243; Wallace, *Soul of the Lion*, 143; Trulock, *Hands of Providence*, 231.

6. Chamberlain, *Passing of the Armies*, 33–34; Wallace, *Soul of the Lion*, 143; Trulock, *Hands of Providence*, 231, 234; OR, Series I, Vol. 46, Pt. I, Ch. 58, p. 847.

7. Chamberlain, *Passing of the Armies*, 34–36; Pullen, *Twentieth Maine*, 244; Wallace, *Soul of the Lion*, 144; Trulock, *Hands of Providence*, 231, 234–35; Gerrish, *Army Life*, 233–34; OR, Series I, Vol. 46, Pt. I, Ch. 58, p. 848.

8. Chamberlain, *Passing of the Armies*, 35–36; Pullen, *Twentieth Maine*, 244; Wallace, *Soul of the Lion*, 144–45; Trulock, *Hands of Providence*, 235.

9. Chamberlain, *Passing of the Armies*, 36–37; Pullen, *Twentieth Maine*, 245; Wallace, *Soul of the Lion*, 145–46; Trulock, *Hands of Providence*, 235–36.

10. Chamberlain, *Passing of the Armies*, 38–39; Pullen, *Twentieth Maine*, 245; Wallace, *Soul of the Lion*, 146–47; Trulock, *Hands of Providence*, 236; OR, Series I, Vol. 46, Pt. I, Ch. 58, p. 848.

11. Chamberlain, *Passing of the Armies*, 39; Pullen *Twentieth Maine*, 245; Wallace, *Soul of the Lion*, 147–48; Trulock, *Hands of Providence*, 237; OR, Series I, Vol. 46, Pt. I, Ch. 58, p. 848.

12. Chamberlain, *Passing of the Armies*, 39–41; Pullen, *Twentieth Maine*, 245; Wallace, *Soul of the Lion*, 148–49; Trulock, *Hands of Providence*, 237–38; OR, Series I, Vol. 46, Pt. I, Ch. 58, pp. 845–46, 848.

13. Chamberlain, *Passing of the Armies*, 42–45; Pullen, *Twentieth Maine*, 245; Wallace, *Soul of the Lion*, 149–50; Trulock, *Hands of Providence*, 239–41; OR, Series I, Vol. 46, Pt. I, Ch. 58, p. 800; Letter from Griffin to promote Chamberlain to brevet major general as of 3/29/1865, Pejebscot Historical Society; Letter to JLC from Stanton dated 7/21/1865, Pejebscot Historical Society.

14. Chamberlain, *Passing of the Armies*, 48–51; Pullen, *Twentieth Maine*, 246–47; Wallace, *Soul of the Lion*, 150–51; Trulock, *Hands of Providence*, 242–45; Grant, *Personal Memoirs of U.S. Grant*, 439–40; Spear, *Civil War Recollections*, 167.

15. Foote, *Red River to Appomattox*, 862–64, 867–69; Bearss, *Fields of Honor*, 381; Grant, *Personal Memoirs of U.S. Grant*, 440–43; Wallace, *Soul of the Lion*, 159; Catton, *A Stillness at Appomattox*, 346–48; Sheridan, *Personal Memoirs of P.H. Sheridan*, 367–68.

16. Chamberlain, *Passing of the Armies*, 54–55; Pullen, *Twentieth Maine*, 247; Wallace, *Soul of the Lion*, 151–52; Trulock, *Hands of Providence*, 246–47; Foote, *Red River to Appomattox*, 867–68; Catton, *A Stillness at Appomattox*, 349; OR, Series I, Vol. 46, Pt. I, Ch. 58, p. 849.

17. Chamberlain, *Passing of the Armies*, 56; Pullen, *Twentieth Maine*, 248; Wallace, *Soul of the Lion*, 152–53; Trulock, *Hands of*

Providence, 247–48; OR, Series I, Vol. 46, Pt. I, Ch. 58, p. 849.

18. Chamberlain, *Passing of the Armies*, 57–60; Pullen, *Twentieth Maine*, 248; Wallace, *Soul of the Lion*, 153–55; Trulock, *Hands of Providence*, 248–51; Gerrish, *Army Life*, 238; OR, Series I, Vol. 46, Pt. I, Ch. 58, pp. 846, 849.

19. Chamberlain, *Passing of the Armies*, 66–67; Pullen, *Twentieth Maine*, 248–49; Wallace, *Soul of the Lion*, 161; Trulock, *Hands of Providence*, 251; Gerrish, *Army Life*, 239.

20. Chamberlain, *Passing of the Armies*, 68–79; Pullen, *Twentieth Maine*, 249–50; Wallace, *Soul of the Lion*, 161–63; Trulock, *Hands of Providence*, 253; Grant, *Personal Memoirs of U.S. Grant*, 443; OR, Series I, Vol. 46, Pt. I, Ch. 58, p. 849.

21. Chamberlain, *Passing of the Armies*, 80; Chamberlain, *Bayonet! Forward*, 102; Pullen, *Twentieth Maine*, 250–51; Wallace, *Soul of the Lion*, 164; Trulock, *Hands of Providence*, 258–59; Foote, *Red River to Appomattox*, 869; Sheridan, *Personal Memoirs of P.H. Sheridan*, 371; Catton, *A Stillness at Appomattox*, 350.

22. Chamberlain, *Passing of the Armies*, 94; Chamberlain, *Bayonet! Forward*, 103; Wallace, *Soul of the Lion*, 165; Trulock, *Hands of Providence*, 259–60; Grant, *Personal Memoirs of U.S. Grant*, 443, 445; Trulock, *Hands of Providence*, 261; Sheridan, *Personal Memoirs of P.H. Sheridan*, 373; Foote, *Red River to Appomattox*, 869; Catton, *A Stillness at Appomattox*, 350–51.

23. Chamberlain, *Passing of the Armies*, 95; Chamberlain, *Bayonet! Forward*, 106; Pullen, *Twentieth Maine*, 251–52; Sheridan, *Personal Memoirs of P.H. Sheridan*, 373; Foote, *Red River to Appomattox*, 870–71; Bearss, *Fields of Honor*, 382–83; Spear, *Civil War Recollections*, 172.

24. Chamberlain, *Passing of the Armies*, 98; Chamberlain, *Bayonet! Forward*, 108–09; Pullen, *Twentieth Maine*, 252–53; Wallace, *Soul of the Lion*, 168; Trulock, *Hands of Providence*, 270; Foote, *Red River to Appomattox*, 871; Bearss, *Fields of Honor*, 384; Sheridan, *Personal Memoirs of P.H. Sheridan*, 374–75; OR, Series I, Vol. 46, Pt. I, Ch. 58, p. 850.

25. Chamberlain, *Passing of the Armies*, 99; Chamberlain, *Bayonet! Forward*, 109; Pullen, *Twentieth Maine*, 253–54; Wallace, *Soul of the Lion*, 168; Trulock, *Hands of Providence*, 271–72; Catton, *A Stillness at Appomattox*, 354; OR, Series I, Vol. 46, Pt. I, Ch. 58, p. 850.

26. Chamberlain, *Passing of the Armies*, 99–100; Chamberlain, *Bayonet! Forward*, 110; Pullen, *Twentieth Maine*, 254; Wallace, *Soul of the Lion*, 169–70; Trulock, *Hands of Providence*, 273–74; Foote, *Red River to Appomattox*, 872; Catton, *A Stillness at Appomattox*, 354.

27. Chamberlain, *Passing of the Armies*, 100–02; Chamberlain, *Bayonet! Forward*, 111; Pullen, *Twentieth Maine*, 254; Wallace, *Soul of the Lion*, 170–71; Trulock, *Hands of Providence*, 274; OR, Series I, Vol. 46, Pt. I, Ch. 58, p. 850.

28. Chamberlain, *Passing of the Armies*, 102–05; Chamberlain, *Bayonet! Forward*, 113, 115; OR, Series I, Vol. 46, Pt. I, Ch. 58, p. 850.

29. Chamberlain, *Passing of the Armies*, 105–06; Chamberlain, *Bayonet! Forward*, 115–17; Wallace, *Soul of the Lion*, 172; Trulock, *Hands of Providence*, 278–79; OR, Series I, Vol. 46, Pt. I, Ch. 58, p. 851.

30. Chamberlain, *Passing of the Armies*, 106; Pullen, *Twentieth Maine*, 256; Trulock, *Hands of Providence*, 275–76, 279; Foote, *Red River to Appomattox*, 873; Bearss, *Fields of Honor*, 387; Catton, *A Stillness at Appomattox*, 355; Grant, *Personal Memoirs of U.S. Grant*, 445–46; Gerrish, *Army Life*, 244–45.

31. Chamberlain, *Passing of the Armies*, 107; Chamberlain, *Bayonet! Forward*, 117–18; Pullen, *Twentieth Maine*, 256–57; Wallace, *Soul of the Lion*, 172–74; Foote, *Red River to Appomattox*, 873–74; Bearss, *Fields of Honor*, 384–85, 388–89; Sheridan, *Personal Memoirs of P.H. Sheridan*, 376; Catton, *A Stillness at Appomattox*, 356.

32. Chamberlain, *Passing of the Armies*, 108–09, 111–12; Wallace, *Soul of the Lion*, 172–73; Trulock, *Hands of Providence*, 280; Foote, *Red River to Appomattox*, 873; Bearss, *Fields of Honor*, 388; Catton, *A Stillness at Appomattox*, 356–57, 365.

33. Chamberlain, *Passing of the Armies*, 114–16; Wallace, *Soul of the Lion*, 174–75; Trulock, *Hands of Providence*, 283; Catton, *A Stillness at Appomattox*, 358.

Chapter 16

1. Chamberlain, *Passing of the Armies*, 135, 137; Grant, *Personal Memoirs of U.S. Grant*, 447–48; Foote, *Red River to Appo-*

mattox, 875–77, 880–81; Bearss, *Fields of Honor*, 389; Catton, *A Stillness at Appomattox*, 360–63; Dowdey and Manarin, eds., *Wartime Papers of R.E. Lee*, 924–26; Trulock, *Hands of Providence*, 286–87; Gordon, *Reminiscences*, 420.

2. Tankersley, *A Study in Gallantry*, 190–91; Gordon, *Reminiscences*, 415, 420–21; Foote, *Red River to Appomattox*, 878, 883–85; Freeman, *Lee's Lieutenants*, vol. 3, p. 680; Bearss, *Fields of Honor*, 389, 391; Eckert, *Soldier, Southerner, American*, 115; Wallace, *Soul of the Lion*, 176; Schaff, *Sunset of the Confederacy*, 57.

3. Grant, *Personal Memoirs of U.S. Grant*, 451–52; Bearss, *Fields of Honor*, 390; Chamberlain, *Passing of the Armies*, 142–46; Pullen, *Twentieth Maine*, 258; Trulock, *Hands of Providence*, 285–86; Gerrish, *Army Life*, 247; Wallace, *Soul of the Lion*, 177; Sheridan, *Personal Memoirs of P.H. Sheridan*, 380; OR, Series I, Vol. 46, Pt. I, Ch. 58, p. 851.

4. Gordon, *Reminiscences*, 423; Freeman, *Lee's Lieutenants*, vol. 3, p. 684; Foote, *Red River to Appomattox*, 888–89; Eckert, *Soldier, Southerner, American*, 115; Douglas, *I Rode with Stonewall*, 315–16.

5. Grant, *Personal Memoirs of U.S. Grant*, 465; Chamberlain, *Passing of the Armies*, 148; Foote, *Red River to Appomattox*, 908–11; Bearss, *Fields of Honor*, 390–93.

6. Grant, *Personal Memoirs of U.S. Grant*, 464–67; Chamberlain, *Passing of the Armies*, 148–50, 154; Catton, *A Stillness at Appomattox*, 368–69; Foote, *Red River to Appomattox*, 911–12, 914; Bearss, *Fields of Honor*, 394; Pullen, *Twentieth Maine*, 259; Trulock, *Hands of Providence*, 287; Sheridan, *Personal Memoirs of P.H. Sheridan*, 380–81; Spear, *Civil War Recollections*, 178; OR, Series I, Vol. 46, Pt. I, Ch. 58, pp. 851–52.

7. Foote, *Red River to Appomattox*, 912, 915; Bearss, *Fields of Honor*, 393; Catton, *A Stillness at Appomattox*, 369–70; Pullen, *Twentieth Maine*, 260; Wheeler, *Witness to Appomattox*, 148, 150–52.

8. Gordon, *Reminiscences*, 424–27; Eckert, *Soldier, Southerner, American*, 115, n.17.

9. Gordon, *Reminiscences*, 427–28.

10. Grant, *Personal Memoirs of U.S. Grant* 472–73; Foote, *Red River to Appomattox*, 915–18; Sheridan, *Personal Memoirs of P.H. Sheridan*, 383; Bearss, *Fields of Honor*, 397.

11. Chamberlain, *Passing of the Armies*, 162; Foote, *Red River to Appomattox*, 918–19; Bearss, *Fields of Honor*, 399; Horn, ed., *Robert E. Lee Reader*, 449; Dowdey and Manarin, eds., *Wartime Papers of R.E. Lee*, 934.

12. Chamberlain, *Passing of the Armies*, 162; Foote, *Red River to Appomattox*, 918–20; Bearss, *Fields of Honor*, 398; Eckert, *Soldier, Southerner, American*, 116–17; Trulock, *Hands of Providence*, 288; Freeman, *Lee's Lieutenants*, vol. 3, pp. 709–10; OR, Series I, Vol. 46, Pt. I, Ch. 58, p. 852.

13. Grant, *Personal Memoirs of U.S. Grant*, 476–77; Foote, *Red River to Appomattox*, 921–22; Bearss, *Fields of Honor*, 400; Catton, *A Stillness at Appomattox*, 372; Wert, *Sword of Lincoln*, 406; Gordon, *Reminiscences*, 432–33.

14. Grant, *Personal Memoirs of U.S. Grant*, 478–79; Chamberlain, *Passing of the Armies*, 167, 169, 189; Foote, *Red River to Appomattox*, 923–27, 929–30, 932–33; Bearss, *Fields of Honor*, 400–01; Catton, *A Stillness at Appomattox*, 373; Horn, ed., *Robert E. Lee Reader*, 436; Dowdey and Manarin, eds., *Wartime Papers of R.E. Lee*, 931–32.

15. Grant, *Personal Memoirs of U.S. Grant*, 481–82; Foote, *Red River to Appomattox*, 930, 932, 936; Sheridan, *Personal Memoirs of P.H. Sheridan*, 390; Freeman, *Lee's Lieutenants*, vol. 3, p. 719; Bearss, *Fields of Honor*, 402–03; Catton, *A Stillness at Appomattox*, 373–75; Eckert, *Soldier, Southerner, American*, 117.

16. Tankersley, *A Study in Gallantry*, 206–07; Foote, *Red River to Appomattox*, 933–34, 939; Freeman, *Lee's Lieutenants*, vol. 3, pp. 724–25; Sheridan, *Personal Memoirs of P.H. Sheridan*, 391; Bearss, *Fields of Honor*, 403; Gordon, *Reminiscences*, 434–36, 443; Eckert, *Soldier, Southerner, American*, 117; Horn, ed., *Robert E. Lee Reader*, 437; Longstreet, *From Manassas to Appomattox*, 623.

17. Chamberlain, *Passing of the Armies*, 171–73; Chamberlain, *Bayonet! Forward*, 222–23; Trulock, *Hands of Providence*, 290–91; Wallace, *Soul of the Lion*, 178–79; Pullen, *Twentieth Maine*, 260, 262.

18. Tankersley, *A Study in Gallantry*, 208–09; Chamberlain, *Passing of the Armies*, 174; Chamberlain, *Bayonet! Forward*, 223, 231; Gordon, *Reminiscences*, 436–37; Eckert, *Soldier, Southerner, American*, 118; Foote, *Red River to Appomattox*, 940; Bearss, *Fields of Honor*, 403–04; Pullen, *Twentieth*

Maine, 263; Wallace, *Soul of the Lion,* 179; Trulock, *Hands of Providence,* 291–92; Wert, *Sword of Lincoln,* 408; Freeman, *Lee's Lieutenants,* vol. 3, pp. 728–29; OR, Series I, Vol. 46, Pt. I, Ch. 58, pp. 852, 1162, 1303.

19. Chamberlain, *Bayonet! Forward,* 144–46; Chamberlain, *Passing of the Armies,* 173–75; Gerrish, *Army Life,* 255–56; Foote, *Red River to Appomattox,* 941; Catton, *A Stillness at Appomattox,* 378; Wallace, *Soul of the Lion,* 179–80; Trulock, *Hands of Providence,* 291, 293.

20. Chamberlain, *Passing of the Armies,* 176–77; Wallace, *Soul of the Lion,* 180–81; Trulock, *Hands of Providence,* 293.

21. Tankersley, *A Study in Gallantry,* 209–10; Gordon, *Reminiscences,* 437–38; Chamberlain, *Bayonet! Forward,* 224; Foote, *Red River to Appomattox,* 941; Freeman, *Lee's Lieutenants,* vol. 3, p. 729; Bearss, *Fields of Honor,* 404–05; Horn, ed., *Robert E. Lee Reader,* 437; Longstreet, *From Manassas to Appomattox,* 624; JBG letter to E. Porter Alexander, dated 3/27/1888, Wilson Library.

22. Gordon, *Reminiscences,* 438–39; Freeman, *Lee's Lieutenants,* vol. 3, p. 733; Eckert, *Soldier, Southerner, American,* 118–19; Tankersley, *A Study in Gallantry,* 211.

23. Gordon, *Reminiscences,* 439; Eckert, *Soldier, Southerner, American,* 119–20; Foote, *Red River to Appomattox,* 943; Freeman, *Lee's Lieutenants,* vol. 3, pp. 733–34; Bearss, *Fields of Honor,* 406; Chamberlain, *Passing of the Armies,* 182–83; John Brown Gordon (hereafter JBG) letter to E. Porter Alexander, dated 3/27/1888, Wilson Library; Supp. to OR, Pt I, Vol. 7, Reports, pp. 793–94.

24. Gordon, *Reminiscences,* 439–41; Freeman, *Lee's Lieutenants,* vol. 3, pp. 734–35; Sheridan, *Personal Memoirs of P.H. Sheridan,* 394; Eckert, *Soldier, Southerner, American,* 120; JBG letter to E. Porter Alexander, dated 3/27/1888, Wilson Library; Supp. to OR, Pt I, Vol. 7, Reports, 793–94.

25. Chamberlain, *Passing of the Armies,* 179–80; Chamberlain, *Bayonet! Forward,* 232; Catton, *A Stillness at Appomattox,* 379; Trulock, *Hands of Providence,* 295.

26. Chamberlain, *Passing of the Armies,* 180–81; Gerrish, *Army Life,* 258; Bearss, *Fields of Honor,* 407; Wallace, *Soul of the Lion,* 182; Trulock, *Hands of Providence,* 295; OR, Series I, Vol. 46, Pt. I, Ch. 58, p. 852.

27. Chamberlain, *Passing of the Armies,* 182–83; Bearss, *Fields of Honor,* 407; Wallace, *Soul of the Lion,* 183; Trulock, *Hands of Providence,* 295–96; OR, Series I, Vol. 46, Pt. I, Ch. 58, p. 1110.

28. Chamberlain, *Passing of the Armies,* 184; Wallace, *Soul of the Lion,* 183–84; Trulock, *Hands of Providence,* 297.

29. Tankersley, *A Study in Gallantry,* 214; Freeman, *Lee's Lieutenants,* vol. 3, pp. 738–39.

30. Grant, *Personal Memoirs of U.S. Grant,* 484–86; Foote, *Red River to Appomattox,* 945; Dowdey and Manarin, eds., *Wartime Papers of R.E. Lee,* 933; OR, Series I, Vol. 46, Pt. III, Ch. 58, p. 666.

31. Winik, *April 1865,* 68; Wheeler, *Witness to Appomattox,* 127.

32. Grant, *Personal Memoirs of U.S. Grant,* 489–90; Foote, *Red River to Appomattox,* 946; Bearss, *Fields of Honor,* 408.

33. Grant, *Personal Memoirs of U.S. Grant* 491–93; Foote, *Red River to Appomattox,* 947–48; Bearss, *Fields of Honor,* 409; Winik, *April 1865,* 187–89; Horn, ed., *Robert E. Lee Reader,* 442.

34. Grant, *Personal Memoirs of U.S. Grant* 493–96; Foote, *Red River to Appomattox,* 949–50; Bearss, *Fields of Honor,* 409; Winik, *April 1865,* 189–91; Horn, ed., *Robert E. Lee Reader,* 443.

35. Gordon, *Reminiscences,* 460–61.

Chapter 17

1. Chamberlain, *Passing of the Armies,* 3, 205; Gordon, *Reminiscences,* 106; JLC Letter to "Sae," April 13, 1865, Bowdoin College (hereafter BC).

2. Gordon, *Reminiscences,* 443, 449.

3. Chamberlain, *Passing of the Armies,* 200–01; Wallace, *Soul of the Lion,* 190.

4. Chamberlain, *Passing of the Armies,* 201; Gerrish, *Army Life,* 263–64; Wallace, *Soul of the Lion,* 191; Pullen, *Twentieth Maine,* 274–75.

5. Chamberlain, *Passing of the Armies,* 201–02.

6. Tankersley, *A Study in Gallantry,* 220–21; Gordon, *Reminiscences,* 448–50; Freeman, *Lee's Lieutenants,* vol. 3, p. 748; Douglas, *I Rode with Stonewall,* 318.

7. Gordon, *Reminiscences,* 450–51, 457; Eckert, *Soldier, Southerner, American,* 125; Foote, *Fredericksburg to Meridian,* 203.

8. JBG telegram to Fanny dated 4/13/1865, Hargrett Library; Gordon, *Reminis-*

cences, 454; Eckert, *Soldier, Southerner, American*, 126.

9. Chamberlain, *Passing of the Armies*, 205–06; Trulock, *Hands of Providence*, 311–12; Wallace, *Soul of the Lion*, 192; OR, Series I, Vol. 46, Pt I, Ch. 58, pp. 730–31, 1011.

10. Chamberlain, *Passing of the Armies*, 207–12; Foote, *Red River to Appomattox*, 986; Pullen, *Twentieth Maine*, 277.

11. Chamberlain, *Passing of the Armies*, 212–14; Gerrish, *Army Life*, 271–72; Wallace, *Soul of the Lion*, 192; Trulock, *Hands of Providence*, 315.

12. Chamberlain, *Passing of the Armies*, 217–19; Wallace, *Soul of the Lion*, 194–95; Trulock, *Hands of Providence*, 315.

13. Chamberlain, *Passing of the Armies*, 219–26; Trulock, *Hands of Providence*, 315–16; Longacre, *Joshua Chamberlain: The Soldier and the Man*, 250–51.

14. Foote, *Red River to Appomattox*, 965–69.

15. Foote, *Red River to Appomattox*, 988–96; Grant, *Personal Memoirs of U.S. Grant*, 514–17.

16. Chamberlain, *Passing of the Armies*, 227–28, 230, 232–34, 238; Gerrish, *Army Life*, 277–95; Pullen, *Twentieth Maine*, 280–81, 283; Wallace, *Soul of the Lion*, 195–96, 198; Trulock, *Hands of Providence*, 317–18.

17. Chamberlain, *Passing of the Armies*, 241, 283–85; Pullen, *Twentieth Maine*, 284–85.

18. Chamberlain, *Passing of the Armies*, 242–45; Wallace, *Soul of the Lion*, 199; Trulock, *Hands of Providence*, 320.

19. Chamberlain, *Passing of the Armies*, 248, 256–57; Pullen, *Twentieth Maine*, 285; Wallace, *Soul of the Lion*, 199; Trulock, *Hands of Providence*, 322–25.

20. Chamberlain, *Passing of the Armies*, 257–71, 276; Foote, *Red River to Appomattox*, 1014; Pullen, *Twentieth Maine*, 286; Trulock, *Hands of Providence*, 326–28.

21. Chamberlain, *Passing of the Armies*, 286–87; Gerrish, *Army Life*, 303, 309; Pullen, *Twentieth Maine*, 289; Wallace, *Soul of the Lion*, 202; Trulock, *Hands of Providence*, 328.

22. Ibid.

Chapter 18

1. Eckert, *Soldier, Southerner, American*, 127–28.

2. Tankersley, *A Study in Gallantry*, 230–31, 255–57; Eckert, *Soldier, Southerner, American*, 128–32, 145; Dunbar, "Political Life of John Brown Gordon," 25; Culpepper, "Political Career of John Brown Gordon," 36–39.

3. Eckert, *Soldier, Southerner, American*, 132–34, 137–39.

4. Tankersley, *A Study in Gallantry*, 239–40; Eckert, *Soldier, Southerner, American*, 140–45; Dunbar, "Political Life of John B. Gordon," 14–21; Culpepper, "Political Career of John B. Gordon," 14–15, 27–28.

5. Eckert, *Soldier, Southerner, American*, 143, 153–56; Gordon, *Reminiscences*, 450–51, 457; Dunbar, "Political Life of John B. Gordon," 42, 44; *Atlanta Constitution*, January 16, 1873.

6. Eckert, *Soldier, Southerner, American*, 158–59, 162; Dunbar, "Political Life of John B. Gordon," 46; *New York Herald*, September 12, 1873; *Atlanta Constitution*, May 15, 1873.

7. Tankersley, *A Study in Gallantry*, 270–74; Eckert, *Soldier, Southerner, American*, 163–67; Cong. Record, 43rd Congress, 2nd Sess., pp. 269–74; *Atlanta Constitution*, January 9, 1875.

8. Gordon, *Reminiscences*, 35–36, 159–60; Trulock, *Hands of Providence*, 366.

9. Eckert, *Soldier, Southerner, American*, 174–81.

10. Eckert, *Soldier, Southerner, American*, 183–86; Trulock, *Hands of Providence*, 353; Dunbar, "Political Life of John B. Gordon," 77–80; Culpepper, "Political Career of John B. Gordon," 76.

11. Eckert, *Soldier, Southerner, American*, 187–97.

12. Eckert, *Soldier, Southerner, American*, 201, 214, 233, 235; *Atlanta Constitution*, May 25, 1880.

13. Eckert, *Soldier, Southerner, American*, 241–46, 259.

14. Eckert, *Soldier, Southerner, American*, 262–63, 266–67.

15. Eckert, *Soldier, Southerner, American*, 268–70; Culpepper, "Political Career of John Brown Gordon," 92; *Atlanta Constitution*, April 30, 1886.

16. Eckert, *Soldier, Southerner, American*, 270–73, 277, 281, 289; Culpepper, "Political Career of John B. Gordon," 107; *Atlanta Constitution*, May 1, 1886.

17. Eckert, *Soldier, Southerner, American*, 291–92, 294; Culpepper, "Political

Career or John B. Gordon," 115–16; *Atlanta Constitution*, July, 8, 1887 and July 23, 1890.

18. Eckert, *Soldier, Southerner, American*, 296–305, 314; *Youngstown (OH) Telegram*, July 11, 1894, Gordon Family Collection, UGA.

19. Trulock, *Hands of Providence*, 330–31.

20. Trulock, *Hands of Providence*, 331–33; Wallace, *Soul of the Lion*, 203; Pension documents, Pejebscot Historical Society.

21. Trulock, *Hands of Providence*, 334–37; Wallace, *Soul of the Lion*, 204, 206.

22. Trulock, *Hands of Providence*, 337, 341; Wallace, *Soul of the Lion*, 204–08.

23. Trulock, *Hands of Providence*, 342–47; Wallace, *Soul of the Lion*, 228–41.

24. Trulock, *Hands of Providence*, 362–63; Wallace, *Soul of the Lion*, 243, 246–47; Welsh, *Medical Histories*, 64, Pejebscot Historical Society.

25. Trulock, *Hands of Providence*, 355–56; Wallace, *Soul of the Lion*, 253–55.

26. Trulock, *Hands of Providence*, 355–57; Wallace, *Soul of the Lion*, 255–59.

27. Trulock, *Hands of Providence*, 356; Wallace, *Soul of the Lion*, 259.

28. Trulock, *Hands of Providence*, 357; Wallace, *Soul of the Lion*, 260.

29. Ibid.

30. Trulock, *Hands of Providence*, 358; Wallace, *Soul of the Lion*, 264.

31. Trulock, *Hands of Providence*, 359; Wallace, *Soul of the Lion*, 260–62, 265–70.

32. Trulock, *Hands of Providence*, 366–67, 369; Wallace, *Soul of the Lion*, 275–82.

33. Chamberlain, *Bayonet! Forward*, 190–202.

34. Eckert, *Soldier, Southerner, American*, 315–18.

35. Ibid., 316–17, 319.

36. John B. Gordon Family Papers, Hargrett Library; Eckert, *Soldier, Southerner, American*, 319.

37. Eckert, *Soldier, Southerner, American*, 320.

38. Eckert, *Soldier, Southerner, American*, 324–25; Stephen D. Lee, in Gordon, *Reminiscences*, xvii.

39. Eckert, *Soldier, Southerner, American*, 327–29; Stephen D. Lee, in Gordon, *Reminiscences*, xvii-xviii.

40. Tankersley, *A Study in Gallantry*, 372; Eckert, *Soldier, Southerner, American*, 338–39; Frances Gordon Smith, "Memorial Sketch," in Gordon, *Reminiscences*, xxi-xxii; *Atlanta Constitution*, January 9–10, 1904.

41. Eckert, *Soldier, Southerner, American*, 339–40; Smith, "Memorial Sketch," xxiii-xxv; *Atlanta Constitution*, January 13, 1904.

42. Eckert, *Soldier, Southerner, American*, 340–341; Smith, "Memorial Sketch," xxv-xxvii; Stephen D. Lee, in Gordon, *Reminiscences*, xviii-xix; *Atlanta Constitution*, January 15, 1904.

43. Eckert, *Soldier, Southerner, American*, 342; Pollard, *Companions in Arms*, 547; Warner, *Generals in Gray*, 111; Stephen D. Lee, in Gordon, *Reminiscences*, xix; *Atlanta Constitution*, January 13, 1904.

44. Trulock, *Hands of Providence*, 367, 369; Wallace, *Soul of the Lion*, 288–94; National Archives, Joshua L. Chamberlain Military Records.

45. Trulock, *Hands of Providence*, 371, 374–76; Wallace, *Soul of the Lion*, 297, 300–01, 305–06, 309.

46. Trulock, *Hands of Providence*, 376–79; Wallace, *Soul of the Lion*, 310–12.

47. Gerrish, *Army Life*, 347; Letter of 3/9/1865 from Ellis Spear to General J.S. Hodsdon, Adj. Gen., Maine, BC.

Afterword

1. Gordon, *Reminiscences*, 76–77; Chamberlain, *Passing of the Armies*, 295.

Bibliography

Books

Alexander, General E. Porter. *Fighting for the Confederacy: The Personal Recollections of General Edward Porter Alexander*. Chapel Hill: University of North Carolina Press, 1989.

Atlanta Georgia Journal 29 (November 1901). "Sanders, Col. C.C."

Bearss, Edwin C. *Fields of Honor*. Washington, D.C.: National Geographic Society, 2006.

Berkley, Henry Robinson. *Four Years in the Confederate Artillery*. Chapel Hill: University of North Carolina Press, 1961.

Buell, Thomas B. *The Warrior Generals: Combat Leadership in the Civil War*. New York: Three Rivers, 1997.

Catton, Bruce. *A Stillness at Appomattox*. Garden City, NY: Doubleday, 1953.

Chamberlain, Joshua Lawrence. *Bayonet! Forward: My Civil War Reminiscences*. Gettysburg: Stan Clark, 1994.

_____. *Passing of the Armies*. New York: Bantam, 1992.

Cullen, Joseph P. "The First Bull Run." In *The Image of War, 1861–1865*. Edited by William C. Davis and Bell I. Wiley. Vol. 1, *Shadows of the Storm*. Garden City, NY: Doubleday, 1982.

Culpepper, Grady Sylvester. "The Political Career of John Brown Gordon, 1868 to 1897." Ph.D. diss., Emory University, 1981.

Desjardin, Thomas A. *Stand Firm, Ye Boys from Maine*. Gettysburg: Thomas, 1995.

Douglas, Henry Kyd. *I Rode with Stonewall*. Chapel Hill: University of North Carolina Press 1940.

Dowdey, Clifford, and Louis H. Manarin, eds. *The Wartime Papers of R.E. Lee*. New York: Bramhall, 1961.

Dunbar, Alice. "The Political Life of John Brown Gordon, 1865–1880." Master's thesis, Emory University, 1939.

Early, Jubal A. *Autobiographical Sketch and Narrative of the War Between the States*. Wilmington, NC: Broadfoot, 1989.

Eckert, Ralph Lowell. *John Brown Gordon: Soldier, Southerner, American*. Baton Rouge and London: Louisiana State University Press, 1989.

Foote, Shelby. *The Civil War Narrative: Fort Sumter to Perryville*. New York: Vintage, 1958.

_____. *The Civil War Narrative: Fredericksburg to Meridian*. New York: Vintage, 1963.

_____. *The Civil War Narrative: Red River to Appomattox*. New York: Vintage, 1974.

Freeman, Douglas Southall. *Lee's Lieutenants*. Vol. 1, *Manassas to Malvern Hill*. New York: Charles Scribner's Sons, 1942.

_____. *Lee's Lieutenants*. Vol. 2, *Cedar Mountain to Chancellorsville*. New York: Charles Scribner's Sons, 1943.

———. *Lee's Lieutenants.* Vol. 3, *Gettysburg to Appomattox.* New York: Charles Scribner's Sons, 1944.

Gerrish, Theodore. *Army Life: A Private's Reminiscences of the Civil War.* Baltimore: Butternut and Blue; Gettysburg: Stan Clark, 1995.

Gordon, John B. *Reminiscences of the Civil War.* Dayton, OH: Morningside, 1903.

Grant, Ulysses S. *Personal Memoirs of U.S. Grant.* Vol. 2. New York: Charles L. Webster, 1886.

Haskell, Frank Aretas. *The Battle of Gettysburg: The Eyewitness Account of Col. Frank A. Haskell.* Sandwich, MA: Chapman Billies, 1993.

Hassler, Warren W., Jr. "Yorktown: The First Siege." In *The Image of War, 1861–1865.* Edited by William C. Davis and Bell I. Wiley. Vol. 2, *The Guns of '62.* Garden City, NY: Doubleday, 1982.

Horn, Stanley F., ed. *The Robert E. Lee Reader.* New York: Konecky & Konecky, 1949.

Krick, Robert K. "Into the Wilderness." In *The Image of War, 1861–1865.* Edited by William C. Davis and Bell I. Wiley. Vol. 5, *The South Besieged.* Garden City, NY: Doubleday, 1982.

Lindsey, David. "The Second Bull Run." In *The Image of War, 1861–1865.* Edited by William C. Davis and Bell I. Wiley. Vol. 2, *The Guns of '62.* Garden City, NY: Doubleday, 1982.

Longacre, Edward G., *Joshua Chamberlain: The Soldier and the Man*, Combined, Philadelphia, 1999.

Longstreet, General James. *From Manassas to Appomattox.* New York: Konecky and Konecky, 1992.

Medical and Surgical History of the War of the Rebellion. Part II, Vol. 2. Washington, D.C.: Government Printing Office, 1876.

Munson, Edward L., M.D. (Major, Medical Department, United States Army). In *The Photographic History of the Civil War.* Vol. 4 New York: The Review of Reviews Co., 1911.

Newman, Ralph G., and Otto Eisenschiml. *The Civil War: An American Iliad.* Secaucus, NJ: Blue and Gray Press, 1947.

Norton, Oliver Willcox. *The Attack and Defense of Little Round Top, Gettysburg, July 2, 1863.* New York: Neale, 1913.

Oates, William C. *The War Between the Union and the Confederacy and Its Lost Opportunities.* Dayton, OH: Morningside, 1985.

Parrish, Peter J. "The Fury of Fredericksburg." In *The Image of War, 1861–1865.* Edited by William C. Davis and Bell I. Wiley. Vol. 3, *The Embattled Confederacy.* Garden City, NY: Doubleday, 1982.

Pollard, Edward A. *Lee and His Lieutenants: Comprising the Early Life, Public Services, and Campaigns of General Robert E. Lee and His Companions in Arms.* New York: E.B. Treat, 1867.

Pullen, John J. *The Twentieth Maine.* Dayton, OH: Morningside, 1957.

Robertson, James I., Jr. "The Bloodiest Day: Antietam." In *The Image of War, 1861–1865.* Edited by William C. Davis and Bell I. Wiley. Vol. 3, *The Embattled Confederacy.* Garden City, NY: Doubleday, 1982.

Schaff, Morris. *The Sunset of the Confederacy.* Boston: John W. Luce, 1912.

Sears, Stephen W. *Landscape Turned Red.* New Haven and New York: Ticknor & Fields, 1983.

Sheridan, Philip Henry. *The Personal Memoirs of P.H. Sheridan.* Da Capo, 1992.

Smith, Everard H. "Back to the Valley." In *The Image of War, 1861–1865.* Edited by William C. Davis and Bell I. Wiley. Vol. 5, *The South Besieged.* Garden City, NY: Doubleday, 1983.

Sorrel, G. Moxley. *Recollections of a Confederate Staff Officer.* New York: Smithmark, 1994.

Spear, Ellis (General). *Civil War Recollections.* Orono: University of Maine Press, 1997.

Tankersley, Allen P. *John B. Gordon: A Study in Gallantry.* Atlanta: Whitehall, 1955.

Taylor, Walter H. *Four Years with General Lee.* Bloomington: Indiana University Press, 1962.

Thomas, Emory M. "The Peninsular Campaign." In *The Image of War, 1861–1865*. Edited by William C. Davis and Bell I. Wiley. Vol. 2, *The Guns of '62*. Garden City, NY: Doubleday, 1982.

Trulock, Alice Rains. *In the Hands of Providence: Joshua L. Chamberlain and the American Civil War*. Chapel Hill: University of North Carolina Press, 1992.

Wallace, Willard M. *Soul of the Lion: A Biography of General Joshua L. Chamberlain*. Gettysburg: Stan Clark, 1995.

The War of the Rebellion: Official Records of the Union and Confederate Armies. Washington, DC: Government Printing Office, 1880.

Warner, Ezra J. *Generals in Gray*. Baton Rouge: Louisiana State University Press, 1959.

Welsh, Jack D. *Medical Histories of Union Generals*. Kent, OH: Kent State University Press, 1996.

Wert, Jeffrey D. *Gettysburg: Day Three*. New York: Simon & Schuster, 2001.

———. *The Sword of Lincoln*. New York: Simon & Schuster, 2005.

Wheeler, Richard. *Witness to Appomattox*. New York: Harper and Row, 1989.

Winik, Jay. *April 1865*. New York: HarperCollins, 2001.

Collections

Bowdoin College, Hawthorne-Longfellow Library, Brunswick, Maine

Emory University, Robert W. Woodruff Library

Library of Congress, Manuscript Division

Maine Historical Society

National Archives

Pejebscot Historical Society, Brunswick, Maine

Southern Historical Society Papers

University of Georgia, Hargrett Rare Book and Manuscript Library

University of North Carolina at Chapel Hill, Wilson Library

Virginia Historical Society

Index

Numbers in ***bold italics*** indicate pages with photographs.

Alexander, E. Porter 52, 57
Amelia Courthouse, Virginia 155, 156
Ames, Adelbert 30, 50, 53, 55, 62, 75, 82, 90
Anderson, George B. 42
Anderson, Richard H. 42, 60, 61, 70, 72, 81, 103, 104, 108, 110, 111, 113, 138, 145, 156, 157, 158
Anderson, Robert 25
Antietam Creek 31, 40, 41, 46, 47, 48
Appomattox Courthouse 134, 157, 159, 160, 162, 164–165, 166, 167, 169, 170, 172, 195; Battle of 159–62; intermingling of soldiers 9–10; salute ***12***, 14
Appomattox River 13, 112, 155, 156, 158, 159
Archer, James 68
Armistead, Lewis 84, 85
Army of Northern Virginia 9, 10, 11, 13, 38, 39, 41, 47, 48, 51, 57, 61, 64, 83, 86, 89, 103, 108, 110, 112, 131, 134, 135, 136, 137, 140, 146, 155, 156, 157, 159, 163, 164
Army of the James 161
Army of the Potomac 9, 11, 12, 30, 32, 37, 38, 39, 40, 41, 47, 49, 51, 56, 59, 61, 62, 67, 71, 74, 83, 86, 89, 92, 95, 102, 103, 108, 109, 110, 111, 112, 119, 131, 152, 161, 163, 164, 171, 172, 174, 175
Army of the Tennessee 96, 136, 171
Atlanta, Georgia 23, 27, 96, 109, 122, 131, ***174***, 176, 177, 178, 181, ***189***, 191
Atlanta Constitution 177, 180
Atlanta University 181
Ayres, Romeyn 142, 145, 146, 147, 149–50, 151, 170

Bangor Theological Seminary 20
Barksdale, William 51
Barlow, Francis C. 36, 45, 105, 107, 188; wounding at Gettysburg and meeting with Gordon 69–70
Barlow, S.L.M. 180
Barnes, James 90, 113
Bartlett, Joseph J. 102, 113, 147, 148, 150, 152, 155
Beasley, William 100–1
Beauregard, P.G.T. 25, 28, 111, 112–13, 171
Birney, David B. 113, 119, 159, 161
Blaine, James G. 184, 185
Blair, Francis P. 134
Bloody Angle 107–8
Bloody Lane (sunken road) ***40***, 42–45
Boston Daily Globe 189
Bowdoin College 18–19, 20–21, 29, 30, 50, 62, 81, 90, 131, 182, 183–84, 186, 192, 194
Boydton Plank Road 132–33, 141–42, 145, 148
Brastow, Sarah Dupee 17
Breckinridge, John C. 110, 120–21
Brewer, Maine 17, 63
Brock Road 96, 98, 103
Brown, Joe 182
Brunswick, Georgia 176
Brunswick, Maine 18, 19, 20, 21, 23, 81, 89, 92, 132, 182, 192, 193, 194
Buck, George Washington 78
Buford, John 67–68
Bull Run, First Battle of (First Manassas) 28
Bull Run, Second Battle of (Second Manassas) 37, 38
Bullock, Rufus B. 177
Burkeville, Virginia 156, 159, 169, 170, 171
Burnside, Ambrose E. 46, 47, 51, 52, 54, 56, 57, 59, 95, 99, 100, 103, 104, 107, 110, 111, 113
Butler, Benjamin 96, 109, 110, 111

219

Campbell, John A. 134
Carter, Thomas H. 128
Castle Rock Coal Company 23
Cedar Creek, Battle of **125**, 126–30
Cemetery Hill 71, 81–82, 84, 87, 100
Cemetery Ridge 71, 72, 81–82, 83–84
Chamberlain, Fanny (Frances Caroline Adams) **19**, 20, 21, 30, 50, 92, 132, 182, 192; death 194; letter from JLC after Gettysburg 87; letter from JLC anticipating death 118–19; marriage 21
Chamberlain, Gertrude Loraine 132, 182
Chamberlain, Grace Dupee 21, 182
Chamberlain, Harold Wyllys 21, 182
Chamberlain, John 74
Chamberlain, Joshua 17
Chamberlain, Joshua L. **4, 18, 192**; appearance 11; commendations by superiors 89–90, 113, **116**; compassion and respect for common soldier and peers 55, 63, 78, 89, 117, 147–48, 150–51; compassion for enemy 48, 145; death 194; humility 102, 150, 161, 178; integrity 185; Medal of Honor **81**, 83, 192; near capture 55, 143–44; wounding 117; *see also* Maine election of 1879
Chamberlain, Sae 167
Chamberlain, Thomas 10, 14, 30, 73, 74, 77, 118, 173
Chambersburg Pike 68
Charlemagne 91, 114, 143, 172, 173
Chickahominy River 33, 34, 35, 36
Cincinnati Enquirer 189
Clark, Hiram 163
Cleburne, Pat 134
Cleveland, Grover 180
Cobb, Howell 134
Cold Harbor 15, 110–12, 120
Colquitt, Alfred 42, 46
Crawford, Samuel W. 142, 145–47, 149, 151–52, 161
Crook, George 124, 125, 126, 127, 128
Culp's Hill 71, 72, 81–82, 83
Custer, George Armstrong 162, 163
Custis-Lee mansion 172

Danville, Virginia 155, 156, 161
Danville Railroad 141, 154, 156
Davis, Daniel F. 184, 186
Davis, Jefferson 9, 35, 38, 64, 68, 94, 103, 134, 135–36, 136–37, 140, 155, 157, 170, 171, 181
Davis, Joseph R. 68
desertion, by Confederates 133, 134, 135–36, 171; Union desertion, execution for 90–91
Devil's Den 72, 73, 81
Dimmock Line 112–13, 139
Dinwiddie Courthouse 142, 145–46, 148–49
Doubleday, Abner 84
Douglas, Henry Kyd 121, 124, 130, 169
Dunning, S.A. 129

Early, Jubal A. 57, 58, 59, 60, 92, 94, 103–4, 108, 110–11, 112; Gettysburg campaign 64, 65, 66, 67, 69, 70, 71, 82; Valley Campaign 120, 121–24, 126, 127–30; in the Wilderness 96–97, 99, 100
Edmunds, George F. 178
8th Ohio 84
83rd Pennsylvania 31, 54, 73–74, 80, 82, 109
Emancipation Proclamation 49
Emmitsburg Road 71–72, 85, 115
Emory, William H. 125–26, 127, 128, 129
Everett, Edward 87
Ewell, Richard S. 28, 103, 104, 105, 110, 128, 136, 146, 156, 157–58; Gettysburg campaign 64, 65, 67, 68, 70–71, 72, 81, 83, 86; in the Wilderness 96–97, 98, 99, 100

Farmville, Virginia 156, 158, 159, 170
Felton, Rebecca Latimer 179
Ferrero, Edward 46–47
15th Alabama 15, 72, 74–75, 77, 79–80
5th Texas 74
1st Minnesota 81
Fisher's Hill 124, 130
Five Forks 141–42, 145–46, 148–49, 151–52, 155–56, 161, 170
Fort Stedman 137–40, 141, 154
Fort Sumter 9, 25, 26, 28
48th Alabama 74
44th New York 31, 73–74, 82, 97, 118
47th Alabama 15, 72, 74–75, 78, 80
Fourteenth Amendment 183
4th Alabama 74
4th Texas 74
Franklin, William B. 51, 54
French, William H. 42–43, 45

Gaines Mill, Battle of 35–36
Garcelon, Alonzo 184–85
Garnett, Richard 84, 85
Gerrish, Theodore 48, 53–54, 76, 89–90, 90–91, 92–93, 174, 194
Gettysburg Address 88
Gibbon, John 10, 11, 84, 85
Glenn, Edwin A. 147, 151
Gordon, Augustus 27, 34, 61
Gordon, Carolina 179
Gordon, Caroline Lewis 181
Gordon, Eugene 27, 121, 180
Gordon, Fanny (Fanny Rebecca Haralson) **21**, 23, 26, 33, 35, 64, 65, 121, 123–24, 138, 155, 169, 170, 180, 187, 191; goes to war 26; nurses husband after wounding 45–46
Gordon, Frank 124
Gordon, John B. **6, 22, 180**; advocating for slavery 23; appearance 10; commendations by superiors 46, 94, 121; compassion for enemy 93–94, 156–57; compassion for his men 33; compassion for Northern civilians 66; death 190–91; humility 34, 178; near

capture 100–1; oratorical skills 13, 23, 43, 97, 106, 168, 177–78; regard for Gordon by his men 64; wounding 44
Gordon, John B., Jr. 180
Gordon, Malinda Cox 21
Gordon, Walter 180
Gordon, Zachariah 21
Grand review 173–74
Grant, Julia 182
Grant, Ulysses S. 9, 10, 11, 16, 65, 109, 114, *116*, 117–18, 119, 120, 121, 122, 130, 132, 133, 134, 135, 136, 137, 139–40, 169, 170, 171, 176, 178, 182; at Cold Harbor 110–12; Petersburg to Appomattox 141–42, 145, 146, 148–49, 152, 154, 155, 157, 158, 159, 160, 162–63, 164–166, 172; promotion to lieutenant general 95; at Spotsylvania Courthouse 103, 104–5, 107, 108; in the Wilderness 96, 99, 101–2
Gravelly Run 142, 145, 147
Gregory, Edgar M. 147, 150, 160–61
Griffin, Charles 10, 11, 62, 89, 91, 96, 97, 109–10, 113, 114, 116, 170, 173; Petersburg to Appomattox 142, 143, 144, 145, 146–47, 148, 149–50, 151–52, 159, 161, 163, 164
Grimes, Bryan 164
Gwyn, Edgar 150

Halleck, Henry 51, 67, 86
Hancock, Winfield S. 58, 71, 84, 85, 96, 98–99, 103, 104, 105–7, 108, 110, 111, 112, 113, 133, 178
Harpers Ferry, Virginia 39, 40, 47, 48, 50, 67, 120, 122
Haskell, Frank A. 85
Hatcher's Run 132, 133, 140, 142
Hayes, Rutherford B. 179
Hays, Alexander 84
Heth, Henry W. 67–68, 70
Hill, A.P. 37, 40, 47, 48, 59, 67, 70, 72, 81, 83, 84, 91, 96, 98, 103, 108, 110, 111, 130, 136, 138, 140, 154, 156
Hill, Benjamin 181
Hill, D.H. 36, 37, 39, 42, 43, 45, 46
Hoke, Robert F. 94, 111
Hood, John Bell 15, 41, 48, 71–72, 115
Hooker, Joseph 41, 48, 51, 54, 56, 67, 95, 96; at Chancellorsville 57–58, 59–60, 61, 62, 74
Howard, O.O. 58, 69, 71, 90
Hotchkiss, Jedediah 126
Humphreys, Andrew A. 133, 141, 145, 157–58, 159, 162
Hunter, David 112, 120, 122
Hunter, Robert 134–35

invasion of Maryland 38

Jackson, Thomas J. "Stonewall" 37, 39, 40–41, 42, 52, 64, 70, 71, 98, 100, 109, 121, 137; at Chancellorsville 57, 58, 59, 61, 62
James River 36, 37, 96, 109, 111, 112, 141, 146, 154, 155
Jerusalem Plank Road 114, 132
Jetersville, Virginia 156
Johnson, Andrew 173, 176
Johnson, Bushrod 146, 154, 157
Johnson, Edward 94, 96, 105, 107, 108
Johnston, Joseph 33, 35, 96, 109, 136–37, 155, 159, 164, 171–72
Johnston, Robert 100, 105

Kemper, James L. 84–85
Kershaw, Joseph P. 124, 127, 129
Ku Klux Klan 176

Last Days of the Confederacy 188–90
Law, Evander 72–73, 74, 79
Lee, Fitzhugh 111, 146, 148, 149, 154, 157, 159, 161
Lee, Robert E. 9, 10, 16, 46, 48, 51, 52, 54, 56, 57, 64, 67, 91, 92, 93, 94, 95, 109, 115, 119, 120, 122, 130, 132, 133, 134, 135, 136–37, 139, 140, 170, 171; at Chancellorsville 58, 59, 60, 61; at Cold Harbor 110–11, 112, 113; at Gettysburg 69, 70, 71–72, 73, 81, 83, 84, 85, 86; in Maryland campaign 38–39, 40–44, 47; in Peninsula Campaign 35–37; Petersburg to Appomattox 141, 145–46, 154, 155, 156, 157, 158–60, 162, 163, 164–66, 167, 172; at Spotsylvania Courthouse 103–104, 105–7, 108; in the Wilderness 96, 98–99, 100, 101–102
Lee, Stephen D. 190, 191
Lee, W.H.F. 157
Lewis, John Sutherland 35
Lightfoot, James 44
Lincoln, Abraham 9, 10, 23, 25, 26, 28, 29, 30, 32, 39, 49, 51, 56, 67, 87–88, 92, 95, 118, 131–32, 134–35, 165, 169, 171, 173, 177, 183, 194; assassination 16, 170, 172
Little Round Top 15, 63, 71, 72–74, **75, 76**, **77, 78**, 80, 81, 82, 83, 84, 86, 89, 90, 91, 97, 185, 192
Livermore, William 50
Longstreet, James 10, 37, 39, 41, 45, 52, 67, 71–72, 74, 83–84, 86, 96, 98, 103, 130, 135, 136; Petersburg to Appomattox 146, 154, 156, 157, 158, 159, 162, 163
Lynchburg Pike 159, 160

Magruder, John 33
Mahone, William 107, 156
Maine election of 1879 184–86; *see also* Chamberlain, Joshua L.; integrity
Malvern Hill, Battle of 36–37, 69
Mansfield, Joseph K.F. 41
Marye's Heights 51, 52, 54, 58, 59, 60, 61, 85

Massanutten Mountain 126
McCausland, John 122
McClellan, George B. 32, 51, 95, 131–32; in Maryland campaign 38, 39, 40, 41, 46, 47, 49; in Peninsula Campaign 32–33, 35, 36, 37
McDowell, Irvin 28, 32, 95
McEuen, Charles I. 145
McLaws, Lafayette 42, 59, 60, 61, 71–72, 81
McLean house 165
McPherson's Ridge 68, 69
Meade, George Gordon 39, 52, 62, 63, 67, 91, 92, 95–96, 109, 113, 114, 117, 119, 148, 170, 178; at Gettysburg 68, 69, 71, 72, 73, 83, 85, 86
Medal of Honor *81*, 83, 192
Melcher, Holman S. 80
Merritt, Wesley 10
Milledgeville, Georgia 20, 23, 26
Mitchell, John 144
Monocacy River 120–21
Moore, A.B 27
Morrill, Walter G. 74, 80, 91–92
Mud March 56, 57
Mule Shoe 104, 105, 107–8

Namozine Road 155, 156
New England magazine 186
New York Tribune 180
Norfolk Railroad 114, 132
North Anna River 109–10

Oakland Cemetery *189*, 191
Oates, John A. 77
Oates, William C. 72–73, 74, 75, 77, 79–80, 81, 83, 91
185th New York 131, 142, 144, 147, 163
198th Pennsylvania 131, 142, 143, 147
Orange Plank Road 96, 98
Orange Turnpike 96–97, 103, 146
Ord, Edward 135, 141, 157, 160, 162

Pace, James M. 170
peach orchard 72, 73, 81
Pegram, John 126, 127, 130, 133
Pendleton, W.N. 10
Peters, William E. 122
Petersburg, Virginia 11, 15, 96, 109, 112–13, 114, 118, 119, 120, 131, 132–33, 134, 135, 136–37, 138, 141–42, 154, 155, 165, 169, 171, 172, 180, 182, 188, 194
Petersburg mine 119
Pettigrew, Johnston 67, 69, 83, 84
Peyton, Green 162
Pickett, George E. 83–86, 110, 113, 146, 148–49, 151, 154, 157
Pickett's Charge 83–86
Pine Grove Cemetery *193*, 194
Pleasant Green Academy 22
Pole Cat Creek 109

Pope, John 37, 95
Potomac River 33, 38, 41, 47–48, 51, 65, 86, 120–21, 173
Prince, Howard L. 74

Quaker Road 142–43, 144, 145, 147, 149, 151, 168, 170

Raccoon Roughs 26–27, 136
Ramseur, S. Dodson 123, 126–27, 129
Rapidan River 57, 91, 92, 93, 95, 96, 101–102, 188
Rappahannock River 51–52, 53, 55, 56, 57, 59, 60, 61, 62, 89, 91–92
Reconstruction 177, 185
Rewalt, Mrs. L.L. 66, 188
Reynolds, John F. 68–69
Rice, James C. 82, 89, 90
Richardson, Israel 42, 44, 45
Richmond, Virginia 27, 32, 33, 35, 36, 37, 38, 46, 51, 64, 67, 94, 96, 108, 109, 110, 112, 122, 130, 132, 133, 134, 136–37, 141, 154, 155, 172
Rives' Salient 11, 15, 114, 118, 119, 131
Rodes, Robert E. 34, 36, 39–40, 42, 44, 46, 64, 68–69, 82, 94, 105, 107, 123, 126
Rohrbach Bridge (Burnside Bridge) 46–47, 48
Roosevelt, Theodore 191
Rosser, Thomas L. 127
Round Top 71, 72–73, 75, *78*, 79, 80, 82, 86

Sanders, C.C. 60
Savage Station, Battle of 36
Sayler's Creek 157–58
secession 23, 25, 165, 183, 189; Chamberlain's view 29, 186; Gordon's view 25–26
2nd Maine 62–63, 74, 77, 89
Sedgwick, John 42, 59, 60, 61, 91, 96, 98, 99, 100, 103, 104
Seminary Ridge 71, 84, 85
Seven Days' Battle 35
Seven Pines, Battle of (Fair Oaks) 33–34, 35, 46
Sharpsburg, Maryland 31, 40, 46, 47, 48, 49, 50, 51, 120
Shenandoah River 126, 127
Shenandoah Valley 28, 64, 65, 96, 109, 110, 112, 120, 121–22, 124, 130, 131
Shenandoah Valley Turnpike 122–23, 124, 125, 127
Sheridan, Philip 96, 111, 112, 172; Petersburg to Appomattox 141, 145–46, 148–49, 150, 151, 152–53, 155, 157, 159, 160–61, 162–63, 164–65; Valley campaign 122–23, 124, 125, 126, 127–29, 130, 131
Sherman, William Tecumseh 96, 109, 131, 136, 140, 156, 165, 171–72, 174, 189
Sickel, Horatio G. 142–43, 145

Sickles, Daniel 72–73
Sigel, Franz 96, 109, 110, 112
16th Michigan 31, 54, 73–74, 109
6th Alabama 27, 28, 33–35, 47, 57, 181; at Antietam 42, 44, 69; at South Mountain 39–40
slavery 19, 23, 24–25, 49, 135, 183; Chamberlain's view 28, 187; Gordon's view 25, 29; slaves as soldiers 134; *see also* Thirteenth Amendment
Smith, Joseph L. 184
Smith, William F. "Baldy" 111, 112–13
Sniper, Gustave 142–43, 144
Sorrel, G. Moxley 98
South Mountain, Battle of (Turner's Gap) 39–40, 46, 48
Southside Railroad 132, 141–42, 146, 152, 154, 155, 156
Spear, Ellis 30, 80, 173, 194
Special Orders No. 191 39, 40, 41
Stanton, Edwin M. 118, 135
Stephens, Alexander H. 134–35
Stoneman, George 58
Stoneman's Switch 51, 56
Stowe, Harriet Beecher 19
Stuart, J.E.B. 41, 52, 58, 60, 62, 67, 108
Sumner, Edwin Vose "Bull" 42, 51, 54
surrender 9, 12–13, 134, 157, 163, 166, 167, 170, 171; Army of the Tennessee 171–72; ceremony 11, 13–15, 168; formal terms of 10; Grant and Lee terms 165–66
Susquehanna River 65–66
Sykes, George 58

Taylor, Walter 134
3rd Alabama 36
Thirteenth Amendment 135, 183; *see also* slavery
Toombs, Robert 46
Tozier, Andrew 77
Traveller 106, 166
Trimble, Isaac 83–84
20th Maine 10, 11, 15, 29–31, 62, 63, 82, 89, 91, 92–93, 96–97, 102, 109, 118, 147, 169, 194; at Battle of Fredericksburg 50, 53, 54, 55; at Little Round Top 73–81, 83, 87, 90; in Maryland campaign 47–48; mustered out 174

United Confederate Veterans 190
University of Georgia 22
Upson County, Georgia 21
Upton, Emory 104–5, 107

Vincent, Strong 73–74, 82, 87, 89

Wallace, Lew 120
Warren, Gouvernor K. 73, 74, 91, 96, 97, 98, 99, 103, 104, 108, 110, 111, 113, 114, 117–18, 132, 133; Petersburg to Appomattox 141, 142, 145, 146–47, 148, 149, 151, 152, 153, 161, 172
Washburn, Israel 29
Washburne, Elihu 169
Washington, D.C. 28, 30–31, 32, 37, 38, 47, 51, 64, 67, 70, 71, 83, 86, 92, 102, 120, 121, 122, 124, 134, 135, 145, 161, 170, 171, 172, 174
Washington Post 180
Weldon Railroad 132
Wharton, Gabriel 127
wheatfield 72, 73, 81
White Oak Road 142, 144–45, 146, 147–48, 149, 150, 151–52, 156
White Oak Swamp, Battle of 36
Whiting's Military and Classical School 18
Wilcox, Cadmus 94, 105, 107
Wilderness 15, 58, 61, 96, 97–98, 101, 102, 103, 110, 128
Winchester, Battle of (Second) 65
Winchester, Battle of (Third) 122–23
Wise, Henry A. 168
Woods, Leonard 18, 19
Wright, Ambrose 82
Wright, Horatio G. 104, 107–8, 110, 111, 119, 121, 126, 127, 130, 157, 159
Wrightsville, Pennsylvania 66, 188

York, Pennsylvania 65–66
Yorktown, Virginia 33

Ziever, Augustus 147

www.ingramcontent.com/pod-product-compliance
Ingram Content Group UK Ltd.
Pitfield, Milton Keynes, MK11 3LW, UK
UKHW041951140426
5217IPUK00015B/753